One Life in the Law
A 60-Year Review

The University of Arkansas News Service

Robert A. Leflar

ONE LIFE
IN THE LAW

A 60-Year Review

To Sandra Aymond,
with our mutual Torts memories —
Robert A. Leflar

The University of Arkansas Press
Fayetteville   1985

LIBRARY OF CONGRESS CATALOGING-IN-PUBLICATION DATA

Leflar, Robert Allen, 1901–
    One life in the law ; a sixty year review.

    Bibliography: p.
    Includes index.
    1. Leflar, Robert Allen, 1901–   2. Law
teachers—United States—Biography.   I. Title
II. Title: 1 life in the law.
KF 373.L42A36   1985   349.73′092′4[B]   84-28017
ISBN 0-938626-40-X   347.300924 [B]
ISBN 0-938626-99-X (pbk.)

To the 1000 judges who by participating in the Appellate Judges Seminars during the last 29 years have evinced their interest in better law and in improving the administration of our legal system.

Contents

Acknowledgments

Though this little book was put together in 1984, some segments of it were first written during the preceding sixty years, then occasionally rewritten. Parts of articles previously published in legal journals are, always with permission, reprinted here, sometimes with only slight changes, sometimes with more than slight ones. I thank the copyright owners, in each case the original publishers noted below, for permission to include here paragraphs and pages copied from my earlier writings, as follows:

The Great and Common Law, 30 Ark. L. Rev. 395 (1977)

The Making of a Good Law School, 20 Ark. L. Rev. 50 (1966)

Legal Remedies for Defamation, 6 Ark. L. Rev. 423 (1952)

Conflicts Law: More on Choice-Influencing Considerations, 54 Calif. L. Rev. 1584 (1966)

Community Property and Conflict of Laws, 21 Calif. L. Rev. 221 (1933)

The Nature of Conflicts Law, 81 Columbia L. Rev. 1080 (1981)

Some Observations Concerning Judicial Opinions, 61 Columbia L. Rev. 810 (1961)

Minimizing State Conflicts of Laws, 1983 Detroit College of Law Rev. 1325

Extrastate Enforcement of Penal and Governmental Claims, 46 Harvard L. Rev. 193 (1932)

No Task for the Short-Winded, 54 Judicature 366 (1971)

The Multi-Judge Decisional Process, 42 Maryland L. Rev. 722 (1983)

Negligence in Name Only, 27 New York Univ. L. Rev. 564 (1952)

Choice-Influencing Considerations in Conflicts Law, 41 New York Univ. L. Rev. 267 (1966)

Honest Judicial Opinions, 74 Northwestern Univ. L. Rev. 721 (1979)

Contribution and Indemnity Between Tortfeasors, 81 U. Pennsylvania L. Rev. 130 (1932)

The Social Utility of the Criminal Law of Defamation, 34 Texas L. Rev. 984 (1956)

Equitable Prevention of Public Wrongs, 14 Texas L. Rev. 427 (1936)

Roger J. Traynor—Exemplar of the Judicial Process, 1971 Utah L. Rev. 1

The Free-ness of Free Speech, 15 Vanderbilt L. Rev. 1073 (1962)

Comment on Contributory and Comparative Negligence, 21 Vanderbilt L. Rev. 918 (1968)

Taught Law Is Tough Law, 8 Wayne L. Rev. 465 (1962)

Tort Law Objectives, in Appellate Judicial Opinions, p. 16 (West Publ. Co., 1974)

The Law Teacher's Place in the American Legal Profession, Journal of Society of Public Teachers of Law, p. 21 (England 1963)

Foreword

What justification, if any, is there for the publication of this little book? What is the purpose?

The answer must be in terms of my obviously immodest desire to record something of my sixty-year life in the law, the law jobs that I've worked at and the principles that underlie that work. I want to set out, as best I can, the ideas and ideals that have sustained me, and show how they tie in with teaching and other law-related work that have constituted my professional life. Perhaps I want to preach a little too, by continuing to advocate those ideas and ideals.

Parts of the book are newly written, and parts are not. A good many of the sections are taken from law review articles that I wrote in years gone by. Some sections are derived from two or three or a half dozen of such articles. Footnotes are omitted, as are most legalistic technicalities, unless the technicalities were what I was talking about. Occasionally I found that what I'd written several years ago had since become obsolete, by reason of intervening changes in the law or in its administration, but not often. Improvements have occurred, but permanent perfection is an ideal seldom if ever realized. In fact, I seldom advocate it. There are plenty of lesser goals to work for, even in the law. The fact that they are lesser ones does not negate their genuine importance.

I am told that a small bit of personal history will be helpful to persons reading the book. This is probably as good a place as any to stick it in.

I was born at Siloam Springs in Arkansas on March 22, 1901. My father was a drayman who always explained that in school he "went through the Fourth Reader." In his youth, before he became a drayman, he was Town Marshal of Alma, Arkansas, then for a time a deputy U.S. Marshal in the Western District of Arkansas and Indian Territory ("Hanging Judge" Parker's court). My mother was a high school graduate and a firm believer in education. I was the oldest of their eight children, and our mother saw to it that all of us, in one way or another, got through high school.

My first marriage, in 1928, was to Doris Drake. Our only child was a foster daughter, Helen, who now lives in Kansas. After seventeen years Doris divorced me, undoubtedly for good cause. Then in 1946 Helen Finger and I were married. We have two sons, Robert B who, like me, is a Harvard Law School graduate now on the University of Arkansas Law School faculty, and Charles, who is a University of Arkansas graduate and an accountant now working for Price Waterhouse in their Dallas office. After 38 years Helen is still married to and living with me, though she too undoubtedly has good grounds for divorce. I will not recount them here.

Other aspects of my personal history can be noted, by anyone who is interested, in connection with the law-related items that compose the book. All of these items deal with matters in which I have been, and am, truly interested. I realize that few if any readers will find them as interesting as they are to me. My hope must be that some will read them and take them seriously.

One Life in the Law
A 60-Year Review

I Personal

Preparing for Law School

I have been asked how it happened that I went to Harvard for my law study, something for which there was no precedent from Siloam Springs and little from Arkansas.

For one thing, there was no law school at the University of Arkansas when I was an undergraduate there. Probably I would have gone to Harvard, however, even had there been one then. The University of Arkansas Law School was started in 1924, the same time I began my law study in Cambridge. In fact, I talked with Dean Julian S. Waterman about my plans in August, 1924, just before I left for Cambridge, and he explained to me his plans for the new law school at Fayetteville. He encouraged me to go forward with my preexistent plans.

My plans dated back to 1916, when I was 15 years old. I had

by then decided that I wanted to study law—to be a lawyer rather than a preacher or a grocer or a drayman. I somehow concluded that five American law schools were outstanding, or at least of most interest to me. These were the University of Michigan, Yale, Harvard, Columbia, and George Washington. I wrote to them for catalogs, not telling them I was still in high school, and I studied all five catalogs in minute detail. Each of them described the courses taught, then named the casebook used in each course and the teacher who taught it. The courses and course descriptions were pretty much the same in all five schools, and so were the casebooks. There were not many casebooks available in those days, seldom more than two for a subject, and only one for the more advanced subjects. The big difference was that for most of the courses the editor of the casebook (at the time I used the word "author") was the man who was teaching the course at Harvard. That came near to making up my mind.

Later, in the University library at Fayetteville, I found the report by Josef Redlich, a world-famous Austrian lawyer and law teacher who had been employed by the Carnegie Foundation for the Advancement of Teaching in 1913 to study legal education in America and make recommendations for improvement of what was by many regarded as a sorry and inefficient, often profit-oriented, system. A similar Carnegie Foundation study of medical education had recently achieved a revolution in that area, very nearly ridding the nation of fly-by-night quack medical schools which disgraced that profession. The Redlich study proposed a comparable method of accreditation for public law schools, with the study of actual cases then being emphasized at Harvard, rather than the lecture method of teaching previously employed in most law schools, as the standard instructional technique. The proposed change in teaching methods caught on much more slowly in law than in medicine, perhaps because public interest in medical services was greater than with lawyer services, perhaps because private political and financial interests were more firmly intrenched in profit-making law schools than in profit-making medical schools. At any rate the modernization of legal education followed that in medical education slowly, but eventually. It had not yet caught up by 1920. It was then that I read the Redlich report. My personal commitment to go to Harvard was reinforced. It simply did not occur to me that I would do anything else. I knew that law study should be a full-time job, not the casual and incidental matter that under-graduate study had been.

During my four undergraduate years at Arkansas my principal concern was with making a living; study was secondary. I received a $150 scholarship in 1919, held janitor jobs during my freshman and sophomore years, and made the Kansas wheat harvest in the summers of 1919 and 1920. During my last two college years my work was largely journalistic. I was the Fay-etteville reporter (stringer) for the *Arkansas Gazette* and the Fort Smith *Southwest American*, and worked in the afternoons, supposedly half-time, at the University's news bureau. I'm sure that I benefitted substantially from several college courses, perhaps in spite of myself; in others I sought for little more than a passing grade and accordingly received minimal bene-fits from them. I was not a serious student but only a course-taker. That was the foolish period of my academic career. At least I made a living as I attended classes with fair regularity.

I did have sense enough to realize that at Harvard I would not be free to devote the bulk of my time to making a living, as I did at Arkansas. I knew that I should go there with enough money to enable me to spend my time studying rather than on penny-earning outside work. Accordingly, I first assured my admission to the Law School, then asked that it be postponed while I earned some money. That request was readily granted. Then I taught school for a year at Stuttgart, Arkansas, ran the

University's news bureau in the summers of 1922 and 1923, and taught a year at John E. Brown College in Siloam Springs.

My John E. Brown College experience was important. It matured me, and taught me how to work in an organized fashion. I was hired to teach journalism and public speaking to high school and junior college classes. On September 1, 1923, when I reported to the Siloam Springs campus, I was informed that part of my duties as journalism teacher was to serve as managing editor of the *Interstate American*, a weekly newspaper published at the College for the local trade area. Student reporters, advertising solicitors, and other helpers were amazingly competent and by the time classes started two weeks later I felt that the job was under control. In late October, however, I was asked also to become managing editor of the *Ozark American*, the College's monthly promotional magazine. That turned out not to be a very difficult assignment, since articles to fill the magazine's sixteen pages were readily available. At Christmastime I acquired a third editorial responsibility, though without title, this time for putting together the *American Evangelist*, a 24-page monthly magazine of which President Brown was the editor. These three journalistic duties continued, along with my five classes, to the end of the school year. The public speaking classes also produced an extracurricular opportunity. Boys in my high school class decided to enter the state high school debate contest, with me as their coach. To my surprise they won every debate in which they took part, first with other Northwest Arkansas high school teams, then in the finals in the spring of 1924 at the University in Fayetteville against the winning teams from other high school districts across the state. After that victory we led a noisy parade down St. Nicholas Avenue in Siloam Springs. By the end of that school year, during which I also taught a Sunday School class at the North Methodist Church, I felt that I knew how to organize my work and time effectively. I thought that if I could handle all the work that I had piled on myself during that year I could take on whatever the future might bring. *

In August of 1924 I was ready to go to law school. A month later I entered upon my life in the law, now continued for over 60 years, and still continuing.

Law School Student

My law school days, like those of many elderly lawyers, are a treasured memory. The memory centers somewhat around classmates who later became judges, law teachers, successful practitioners, and politicians. (Most of them have now passed on.) The memory centers still more on the teachers who conducted our classes. Some of them were great teachers. Less of my memory stays with what I learned during those three years.

The first teacher we met was Edward H. ("Bull") Warren, for Property I. There were 265 of us, exactly half of the 1924 entering class, in the room. What happened has been commemorated, under fictional names, in a much later moving picture. Apparently it happened every fall, year after year. Smiling broadly, Warren greeted us in friendly fashion, expressed the hope that we would enjoy law study, urged us to work together as friends with our fellow students, then said, "Now, shake hands with the man on your right." We did as he said. Still smiling: "Turn and shake hands with the man on your left." We did it, and nearly all of us were smiling too. "One of the three of you will not be back here next year!" he thundered. At that, we sobered up and went to work. Warren

* A 1981 honorary Doctor of Letters degree from John Brown University, as the erstwhile College is now named, brought back to mind the marvelously busy 1923–24 year that I spent there, as well as my memory of the marvelous personality of the founder and original President John E. Brown.

was not a great teacher, though he was one we always remembered. His learning was simplistic, doctrinaire, looking mostly to the past, largely misreading the present, and having little to do (as we later realized) with the future. He was good as a teacher of elementary property law, which was a kind of socioeconomic history derived from late medieval England. He also taught the course in Corporations which many of us, even in the mid-twenties, felt was based on antiquated theory. Perhaps he was a superior educator, since our rejection of his ideas led us to think a little for ourselves. I doubt, though, if that was what he had in mind.

I thought that Samuel ("Sammy") Williston, author of the multi-volume treatise on contracts and of books on other commercial law subjects, was our best teacher. He was genial, sharp, and always had a point to make. His points were clothed in factual illustrations which made them clear and sensible. Men who were hooked on the horns of one of his temporary dilemmas still enjoyed the process because he was so good natured about it and so convincing in the end. The law of contracts has moved beyond him since his time, but he taught it effectively as it was then. He was truly a great teacher.

For me Felix Frankfurter was not one of the "greats." For others he was. He was good with seminars, not with large classes. Even when he had a large class he conducted it as a seminar, with the active participants limited to those usually seated in the front rows who held up their hands and volunteered their reactions to his questions. His classes were conversations with these volunteers. Unfortunately, I was never much inclined to hold up my hand. In a Frankfurter class I became an observer, not a participant.

I had only one course under Frankfurter. That was Municipal Corporations. I assumed that it would be a course in local government, perhaps dealing with interrelationships between cities and other governmental levels, with different forms of municipal government, and with administrative problems arising within the varied areas of municipal activity. I was wrong. Almost the entire semester was devoted to questions concerning municipal liability in tort, a topic to which I now regularly give a part of one class hour in my course on Torts.

The Frankfurter semester started with the old English rule that governments could not be sued without their consent ("The King can do no wrong"), then a comparison of municipal corporations with private corporations which are liable under ordinary tort law principles for injuries inflicted by their employees, and finally the devices by which the old rule was being eroded so that tort recoveries could in recent years, in some states, under special circumstances, be secured against a city. The principal circumstance in which it was suggested recovery might be secured was that in which the tortious injury arose out of the city's engagement in what were called proprietary (street cars, water and light plants) as distinguished from governmental (police, fire department) activities. We spent between three and four weeks on that distinction, arguing about whether charges for admission to parks, or sales of ice cream cones in the park, or tuition charged for certain school courses, made them proprietary rather than governmental.

Professor Frankfurter, in planning his course, obviously made a poor guess as to the law's future growth in the municipal tort area. Today's law has practically forgotten the distinction between proprietary and governmental activities, always an artificial one. The availability of liability insurance or its self-insurance equivalent, scarcely mentioned during the Frankfurter semester, has come to be all-important. What we learned that had permanent value was that the law does change and that it is characteristic of the judicial process that changes often are achieved by minute and barely logical distinctions which can be abandoned when a distinction has been carried so far that its absurdity is apparent to nearly everybody.

The trouble was that we were made to feel that the distinctions were themselves important, that it was the law's function to develop such distinctions, and that our job as lawyers was to become adept at developing them, as the means by which needed change in the law might be achieved. Frankfurter had a reputation as a liberal and a reformer. He recognized that law must change to meet the needs of new times. But he believed that change should be slow, barely perceptible, so that judges could deny that they were making changes. He was a traditionalist, though in the slightly hypocritical sense of insisting that established standards and approaches ought always to be followed while at the same time suggesting techniques and devices for achieving desired results within the established norms.

Dean Roscoe Pound was one of my heroes. (I do not have many.) His Jurisprudence course was primarily for graduate law students, but he gave me permission in 1926, as a third-year man, to enroll for it. There were about 35 of us in the class, all but two of the others being law teachers elsewhere or older lawyers who wanted to become law teachers. Pound was undoubtedly the most learnedly comprehensive scholar I had ever known. The breadth of his knowledge and his ability to correlate the variety of influences that have affected and can further affect not only the common law but any or all of the world's legal systems, summed up in his sociological jurisprudence, gave me for the first time a view of the law's forest as against its little groves of related trees. For me it was an intellectual experience beyond all others.

Not only was Dean Pound, then in his prime, one of the world's truly great scholars, he was one of the most human, and humane, of men, and one of the most efficient. He liked to get acquainted with students, to help them individually, and to join them in their social functions. He remembered them after they were graduated, and continued to help them. And he himself, as Dean, really ran the Law School. He had one exceedingly competent secretary, who had been with him for years. There were no associate deans or assistant deans. All the School's problems came to him, and they were solved. On top of that, when some emergency left a scheduled course without a teacher, he would meet the class himself, and teach well. Pound was a giant above most giants.

Austin W. Scott (Scotty) was, after Williston, the best of my teachers. We had both Civil Procedure and Trusts under him. No one slept in his classes, nor was time wasted in them. He kept us busy, and busy at thinking. Like Pound and Williston, he lived to a great old age, close to the century mark, and was active almost to the end. In addition to serving as Reporter for the Restatement (Second) of Trusts, he was Associate Reporter for the Restatement (Second) of Conflict of Laws, and one of my most satisfying bits of continuing legal education came when, as one of the advisers for the Conflict of Laws Restatement (Second), I worked under him on that project in 1966–71. He was still vigorous in June of 1977, when he helped to host the 50th anniversary party for our class of 1927.

The other Law School teacher who influenced me substantially was Joseph H. Beale. His principal subject was Conflict of Laws, which in time became my principal subject. He developed Conflicts as a law school course, and came to feel as if he owned it. His classroom approach was based on a formal logic that always sustained his conclusions, and he never lost an argument with a student. We may have felt unhappy with some of the conclusions, but we accepted them. There seemed to be no logical alternative.

By the time I came back in 1931 to work for my S.J.D. I had been teaching Conflict of Laws for four years, and had found time to read some of the questioning literature that we had not been encouraged, nor had the time, to read five years earlier. Beale, as the leading American authority, was Reporter for the first Conflict of Laws Restatement. Dissent among the committee of advisers had come out into the open. The dissenters did not take over; they resigned.

In 1931–32 Beale was putting the Restatement into final form. His Conflict of Laws seminar for that year was planned as a review of the tentative Restatement sections. I, of course, signed up for the seminar, along with some 25 other graduate students. It afforded my first student experience in real controversy. As we took up the Restatement sections, most of the students undertook to agree with the professor's views by applying Bealian methods of analysis. I found myself dissenting. That, it turned out, was just what Beale wanted. He needed someone to present opposing views, and encouraged me to do so. He helped me constantly with the writing that I had to do, suggested to the Harvard Law Review that it publish one of the pieces I wrote for him, and made me think that some of the Restatement sections were revised on the basis of my comments. I came to realize that the teacher I had regarded as a harsh and scholarly autocrat was really a kind and gentle man.

Another seminar that I signed up for at the same time was on Torts law, which I'd been teaching for four years and intended to continue. The seminar was listed in the catalog as being offered by Professors Seavey, Thurston, and Magruder, all of whom taught sections of the first year Torts course. Seavey was in charge. I was already acquainted with Seavey who, though he was still teaching at Yale when I was an undergraduate law student, had known my then father-in-law when both of them had taught in Chinese Imperial University at Tientsin earlier in the century. I visited him to find out plans for the seminar. He told me that I was the only person who had signed up for it, and that the three of them were not about to spend two hours each week talking with me alone about torts. Instead, he said, he would keep me busy writing on topics he would suggest (three subsequently published articles were the result) and that he would take me to lunch on Thursdays at the Faculty Club where we would sit at a round table regularly occupied by Law School teachers whom he would ask to talk about torts. We did that each Thursday. Needless to say, they did not talk torts all the time, or much of the time; they talked about whatever interested them. Regardless of topics discussed, it was a marvelous educational hour each week.

By mid-April my thesis had been accepted and my three-hour oral examination before Pound, Beale and Seavey had turned out to be a pleasant though lively conversation about matters in which I was interested. My graduate year was practically ended well before the school year was over. It was a good year.

Law school is much more than scheduled courses taught by faculty members. Most important of all is the reading and thinking done on the student's own initiative, entirely apart from required or even suggested outside reading. Of almost equal importance are the contacts with fellow students. They may be thought of as "bull sessions," but when they relate to the law—and an amazing proportion of the talk among law students does relate to the law—they are part of the process of legal education. Typically, such conversations attempt to clarify what was said in the classroom, or go beyond what was said there.

Henry Friendly was from the beginning the top man in our class, and his brilliance soon made him known to all of us. We listened to Henry's words as carefully as we listened to most of the professors, sometimes more carefully. The fact that he was later recognized as one of the nation's ablest appellate judges was no surprise to any of us. Livingston Hall, who later became Vice-Dean of the Law School, was almost as good. Erwin

Griswold, one year behind us, was known to most of us, and his later service as long-time Dean of the Law School, then as Solicitor General of the United States, was in a way predictable. Both Lewis Powell, later a Justice on the United States Supreme Court, and Paul Freund, did their graduate law work in the same year (1931–32) as I did. Most of the classmates with whom we talked all kinds of law were, of course, more ordinary men who in due time became typical practicing lawyers, law teachers, and judges. We educated each other. For physical exercise I took long walks, usually with classmates, most often around Fresh Pond in Cambridge, but at times to places like Lexington and Concord. These afforded time for a lot of legal theorizing.

In June of 1925, at the end of my first year of law study, I hitchhiked back to my parents' home in Siloam Springs, and spent most of the summer working and studying in lawyer A. L. Smith's office there. (The hitchhike took eight days, and I saw a lot of country.) Smith was a good country lawyer, and really helped me. He took me with him on trips to court, let me sit in on client interviews, and had me write memoranda for him on legal issues that arose in his cases. I also had long visits with the four other Siloam Springs lawyers. These were all informative. In September I hitchhiked back to Cambridge.

I had saved enough after graduation from college to see me through the first two years of law school. At the end of my second year, though, I found myself very nearly, but not quite, broke. I needed more money. Tuition charges, then only $200 annually, were taken care of by a scholarship based on grades. I decided to take a chance on earning something during the coming school year, and spent the summer working up the next year's courses so that I would have free time for outside work during the school year. During that summer I abstracted all the cases in the casebooks that would be used during the coming school year in the courses on Conflict of Laws, Corporations, and Constitutional Law. The plan worked. I then got a job that provided my meals in a nearby restaurant patronized largely by law students, where I had already been eating occasionally. And I did a lot of tutoring, both of groups and of individual students, in second-year courses, at hourly rates a good deal higher than were being paid for manual labor. When June came I even had enough money left to enable me to ride back to Arkansas on the passenger trains. Then I spent the summer of 1927 working on the courses that I was scheduled to teach at the University of Arkansas Law School in September.

Post-Law School Career

In February, 1927, when I was nearing the end of my three years in law school, Dean Julian S. Waterman wrote me that there was a vacancy at the beginning level at the new University of Arkansas Law School, and invited me to apply for it. I did, and in due time President John C. Futrall appointed me to the position of Instructor at the salary of $2500 a year. It took me less than a minute to accept. At almost the same time Dean Roscoe Pound called me to his office and said, "Leflar, I have a job that I'll recommend you for. It's with a good law firm in Honolulu. You'll like it out there in Hawaii." I had to tell him that I had just taken the Arkansas job, and that I really wanted to go back home in any event.

That was that. I began my law teaching career in September, 1927. I have many times wondered what my life would have been like had I gone to Honolulu. At least it would have been different. A classmate named Charles Adley Gregory took the Hawaiian job, and stayed with the firm, I think, the rest of his life. In the 1960s he came to Fayetteville for a visit, and assured me that his life out there had been good. His life and mine, though, could not have been the same. I still wonder, now and then, what mine would have been had I gone in that other direction.

For the next four years I taught at Arkansas, and enjoyed the work. Then I received leave of absence for my year of graduate law study (1931–32) under a Harvard fellowship. At the end of the year the leave was extended so that I could take a visiting professorship at the University of Kansas Law School, on the sound theory that this broadened experience would make me a better teacher at Arkansas. In September 1933, in the depths of the great depression, my return to Arkansas, now with the rank of "full" professor, was at the salary of $2457.45 a year. All Arkansas salaries had been reduced on some kind of a percentage basis. The Kansas experience paid off in another way, however. Later in the year Kansas asked me to join their permanent faculty, and I was tempted, but President Futrall found a way to add $1542.55 to my Arkansas salary. Though this did not equal the Kansas offer, the advantages of staying at home made it more than equal.

Interesting Arkansas activities increased during the next few years. I was teaching criminal law then, and Governor J. M. Futrell named me to a commission headed by the late Abe Collins of DeQueen, Arkansas, to update the state's laws in that area. We undertook to tighten, not lighten, them. The constitutional amendment and initiated act that we sponsored, both adopted at the 1936 general election, were not designed to protect defendants; their purpose for the most part was to aid prosecuting attorneys in convicting guilty criminals. During the same years I wrote and published a little book titled *The Arkansas Law of Conflict of Laws*.

A visiting professorship at the University of Missouri Law School in 1936–37 did not much interfere with the Arkansas activities, though it did produce a decision not to accept a Missouri proposal to divide my time half-and-half between the Arkansas and Missouri law schools. It also created an opportunity for Bill Fulbright to return to Arkansas and teach my courses while I was at Missouri, thus opening up for him the great career with which we are all familiar. I have often thought that creating this opening for the future Senator Fulbright may well have been the single most important contribution of my lifetime to the welfare of the state and nation.

Law school enrollment dropped off to almost nothing during World War II. Many law teachers engaged temporarily in other work. Mine was as an attorney for the War Relocation Authority, the federal agency that had charge of persons of Japanese ancestry who were removed by the military from California and other western states in 1942. Many of us in the agency felt substantial sympathy for the evacuees and tried to get them out of the relocation centers as quickly as possible, though they could not yet return to their homes on the west coast.

Dean Julian S. Waterman died at Fayetteville in September, 1943. Marion Wasson, representing the University of Arkansas Board of Trustees, telegraphed me at once and asked if I was interested in the deanship. I was, but felt that I could not break away overnight from my federal agency duties. The conclusion was that the Board named me Dean at once, but gave me a leave of absence for a year to finish up my work in Washington. Professor Edward B. Meriwether was made Acting Dean. I returned when school commenced in 1944, though for another year I spent part of my time as a "public member" of the Regional War Labor Board in Kansas City. It was not until the war ended in 1945 that law school teaching was really resumed in earnest.

The next few years were good ones. Returning students were more mature. We hired able new teachers, expanded the curriculum, and started the Arkansas Law Review as a scholarly legal journal for the bar. Enrollment increased, as did the quality of the student body. Earlier graduates of the Law School began to be the state's leading lawyers, judges, and public officials. As chairman of the Arkansas Statute Revision Commission I helped to bring out a new and more comprehensive edition of the Arkansas Statutes. I was named an Arkansas member of the National Conference of Commissioners on Uniform State Laws in 1945, eventually becoming a "life member." Serving as chairman of the University's athletics committee and as President of the Southwest Athletic Conference in the late 1940s was also interesting.

The School for Legislators that the Law School conducted at Little Rock each two years, beginning in 1936, was a valuable experience for me. Dean Julian Waterman directed it the first time, in December of that year, then in 1938 turned it over to me. It was conducted for newly elected members of the House and Senate, with experienced Senators and Representatives as faculty members. Most of the School's work simulated regular sessions of the House of Representatives, with bills introduced, amendments offered, a wide variety of motions made, and other typical activities undertaken as if the House were in session, but with the difference that each piece of business was at once explained by a faculty member. Constitutional and statutory provisions governing legislation, the House and Senate rule books, a bill drafting handbook, and similar materials were worked into the discussions. The Director's job was to see that the faculty members all had their assignments and were ready to speak their parts in the two-day stage performance that purported to cover the technique of an entire 60-day legislative session. I came to feel almost like a legislator myself, and in a sense almost became one when the Legislative Council was created in 1947 with a provision that the Dean of the Law School should be an assistant to the Council.

When in the summer of 1949 Governor Sid McMath appointed me Associate Justice of the Arkansas Supreme Court to fill out a deceased Justice's unexpired term, I realized that I had to relinquish my legislative activities. The separation of powers became a controlling principle, despite the fact that working with legislators may have been more fun than working with Supreme Court Justices. During my year and a half on the Court I continued to serve as Dean of the Law School, though I collected only one salary—the Supreme Court salary, because it was bigger. After that experience I spent the summer of 1951 soliciting money, mostly from lawyers, for the construction of a new Law School building. Nearly $100,000 was pledged, the Board of Trustees appropriated some more, and Waterman Hall was built. (For me, begging for money was not an enjoyable activity.)

About this time I began to receive offers from other law schools. I turned down a higher-paying deanship in another state, spent a pleasant summer as a visiting professor at the University of Colorado, then again on leave of absence taught at New York University for the school year 1952–53. They asked me to stay there. New York University, under the leadership of Arthur Vanderbilt and Russell Niles, was beginning to become one of the nation's ten great law schools. After another semester back home I resigned as Arkansas dean (1954) and began to divide my time between Arkansas and N.Y.U. as a regular member of both faculties, sometimes for a full year but usually for a semester at one place and then the other. It was in 1959–60 that I taught in New York on Mondays and Tuesdays and in Fayetteville the latter part of each week. The airlines were cooperative, and I did not miss a class, nor was I late for class, a single time at either law school.

During these years I also did some labor arbitration, holding hearings and deciding disputes between corporate employers and organized employees represented by their labor unions. These disputes normally involved application of collective bargaining contracts to an infinite variety of fact situations most of which were not specifically covered by the contracts. Lawyers often appeared for both sides, but not always. Management officials and union officers sometimes presented the cases. Witnesses were heard and arguments made in orderly fashion, much as in trial courts sitting without a jury, though less formally. Written opinions explaining the arbitrator's decisions were customary, and many of these were, and still are, published in bound volumes by a national reporting service. A kind of common law of labor relations, based on opinions as precedents that were persuasive but not binding in future disputes, developed nationally. Working as an arbitrator was interesting and on the whole useful, but it required long trips to all parts of the country, and in the early 1970s I ceased it altogether.

Another interesting job which I held for about three years in 1972–74 was as trustee of the majority stock ownership in the greyhound racing track at West Memphis, Arkansas. There were stockholder controversies and even allegations of Mafia connections at the time. Governor Dale Bumpers and the State Racing Commission, as well as embattled stockholders, asked me to take the trusteeship. Becoming the legal owner, in a way, of one of the nation's biggest dog racing operations was a challenge, and I did a lot of checking on the facts. In the end the disputes were settled fairly and satisfactorily, and I turned the stock back to its true owners. The dogs still run.

The first of the Appellate Judges Seminars was held in the summer of 1956, and I have had responsibilities in them ever since. Requests for surveys and analyses of state appellate court systems came as a consequence of the Seminars. One of these was from the Washington Court of Appeals in 1977. I first studied that court's constitutional and statutory background, its procedural rules, its earlier and recent opinions and its internal practices, then spent five days interviewing all the judges of the court's three divisions, court staff members and other knowledgeable persons. After that I prepared a fairly comprehensive report, published in the state's bar journal, commenting on various aspects of the court's operation and suggesting some improvements, most of which were subsequently implemented. Another survey was made of the entire Pennsylvania appellate system, in 1978. In this one, the American Judicature Society contracted with the state's Supreme Court to conduct the study, then arranged with several of us to do the work. Our report, published as a 66-page brochure, received considerable attention but not much implementation in Pennsylvania. Surveys and recommendations concerning judicial organization in the Commonwealth of Maine, conducted through the Institute of Judicial Administration, were much more warmly received. I genuinely enjoyed visits in Wisconsin and Minnesota, in connection with the establishment of the new intermediate appellate courts in those progressive states. Shorter visits to other states may or may not have been helpful to their courts and judges.

The treatise on the American law of conflict of laws, first published in 1959, came out in revised editions in 1968 and 1977. My centennial history of the University of Arkansas (*The First 100 Years*), a true labor of love, came out in 1972, just fifty years after my own commencement in the semicentennial class of 1922. The book *Appellate Judicial Opinions*, 'originally proposed by Judge Warren E. Burger, then sponsored by the Advisory Council for Appellate Justice and the Institute of Judicial Administration, finally appeared in 1974. The little companion volume, *Internal Operating Procedures of Appellate Courts*, was published by the American Bar Foundation in 1976. Both are used as reference texts in the Appellate Judges Seminars.

At age 67, in 1968, in accordance with University rules, I was placed on half-time status at Arkansas for the next three years, though I continued to teach a full schedule. Then in

1971, after teaching the fall semester without pay, I was retired completely. After that I taught a semester at the University of Oklahoma, a year at Vanderbilt in Tennessee, and another year at Oklahoma. Then I was un-retired at Arkansas, and have been back at Waterman Hall since 1974, teaching Torts, Conflict of Laws and Jurisprudence, though by my own choice collecting no salary checks. I do continue to get paid for my work at New York University, now in the summers only.

One of my major interests over the years has been the improvement of Arkansas' law and legal system, particularly as they are controlled by the state's Constitution. I had spoken and written, sometimes impartially, about various proposed constitutional amendments. Finally, in 1967, Governor Winthrop Rockefeller named me to a 30-member Constitutional Revision Study Commission, of which I was elected chairman. Our report in 1968 dwelt on the need for a new and modernized state constitution, and recommended that a constitutional convention be called to draft such a document. One was called. I was elected as a Washington County delegate, then elected president of the 100-delegate convention. We drafted an excellent constitution which was submitted for adoption at the November, 1970, general election, and was defeated. Other unsuccessful efforts at constitutional revision were made during the next decade. Some amendments, however, were adopted. Then in 1978 the people voted to hold another constitutional convention and elected another 100 delegates, only a few of whom had served in the 1969–70 convention. I was again a Washington County delegate, and was once more elected president of the convention when the delegates met. Again a good state constitution was drafted, with provisions designed to make it more popularly acceptable than the 1970 document had proved to be. This proposed constitution was submitted to a vote by the people at the November, 1980, general election, and was defeated. It is unlikely that another constitutional convention will be held soon. A refreshing fact, however, is that constitutional amendments adopted, after both 1970 and 1980, have included several of the controversial provisions that earlier caused defeat of the longer documents. The combined voting opposition to a dozen reforms constituted a majority, though any one of the proposed changes would by itself probably receive majority approval. It is evident now that constitutional reform in Arkansas, at least in the near future, will have to be on a piecemeal basis.

Retirement

The operation of compulsory retirement rules can always stir up conversations, and often arguments, in an academic gathering. Probably it can have about the same effect in any group of employed persons, whether they be corporate officials or workmen, civil service personnel, partners in law firms, or whatnot.

When I have been in such gatherings, two questions have usually been put to me. One is the obvious: What retirement rules do you think are right for colleges and universities? The second, more personal: Why do you keep on teaching, substantially full-time, without pay, long after you have reached retirement age?

My answer to the first question has bearing on the second. I believe in retirement rules, but I believe also that there should be room for wise discretion in their administration. And the rules should not specify any single invariable age for retirement. Probably 60 is the earliest practicable age in academia. I have known dozens of professors, some in every academic discipline, who by age 50 had quit thinking, quit producing, and ceased to be good teachers. They should have been terminated then. By age 65 more have arrived at that condition, and by age 70 most have reached it, or are near to it. Some, however, have not, and may be good for more years of useful work. They may even be better than they were in earlier years, perhaps in research, possibly in teaching, conceivably in both. Such men and women should be kept on, not for their own sakes, but for the value of their continuing labors to society and, specifically, to their students.

Who should decide whether a teacher is to be retired at 60, at 65, at 70, or kept on after the usual top retirement age? Certainly not the individual faculty member, who will often be the poorest judge of his own capacities. True, no person should be kept on against his will; that would be self-defeating. Apart from that, administrative discretion should be the answer. It should not be unlimited discretion. The views of colleagues who know the individual's work should be systematically collected and analyzed, with careful evaluation of possibly prejudiced or too-friendly responses. Deans, chancellors and presidents would have to make final decisions.

Typically, academic administrators would not—do not—like this kind of responsibility. They prefer easy decisions, the kind that can be based on the calendar, without exercise of a judgment that might be questioned. But any clerk can figure ages by the calendar; that is not why we pay high salaries to administrators. We pay them to make hard decisions on matters important to their areas of academic responsibility. Within these areas, there are few matters more important than the research and teaching performances of senior faculty.

Now, the second question asked of me almost answers itself. I like my work, I think it is important, and I'm willing to continue it. If one enjoys his work, prefers it to available alternatives, he would be foolish not to continue it if offered the opportunity. The absence of salary can be compared with similar minimum income available to persons engaged in other retirement activities in the community where one wishes to live. Other considerations may also be relevant, and all of them must be balanced together. Above all, I must realize that the choice is not, nor has been, really mine. I can and will continue only so long as, from year to year, the members of the Law School faculty (who know me and my work) declare in my absence that they wish me to continue. I can only say, "I'm willing."

II Special Activities

Appellate Judges Seminars

Bringing Supreme Court judges back to law school was, in its inception, a questionable undertaking. Yet the Appellate Judges Seminars at the New York University School of Law have been one of the most effective continuing legal education programs in the United States. Other judicial education systems for other judicial levels have been modeled on them. More than a thousand appellate judges, from every state in the Union and from every United States Court of Appeals, have been members of the seminars. On many state supreme courts every judge has attended, and new judges in these states are almost routinely expected to enroll. For presumably good reasons, Justices of the United States Supreme Court were never invited to become student members of the Seminar, though three alumni, Warren E. Burger (1957), Harry A. Blackmun (1961) and John Paul Stevens (1975) were later named to that court.

When the seminar was being planned, and when it first met in July of 1956, all of us who were responsible for it were doubtful. We did not know whether supreme court justices would come back to law school and work seriously at their assignments. We had in mind a remark made by our former law school dean, Chief Justice Arthur T. Vanderbilt of New Jersey, while he was Chairman of the Conference of State Chief Justices: "All those old boys really want to talk about is salary increases!" That was not the kind of discussion that we contemplated.

The idea for the Seminars came from Judge Frederick G. Hamley, then Chief Justice of the state of Washington. In May of 1955 he wrote to Dean Russell D. Niles of the School of Law proposing the experiment. His letter emphasized both the importance of appellate judges being aware of current writing and thinking in all fields of the law and the need for acquainting new judges with new developments in both substantive law and judicial administration. Dean Niles, after consulting with the faculty, expressed interest in the project. Then at Philadelphia in August 1955, Judge Hamley devoted an address before the Section on Judicial Administration of the American Bar Association to the Seminar project. The response there was favorable.

In the meantime, Dean Niles had asked me to sit in on the discussions, primarily because I was the only member of the NYU faculty who had ever served as a supreme court judge. We concluded that, despite our doubts, we ought to make a serious effort to establish the program. In the fall of 1955 Dean Niles and I prepared a mimeographed prospectus explaining the plan, to be sent to all the state chief justices and the chief judges of the United States Courts of Appeals, with the request that they distribute it to their colleagues. It informed them that the first twenty qualified applicants would be accepted for the 1956 seminar. Attached to the prospectus was a list of some twenty topics that might be discussed in the seminar; applicants were asked to check the topics in which they were most interested.

Neither Dean Niles nor I felt comfortable about signing the letter inviting high court judges to come back to school. Judge Hamley solved that concern for us by agreeing to send out the prospectus over his signature from his chambers in Olympia (Washington). Nineteen applications came in, from sixteen state supreme court justices and three United States Court of Appeals judges. These nineteen were the student members of the first seminar, which met in July of 1956. Judicial faculty members included Justice Walter V. Schaefer (former Northwestern University law teacher) of the Illinois Supreme Court, Chief Judge Charles E. Clark (formerly Yale Law School dean) of the Second Circuit Court of Appeals, Judge Herbert F. Goodrich (former University of Pennsylvania Law School dean) of the Third Circuit, and Judge Hamley, who had in the meantime been named by President Eisenhower to the Ninth Circuit Court of Appeals. Several NYU Law School faculty members were assigned to special topics. I had been made Director, and also served as a faculty member. The judicial faculty members and I regularly participated in all seminar sessions, others only in the sessions for which they were responsible. Thus there were usually about 25 participants in each seminar session. Neither newspaper reporters nor visitors (despite numerous requests) were admitted. The sessions were altogether for the participating judges. This arrangement has been retained ever since.

At the close of the 1956 seminar the members were polled confidentially as to whether the program should be continued. The result was unanimous in favor of continuance, and the members undertook to encourage other judges on their courts to attend. The Law School committed itself to another seminar in 1957.

The faculty in 1957 and thereafter was changed to give greater emphasis to state courts. Chief Justices Roger J. Traynor of California and Frank R. Kenison of New Hampshire began long periods of service, as did Justice William J. Brennan, formerly of the New Jersey Supreme Court, now on the United States Supreme Court. Schaefer continued to serve for many years, as did Hamley.

The question is often asked: What topics do you discuss in these seminars? The topics discussed are selected by the members of each seminar anew, from a longer list of topics submitted to them in advance. It is true that most of the same subjects are selected each time, and we know beforehand pretty well what they will be. The outline of topics in one of the middle years is fairly typical:

1. JUDICIAL ADMINISTRATION BY APPELLATE COURTS (4 or 5 sessions)
    A. *Internal Administration of the Court.*
        (1) "Breaking in" the new judge (acquainting him with the internal history and practices of the court; specific orientation techniques).
        (2) Efficient and appropriate use of law clerks and other professional assistants: their selection, tenure, pay, and duties; use of clerks for criticism and analysis of draft opinions; relationships between judge and law clerk; special need for assistance in handling increasing mass of indigent prisoner appeals; assistance from other staff employees.
        (3) Efficient use of the court's own manpower: (a) relative efficiency of courts with different numbers of judges; (b) splitting the court into panels or divisions and correlating their work; (c) desirability

and value of intermediate appellate courts, allocation of functions between intermediate and top appellate courts; (d) use of retired judges, trial judges, commissioners as "extra judges."

(4) Form of appellate records (excessive and useless printing costs): (a) function of record and transcript; (b) abstracted material; (c) form, content and length of briefs.

(5) Status of appealed cases: (a) discretionary selection of cases for appellate review, selection of cases for full-dress opinions, memorandum and *per curiam* opinions; (b) advancing cases of special public importance, other bases for categorizing cases for special handling; (c) time interval between hearing case and handing down opinion, majority and dissents together; (d) withholding less important opinions from publication (the growing law library problem).

(6) Hearing and determining cases: (a) advance or later reading of briefs; (b) pre- and post-submission conferences; (c) oral argument, its function and value; function of questions directed to counsel; (d) the decision conference, when it should be held and how it should be conducted; (e) assignment of cases: when case should be assigned, method of assignment—by presiding judge, by various rotation techniques, or to "specialist judges," reassignments, same judge writing for both majority and dissent; (f) the opinion conference: pre-circulation of drafts and redrafts, avoidance of "one-man opinions"; (g) techniques for achieving improvements in brother judges' opinions; (h) keeping court's docket current.

(7) Extrajudicial conduct (misconduct): (a) outside

employment ("moonlighting"), important public service assignments, arbitration of labor disputes, relations with former clients and law partners; (b) political relationships, campaigning for office, non-judicial offices, (c) charitable fund-raising, membership on boards of charitable and other civic organizations; (d) private business relationships, investments, membership on corporate boards; (e) personal associations, contacts with lawyers, with prospective litigants, serving as character witness for friends, wife's associations; (f) laziness, inefficiency, failure to perform duties—what colleagues can do about this; (g) sanctions: impeachment, special courts or commissions on the judiciary; internal pressures.

(8) Disqualification for particular cases: relationships requiring it, justifying it; sound standards.

B. *Administration of an entire judicial system*: integrated court systems, court administrators, correlation with work of intermediate appellate divisions, assignment of trial judges, control over congested trial dockets, collection and publication of judicial statistics, checkup on actual performance of trial judges, the rule-making power as applied both to the internal operation of lower courts and to procedural law applicable throughout the judicial system, judicial councils and conferences.

C. *Appellate courts as supervisors of the legal profession*: integration of the bar or other control of bar organization, enforcement of codes of legal ethics, client-reimbursement funds or insurance, prevention of unauthorized practice of law, rule-making power as to law practice generally, control over disciplinary proceedings, admissions to the bar.

D. *External relationships*: with the legislature, on institutional matters and on law generally, with legislative councils and law revision commissions on improvement of the law, with the press in reporting cases and in public relations, with the law schools in all areas where their activities touch the work of the courts, with agencies administering programs of continuing legal education for bench and bar, with the variety of bar organizations, with other agencies.

2. NATURE AND FUNCTION OF THE JUDICIAL PROCESS (3 sessions)
   (a) The function of precedent under *stare decisis*, the problem without precedent, the creative function of appellate courts and the proper limits of this function, making "new law."
   (b) *Techniques of overruling and distinguishing*: narrow distinction of the new case which takes it outside the established rule, narrow distinction of the old case leaving little or nothing of the old rule; non-citation of a relevant precedent; outright overruling based on changed conditions, on the lessons of experience, on later authorities in opposition; are there other acceptable reasons for overruling; how is the problem different from that which confronts a legislature when it is considering a new statute?
   (c) *Prospective overrulings*: when is retroactivity unfair— compare property, contract and torts cases in terms of reliance on past decisions; techniques: the *caveat* device (*dictum* only), giving benefit of change to present litigant but prospectively only to others, setting future date to permit legislative action; effect of making courts readier to overrule old decisions; special appropriateness of this technique in constitutional overrulings.
   (d) *Sua sponte* consideration of unargued issues: request

that counsel brief the unargued issue; compare cases where issue was noted by counsel but inadequately understood or briefed; asserted right of counsel to conduct case in their own way with issue omitted.

(e) *Relation of court and legislature:* the separation of powers, what constitutes "judicial legislation," potentialities of statutory "interpretation"; statutes as precedents (reasoning by analogy from statutes, as from prior cases) sustaining results beyond the letter of the statute.

(f) *Unstated grounds for decision:* the confusion they produce, possible justification for, the process of discovering the unstated grounds, types of cases in which they may exist.

(g) *Judicial notice of socioeconomic facts which may affect decisions:* when affirmative evidence required, "Brandeis briefs," common observation of facts bearing on controversial socioeconomic theories, reliability of sources.

3. OPINIONS (4 or 5 sessions)

(a) *Critique of quality* of judicial opinions; efficient use of law clerks, library and other facilities, exchange of ideas and materials among members of court; advance reading of briefs; conference procedure, rewriting of draft opinions; concurrences and dissents, per curiams; printing of opinions, use and function of oral argument, delayed rendition of opinions.

(b) *Style in Judicial Writing:* Principles of effective writing; judicial writing as a branch of expository writing, special characteristics, values to be achieved; comparison of relevant literary styles; use of citations, quotations; footnotes.

(c) *What a Law Editor Looks for in Judicial Opinions:* e.g., what does a West Publishing Company editor find that is helpful, or difficult, in judicial opinions; suggestions for technical improvement in organization and writing.

(d) *What a Newswriter Looks for in Judicial Opinions*: Effective preparation of opinions from the point of view of a newspaper reporter who is a lawyer also.

4. STATE COURTS AND THE FEDERAL SYSTEM (2 sessions)
Implementation of "the law of the land," state and federal courts as a "national" judicial system, state judicial independence; Congressional power, "preemption," new U.S. Supreme Court decisions affecting state court problems in both civil and criminal areas, and in labor law.

5. SPECIAL AREAS OF APPELLATE REVIEW.
(a) *Appellate Review in Criminal Cases*: (3 sessions) Concept of "harmless error"; life sentence and death cases compared with others; finality of fact findings below, new issues on appellate review; insanity defense; enforcing minimum requirements of due process, such as right to counsel, prompt arraignment, etc.; search and seizure; post-conviction procedures (Uniform Act, habeas corpus, coram nobis, review in federal courts); double jeopardy; correlation with federal constitutional requirements generally.

(b) *Appellate Control over the Judge-Jury Relationship*: (1 session) Review of instructions; re-examination of evidence on appeal; form of transcripts and records; directions on remand.

(c) *Free Press and Fair Trial*: (1 session) What courts can do to guarantee both. Are controls over the press constitutionally permissible, and if so, desirable? Use of contempt power to discipline lawyers, both prosecutors and defense counsel, who attempt to influence the public and prospective jurors before and during trial.

Reversals because of prejudicial reports in news media.

(d) *Appellate Review of Decisions of Administrative Agencies*: (1 session) Workmen's compensation, licensing agencies, regulatory commissions, local and state tax collecting bodies, zoning appeals, separation of powers; etc.

6. SPECIAL AREAS OF GENERAL LAW.

(a) *Current Trends in Accident Law*: (2 sessions) Shifts in meaning of negligence, insurance as a practical factor, declining defense of contributory negligence, new types of "accidents" in a mechanistic society, "products liability"; procedural devices for changing substantive law; the changing concept of "proximate causation" and its corollaries; comparative handling of negligence under other legal systems, shifts from courts to administrative agencies for trial of claims.

(b) *New Developments in Conflict of Laws*: (1 or 2 sessions) New choice of law theories in the courts; expanding bases for judicial jurisdiction ("long-arm" statutes), narrowing federal constitutional limitations; current reevaluation of the field.

(c) *Appellate Control Over the Rules of Evidence*: (1 session) Deliberate overruling or modification of old rules; judicial promulgation of "Rules of Evidence"; the Uniform Rules.

(d) *Principles and Techniques of Statutory Interpretation*: (1 session) Analysis of rules and techniques as related to interpretation, uniform acts, application of interpretative standards to typical modern statutes; common law techniques applied to statutes.

(e) *Current Trends in Property Law*: (1 session) Trusts, wills, estates, future interests; recent statutory changes; current movements for simplification and reform of conveyancing practices; the conflict between "property rights" and "human rights."

For each of the topics, an advance reading list is distributed to all the members of the seminar, with the request that they read listed items before they meet together. At the seminar itself, a more comprehensive reading list is distributed to the members, with the suggestion that they can use it to pursue further the areas of study taken up during the seminar.

Judge Warren E. Burger, then on the District of Columbia Court of Appeals, was a member of the 1957 Seminar. Near the end of the session he asked me about the future of the program, and whether it was securely financed. I had to tell him that it was not, that questions had been raised as to the indefinite use of Law School funds for its support. He then asked for permission to approach an anonymous possible donor. Permission was readily granted. A continuing gift which, since 1958, has paid approximately half of the program's cost was the result. For years the donor asked not to be publicly identified, but eventually it came to be known that it is the West Publishing Company, the principal American law book publisher and the publisher of practically all appellate judicial opinions in the United States. The rest of the cost has been borne by the New York University Law School Foundation, and the program has been administered through the Law School's Institute of Judicial Administration. A second seminar, also two weeks in length but conducted for judges of state intermediate appellate courts, was established in the 1960s and is operated similarly by the same staff though with a separate judicial faculty. So far as is now known the two seminars will be continued indefinitely.

Though the seminars are primarily designed to serve the interests of judges on state and federal appellate courts in the United States and Puerto Rico, a limited number of judges from other nations have been invited to attend. Apart from the foreign judges' own learning experience, their active participation benefits our judges who are enabled to compare our rules and procedures with those employed in the foreign courts. The largest outside participation has been by Canadian judges. For more than twenty years two appellate judges from Canada have each year been members of the seminar. A committee of Canadians, alumni of the seminar, select the two. Four of those chosen have come from the Supreme Court of Canada, and two alumni subsequently became Chief Justices of Canada. All of the high courts of the Canadian provinces have been represented. Judges from the top courts of England, Ireland, the Philippines, and a number of other countries have taken part.

One facet of the Seminar program which apparently has much to do with its acceptance is its intimate informality. Seminar members are treated like intelligent human beings, no longer local gods. The judges, often with wives and families, and faculty judges as well, are housed together in law school dormitory rooms and apartments. They see each other constantly. Social events at the beginning and throughout each seminar give everyone an opportunity to know everyone else. Discussion groups are encouraged. Wives (or husbands) and families get to know each other quickly also, both through the social events and in the course of an early get-acquainted tour of the Greenwich Village area conducted by Helen Leflar, who has become a semiprofessional tour guide for that part of New York City. Finally, reunion parties for alumni, held each year at American Bar Association conventions, regularly bring a hundred or more together to renew old friendships.

If most American lawyers had been asked thirty years ago whether it would be possible to have appellate judges go back to law school and work hard at their studies there, they would have laughed at the idea. English and European lawyers and judges still don't believe it can happen. Yet it has happened. The Seminar program for American and Canadian judges has been amazingly successful, as a serious and hard-working effort at continuing legal education. At least half of all the appellate judges in the United States have participated in the program.

"Free-as-the-Birds Committee"

An interesting bit of legal history, still relevant today, goes back to 1970. It has to do with problems in the federal judicial system at all levels, particularly as they grow out of the tremendous increase in both civil and criminal cases filed in the district courts and the consequent increase in the number of appeals taken up to the Circuit Courts and ultimately to the Supreme Court. There was a fear that the quality of federal justice was breaking down under the overload. That fear has not lessened since 1970.

On December 15 of that year I received a phone call at Fayetteville from Chief Justice Warren Burger asking me to serve on an academic committee which he was appointing to study these problems as they related to civil litigation. I, of course, agreed to his request. The other members of the committee were Alexander M. Bickel of the Yale Law School faculty; Delmar Karlen of the Institute of Judicial Administration at New York University; Arthur R. Miller of the Harvard Law School; Dean Russell D. Niles of the New York University Law School; Herbert Wechsler, Director of the American Law Institute and Columbia professor of law; Jack B. Weinstein, United States district judge and former Columbia law professor; and Charles Alan Wright of the University of Texas Law School. Judge Alf Murrah, Director of the Federal Judicial Center, sat in on most of our sessions.

The Committee held its first meeting at the Federal Judicial

Center offices in Dolley Madison House in Washington on Saturday, January 30, 1971. The Chief Justice met with us. He explained that he was not asking us to make recommendations for change in the system; rather, he asked us to identify and briefly describe possible changes that might conceivably have merit, leaving it to others later to study our list of possibilities and make recommendations concerning them. Ours was to be an unpublicized study, without political or other limits on what we came up with. Before he left us, he suggested that we think of ourselves as the "Free-as-the-Birds Committee." Then, as he opened the door to depart, he named me chairman of the committee. I was surprised, but the other members acted as though they knew what he was going to do. At any rate, we went on from there.

Five months and five meetings later, and after uncounted reams of correspondence, we turned our report over to the Chief Justice. There are copies of this June 30, 1971, report in the University of Arkansas Law Library and, presumably, in the Supreme Court archives. It may be interesting to note some of the possibilities described in the report, partly to see what, if anything, has happened to them. Brief summaries will have to suffice:

1. Court time is wasted by lawyers who file non-meritorious cases or employ non-meritorious delaying procedures in cases that do have merit. Better means might be devised for quick sifting out of these valueless minutiae, and discouraging penalties might be imposed on lawyers responsible for them. Preliminary hearings and summary judgments are possible, but little has actually been accomplished in this area.

2. Appeals are often taken when there are no real grounds for appeal, perhaps merely to delay final judgments. A screening system operated by an appellate court's legal staff, with memoranda identifying and evaluating issues raised so that the court can render quick affirmances, perhaps without formal

opinions, on appeals in which no real error appears, is possible. Some courts are now employing systems of this sort.

3. Para-judicial personnel (court employees) can attend to some clerical and mechanical tasks that have traditionally been performed by the judges themselves. This is happening.

4. More speedy and accurate information retrieval concerning the status of cases and of a court's work generally can enable the court to proceed more efficiently. Maintenance of complete records and statistics by use of modern computers adapted to judicial needs, replacing old-style, handwritten record books, is increasingly common today.

5. Jury trials take longer than trials heard by a judge without a jury, and it is possible that fact-findings by an experienced judge are more reliable than jury findings. For these reasons jury trials have been largely eliminated in civil cases in English courts. A constitutional amendment would have to be adopted if this change were to occur in our federal courts, but there are some quasi-administrative matters to which the constitutional guaranty of jury trial does not apply yet which are now heard by juries.

6. Conduct of jury trials could be made more efficient. A six-member jury takes a little less time and is a little less expensive than a twelve-member one. The time used in selecting jurors could be shortened. The requirement of unanimous verdicts sometimes results in hung juries and retrials of entire cases. These difficulties are being dealt with. Six-member juries are allowed in many districts today. Verdicts by five-sixths jury vote are allowed in several states. Federal judges usually take over and shorten the questioning (*voir dire*) of prospective jurors. Alternate jurors are selected to replace regular jurors who may become incapacitated in the course of long trials, so that the trial will not have to be started all over again.

7. Formal pleadings and motion procedures, which govern the conduct of trials, can be further simplified. In early En-

glish courts pleading became a complex art, too often more important than the facts or even the law. American courts have pulled away from that attitude, but there is still room for improvement.

8. Modern audio-visual techniques can be employed in the courtroom. Witnesses otherwise unavailable, or whose personal presence on the witness-stand is unimportant, can be heard on videotape. Transcripts can be taped more reliably than taken in shorthand. The work of court reporters can be speeded up. This sort of modernization is actually occurring in some courts today.

9. Three-judge trial courts might be eliminated. Under federal law, three judges are called to preside at the original trial of certain types of cases, even with juries. This not only wastes judge time but often trial time as well. Realistically, only one judge can preside over a fact-finding trial. This law is unchanged, but the practice is diminishing.

10. It was suggested that the eleven (now twelve) separate U.S. Circuit Courts of Appeals might be combined into one. This would do away with the circuits, set up one central administrative office, make the judges assignable anywhere in the nation (though still appointed from local areas), still ordinarily sitting in three-judge appellate panels but with *en banc* hearings before five- or seven-judge national panels. Thus the Court of Appeals would become a national rather than a local court, with greater likelihood of uniform decision throughout the nation, largely relieving the Supreme Court of cases involving legal divergencies between circuits. The federal district courts could take care of local concerns insofar as these were relevant. This suggestion died forthwith. It has not been pursued.

11. The procedure for reassigning federal district judges from one district to another throughout the nation could be simplified. Such reassignments are needed when local district

judges are disqualified in particular cases, or physically incapacitated, when some district dockets are overloaded so that
the local judges cannot handle all the cases while the dockets
in other districts are light, and for other good reasons. Transfer
of judges within a circuit is not unduly difficult now, but transfer between circuits is cumbersome.

12. The relation between oral and written procedures could
well be reexamined. Time could be saved, without loss of
effective presentation, by replacing various papers, even including briefs and opinions as well as motions, with oral statements (which would be transcribed for the record). Con-
versely, testimony of some witnesses could be in writing, in
affidavit form, and documents or papers seen in advance by
opposing parties could be received in evidence without the
oral testimony of authenticating witnesses.

13. Lawyers could often do a better job of trying their cases.
Good trial lawyers need and possess special skills. They at least
need to understand the niceties of trial procedure. Ordinary
law study does not give them that specialized understanding. It
does not come automatically with admission to the bar, any
more than membership in the bar assures competence in a
dozen or three dozen other legal specialities in which limited
numbers of lawyers practice. The conduct of court business
would be improved if special training, as by internship under
competent practitioners, were required of all lawyers who undertake to try cases in the federal courts. This requirement
could be applied to new assistant United States attorneys handling government cases as well as to lawyers in private practice. It might be worthwhile for the federal judiciary to establish schools offering short courses (of at least a month's
duration, not just two days) for would-be federal trial lawyers.

14. There may be a need to establish different judicial procedures for particular classes of cases that are increasingly appearing in the federal courts. Some state courts have set up

separate "tracks" for types of cases with peculiar characteristics. The Federal Rules of Civil Procedure, first promulgated in the 1930s and regularly updated since then, provided for no such special handling of unique types of cases. A few areas involving separate bodies of law, such as bankruptcy and taxation, are directed to special tribunals, and there is a distinctive procedure developed for trying complex, protracted, and multidistrict litigation. The procedure was, and is, the same for all regular filings, however. In recent years large numbers of civil rights, reapportionment, antitrust, consumer protection and environmental cases, plus other classes of litigation that have common features, are being filed, and it might be possible to establish "tracks" employing procedures peculiarly appropriate to one or another or even each of these. Speedier than average disposition of cases placed on some of the "tracks" might be justified.

15. Some types of cases that are now being tried in federal courts might be handled instead by administrative agencies, just as the state workers' compensation commissions hear employee injury claims. Such claims under the Federal Employers Liability Act, the Federal Tort Claims Act, and similar statutes could be heard by a federal workers' compensation commission, and comparable administrative tribunals could be established to hear cases based on statutory claims in such areas as pollution control, auto safety standards, consumer protection, and other old and new fields of federal regulation that are now administered through the courts.

16. Many orders issued by presently existent administrative agencies are not self-operative, but have to be enforced by new proceedings brought in the courts. Thus reparation orders issued by the Interstate Commerce Commission or by the Secretary of Agriculture under the Perishable Commodities Act have to be enforced by civil suits for damages based on the or-

ders. They should be self-operative, with the burden of seeking judicial review placed on parties subject to the orders.

17. Under some old laws, double or even triple judicial review of some administrative agency orders is authorized. The order can first be attacked in federal district court, then that court's decision appealed to the circuit court of appeal, then even taken up by certiorari to the Supreme Court. Since there was a hearing held and record made before the administrative tribunal, one appeal on that record should be enough. Duplicate review in the district court and the circuit court is unnecessary and wasteful. Direct review in the court of appeals should suffice.

18. The law could go further than it does by way of encouraging the use of private arbitration and other extrajudicial agencies for the settlement of civil disputes. Areas in which such out-of-court settlement procedures might be established could include malpractice claims between doctors and patients, refund claims by customers against retailers, insurance claims, and landlord-tenant claims.

19. From time to time a volume of cases in some new or unique technical area may suddenly develop, or a new kind of complex legal problem may be presented by cases filed in scattered federal districts. A new expertise is called for, to assure wise decisions and sound uniform precedents in the new area. No permanent specialized courts, such as the Tax Court or bankruptcy judges, are needed, but a temporary specialization to establish the new body of law would be useful. This could be accomplished by an authorization to a central administrative office to assign sitting judges to a temporary bench to which all such pending cases would be assigned. After the precedents were settled the temporary bench could be disbanded.

20. The proper scope of federal jurisdiction, particularly as it affects the division of jurisdiction between state and federal

courts, is and always has been a controversial subject. Federal jurisdiction in cases in which the parties are citizens of different states (diversity jurisdiction) provides a great proportion of all cases heard in federal courts. It came into existence because of a fear, possibly now outdated, that state courts would favor their own citizens against "foreigners." If diversity jurisdiction were eliminated, as has been seriously proposed, the current overload on federal courts would be taken care of. But it would merely be transferred to state courts which, for the most part, are similarly overloaded.

It has also been suggested that many minor claims based on federal law, now heard in federal courts, could just as well be tried in state courts. That is probably true. But that again would merely relocate the overload. The ultimate question on both jurisdictional areas ought to be: Which courts can, or will, most fairly and conveniently exercise the jurisdiction? Undoubtedly some types of cases, especially those involving interests that are primarily local, could well be handled in state courts, but there are others including some tried now in state courts (multi-state and multi-party litigation) that really ought to be in the federal courts. The present allocation of jurisdiction is far from ideal. There could be some improvement in this area if control over federal jurisdiction, within fixed outer limits, were made a part of the Court's rule-making power, as with the Rules of Civil Procedure, instead of being left to Congress where there is only minimal interest in matters of judicial jurisdiction.

21. A criminal act will often give rise to civil liability to injured persons as well as to criminal liability. Or civil liability may be sustainable though a jury may conclude that the higher burden of proof required for a criminal conviction has not been met. The same evidence, however, is relevant on trial of both causes, and the dispostion of one of them may even be

relevant to the disposition of the other. The present theory is that the two matters are altogether separate, so that two complete and independent trials must be conducted. Consideration might be given to developing a procedure for determining both civil and criminal responsibility in one trial.

22. Long-range plans for needed changes in the judicial system should be studied and prepared in advance, so that modifications and improvements can be initiated with fair promptness when the need becomes urgent, rather than waiting until then to consider what might be done. The past tendency, a characteristically human (political) one, has been to wait until a crisis is upon us, then start seeking a solution. Most crises can be foreseen. That is true and for some time has been true of the increasing overload of federal cases. We even know, or at least statistics can be made available to tell us, the kinds of cases that are making up the increase, and the districts in which the bulk of them are being filed.

A system for prediction of workloads coupled with an analysis of workload capacity of sitting judges is essential if new judgeships are to be created when they are needed. Impending vacancies, occasioned by retirement or physical incapacity, should be brought to the attention of the appointing authority so that prompt appointments can be made and cases will not be left to lie idle on the docket because there are no judges to try them. The work of the judiciary cannot be likened to that of a huge business corporation, insofar as the decisional process, its principal function, is concerned. But the business model is appropriate where record keeping and organizational planning are involved. A judicial system needs to plan for next year's workload just as an expanding business needs to plan ahead. Well-managed businesses do this, as do most other public, as well as private, organizations and agencies. The judiciary in general does not, though it could. This is work that could be performed by a central administrative office vested with adequate authority and operating wholly apart from the courts' judgmental functioning.

Several of the possibilities enumerated in the report were not immediately feasible; some perhaps will never be. The report was turned over to the newly created and widely publicized Freund Committee, as a starting point for its more advanced deliberations. Three members of the "Free-as-the-Birds" group, Bickel, Niles and Wright, were on the new seven-man committee headed by Professor Paul A. Freund of the Harvard Law School. A part of the Freund Committee's ultimate report is summarized in 59 American Bar Assn. Journal 139 (Feb. 1973). It produced little in the way of affirmative change in the federal judicial system.

Correlation of record keeping has improved. Statistical information concerning court dockets and overall performance is far more complete now than formerly. Some internal procedural requirements have been simplified. Yet Chief Justice Burger, in 1985, pointed out again the fact that overload on his court has not lightened but has continued to increase rapidly. He proposed the temporary creation of a new Court of Appeals bench just below the Supreme Court to decide issues upon which there is conflict between circuits. The uncertain law on these issues ought to be clarified, but the Supreme Court must deny certiorari on cases presenting them because there are more important and urgent national issues that demand its attention. There is today little likelihood that the Chief Justice's proposal will be implemented. Congress has other problems on its collective mind. The specific difficulty toward which his proposal was directed still remains, as do comparable problems in the lesser federal courts.

The fact is that similar problems exist in many if not in most state court systems, and similar solutions are for them equally available—or unavailable. These are among the problems that are discussed in the sessions on judicial administration in our Appellate Judges Seminars. Occasionally a top court can do something about some of them, and when that is possible a study such as that made by the "Free-as-the-Birds Committee" may lead to tangible reforms. Too often it will merely cause judges to shake their heads and say "I wish we could do something about that!" The general public shares that wish.

Code of Judicial Conduct

Judges, like ministers of the gospel (and Caesar's wife) are supposed to conduct their lives on a higher ethical level than ordinary citizens. "A judge must avoid all impropriety and appearance of impropriety. He must expect to be the subject of constant public scrutiny."—Code of Judicial Conduct, Canon 2, Commentary (1972). He is not as free as are ordinary human beings. Among public officials in the United States, judges stand as a breed apart. They are more trusted and relied upon than legislators, more than most members of the executive branch of government. Greater finality is attached to their work. The courts are accepted as the ultimate arbiters of all kinds of disputes—in fact, of all disputes.

Most of us believe that this trust is deserved. At least we know of no better system for final determination of rights and wrongs, determinations which in our society have to be made somehow, by human beings, who should presumably be superior human beings. By calling them "judges" we both make them superior and assert that their superiority is justified. They are still, however, human beings, and as such, sometimes fall down on the job, morally and otherwise.

If we look back a century or two or three, both in this country and in ancestral England, we find that little was done about unethical judicial conduct. The response to it was thankfulness that it did not happen very often, almost thankfulness that it could usually be covered up when it did happen. There was no machinery for dealing with it. If a judicial culprit actually violated the criminal law he could be convicted of his crime and sent to prison, but for more than one reason that seldom resulted even in raw cases. And non-criminal conduct inappropriate for judges could not be reached by any known official sanctions. In fact, there were no official statements, no promulgated rules, formally describing and forbidding inappropriate conduct. The general view was that honorable judges not only abhorred wrongdoing but established standards for themselves so much higher than those prevailing in other groups that any ordinary set of rules would tend to lower rather than improve the levels of ethical performance.

It was not until 1922 that an American Bar Association (ABA) committee headed by William Howard Taft, former Circuit Judge and President, soon to be Chief Justice, was named to draft Canons of Judicial Ethics. The Code was completed in 1924, then formally approved by the Bar Association and in subsequent years adopted by the courts in most states. Yet the 1924 Code was so vague and general that it was almost useless as far as providing practically enforceable rules was concerned. It was too much like a bland sermon or Sunday School lesson; it did little by way of laying down clear rules or imposing tangible sanctions. The limited applicability of the criminal law remained as the principal legal remedy, one available only in cases of rank misconduct.

In 1969, almost fifty years later, the ABA concluded that the 1924 canons were outdated, that current conditions and problems required their revision with greater specificity and comprehensiveness. A 14-member committee was established in August, 1969, to draft the needed rules. The committee was headed by Chief Justice Roger J. Traynor of California, prob-ably the most respected judge in the United States at the time, and included other outstanding judges from all levels of the judiciary and well-known practitioners. Among the latter were two former ABA presidents, Whitney North Seymour, known as "the Dean of the New York bar," and Edward L. Wright of Little Rock, Arkansas. I was also named to the com-mittee. Other members were Justice Potter Stewart, U.S. Su-preme Court; Chief Judge Irving Kaufman, U.S. Court of Appeals, Second Circuit; Chief Judge Ed T. Gignoux, U.S. District Court, Maine; Justice James K. Grove, Colorado Su-preme Court; Judge Ivan Lee Holt, Circuit Court, Missouri; Judge George H. Revelle, Superior Court, Washington; Walter Armstrong, Jr., Memphis, Tennessee; E. Dixie Beggs, Pen-sacola, Florida; William L. Marbury, Baltimore, Maryland; and W. O. Shafer, Odessa, Texas. We met at once, then fre-quently, over a three-year period. The problems we worried about, and purported to decide, illustrate the difficulties inher-ent in laying down fixed rules identifying limits on ethical conduct. It is easy to frame moral generalities, but an exact dividing line at the outer edge of what common sense does or does not permit is hard to locate.

We issued a preliminary report in June, 1970, and sent cop-ies of it to 14,000 persons, then issued a tentative draft of "Canons" in May, 1971. From these two preliminary publica-tions we received more than 1000 responses suggesting partic-ular revisions and provisions, many of them from committees of state and local bar associations and other groups. In January, 1972, the committee presented its Proposed Final Draft to the ABA House of Delegates for public discussion and debate. A few further improvements were then made in the document. The final Code of Judicial Conduct was published in June, 1972, and formally promulgated by the ABA House of Dele-gates in August of that year. Since then it has been substantially adopted in all the fifty states, though a few modifications of controversial segments appeared in a dozen or more of the states.

What provisions were particularly controversial? One addressed the question of what financial interests ought to disqualify a judge from sitting on a case. The answer was that any such interest, "however small," is a basis for disqualification. All parties to a case may, however, waive the disqualification, so that the expense and delay involved in securing outside judges, especially in rural districts with only one or two judges on the court, can be avoided if the parties trust the sitting judge—as they often do.

Another provision had to do with what is, and is not, permissible extrajudicial conduct for judges. They "may write, lecture, teach and speak on nonlegal subjects" and "concerning the law, the legal system, and the administration of justice," and a judge may engage in other outside activities which "do not detract from the dignity of his office or interfere with the performance of his duties." Judges may participate in civic and charitable activities but should not solicit funds for even the worthiest of them; no prospective contributor should be subjected, nor fear that he is being subjected, to the kind of pressure that a judge might conceivably exert. "Neither a judge nor a member of his [immediate] family . . . should accept a gift, bequest, favor, or loan" from anyone except in very limited and specifically enumerated circumstances. Judges should not accept appointment to governmental committees or commissions established to deal with matters outside the legal system, nor may they work as arbitrators. Obviously they must not practice law. They should regularly file public reports setting forth all compensation received for any extrajudicial activity, and such compensation must not exceed that which would normally be paid to a non-judge for the same services.

A provision that has not been adopted in some states bars any judge from serving "as an officer, director, manager, advisor, or employee of any business," including banks and other financial institutions. There are businesses whose patrons include lawyers and prospective litigants who seek the favor of judges. This can be true even of a shoe store. A judge actively holding himself out as being engaged in or profiting from a business can be charged with suggesting to persons who might come before his court that they would do well to patronize his firm rather than a competitor's. Judges who would disdain such partiality are nevertheless subjected to snide comments and are made to look bad before the public when they have such business interests. There are other types of investment available to them. Most judges and most states have agreed that this prohibition is a sound one, despite some protests. For example, a group of Louisiana judges in 1980 asked the Supreme Court of Louisiana to amend the canons by deleting the prohibition against judges serving as officers or directors of financial institutions. Chief Justice John Dixon asked me to present the ABA view on the matter at an informal hearing before the Court on December 5, 1980, in New Orleans. On July 2, 1981, the Court by a 4-3 vote denied the request to delete. "A judge must avoid all impropriety and appearance of impropriety. He must expect to be the subject of constant public scrutiny. He must therefore accept restrictions on his conduct that might be viewed as burdensome by the ordinary citizen and should do so freely and willingly."

Political relationships cause more concern than almost any other facet of a judge's life, particularly in states that do not employ a system of merit selection. Political considerations can be minimized, but assured avoidance of them has not been achieved. Perhaps it never will be. But a judge who becomes a candidate for non-judicial office must vacate his judgeship immediately. He must not publicly endorse candidates for public offices. And when he is a candidate for election to a judgeship he "should not himself solicit or accept campaign funds," and when a committee does this for him: "Unless the candidate is required by law to file a list of his campaign contributors, their names should not be revealed to the candidate." Needless to say, this is a proscription that is applied to no candidates except for judgeships.

There is another provision in the canons as to which an interesting dispute—interesting to me, at least—developed. The provision has to do with the means by which a judge may study up on unfamiliar legal problems presented in cases pending before him. It goes without saying that judges, both trial and appellate, have to do this all the time. No human being can know all the law, and counsels' briefs are not always complete or completely reliable. The narrow question is whether it should be permissible for a judge, in the course of his research, to consult an expert in a specific field of law, such as a law teacher who specializes in that subject in his law school teaching. Certainly the judge is free to consult that expert's written books and articles in legal periodicals; he is expected to do that. That is why he has a law library. But Judge Traynor announced a view that to consult the expert himself, out of the presence of counsel and without giving counsel an opportunity to respond, violates the adversary character of the common law judicial process and should be prohibited. I disagreed. Judge Traynor's view prevailed, however, by a fairly close vote, and is included in Canon 3A(4) which bars a judge from discussing problems in a case with anyone except judicial personnel. If the judge wants to avail himself of another's knowledge of the law, let the judge invite the expert to file an *amicus curiae* (friend of the court) brief.

I suppose that my contrary reaction was based largely on my own past experience. I have filed *amicus* briefs, but only a few times. They were somewhat expensive, and were a lot of trouble. I filed them only in cases about which I felt strongly. I would not go to that trouble and expense for a case in which I had no interest beyond the fact that some judge wanted, as he would say, "to pick my brains." And the fact is that over the last half-century I have been asked by judges both in Arkansas and from a dozen other states, a hundred times, to explain conflict of laws and other legal perplexities that they said were bothering them in pending cases. I had no sense of partaking in unethical judicial conduct since I did not even know who were the litigating parties, nor did I care.

My past experience went even further in the same direction. While I was a Justice on the Arkansas Supreme Court I was assigned to write the opinion in a complex case possibly involving contingent or shifting future interests, allegedly created many years ago, in real property. My knowledge in that legal area was negligible, as was, I fear, that of my colleagues on the Court. I discussed the issues with my colleagues, studied all the cited cases, read several chapters from books in the library, and still was not satisfied that I understood or had even found the relevant law. I came up to Fayetteville for the next weekend, visited for three hours with Ed Meriwether who taught Future Interests at the Law School, "picked his brain" for the whole time without identifying the parties to the case or their counsel. Then I sat down and wrote the opinion, reasonably confident that I knew what I was doing. The Court approved it unanimously.

Was my conduct unethical? That possibility did not even occur to me in 1950. Yet in 1971 I saw Judge Traynor's point, though I disagreed. And now, in 1984, the prohibition is part of the Code of Judicial Conduct in Arkansas and in most other American states. What does that prove? Well, it at least proves that issues sometimes have to be decided one way, and the decision has to be accepted even though there was room for difference of opinion and it was not decided my way. But it does not prove that the decision was wrong.

It is not easy to formulate clear conclusions regarding sound practice in drafting rules to control conduct. There are situations for which it is desirable to have hard and fast clear rules covering all possible facts, marginal ones included. The exercise of immature and clouded judgments may need to be controlled. This is most apt to be true for conduct as to which ethical standards are so clear that there is little room for argument about them, or ethical standards which are substantially irrelevant to the available choices. When ethical requirements are vague or marginal, however, and there is no other justification for a rigid rule, a broader and less exact one may be preferable. Detailed prohibitions that seem irrelevant are likely to be ignored.

There is a related matter which should be mentioned here. This is that a code of conduct can be flouted by the few "bad guys" who choose not to obey it voluntarily, unless there is some official procedure set up for enforcement and punishment of violations. The Code contains no such procedures. It is not self-executing. In 1975 a committee of the American Bar Association's Appellate Judges Conference was set up to draft, and in 1978 it promulgated a final draft, of Standards Relating to Judicial Discipline and Disability Retirement. Chief Justice Duke Cameron of Arizona was overall chairman of the committee and Chief Justice Ben F. Overton of Florida was chairman of the subcommittee on Judicial Discipline. I served on that subcommittee also. Other members were Justice John Todd, Minnesota Supreme Court; Judge Florence Peskoe, New Jersey; and Roland Nachman, Montgomery, Alabama. The then ABA President, Shepherd Tate of Memphis, Tennessee, sat with the subcommittee at times. One of its two-day sessions held at Fayetteville, Arkansas, may have been

the only American Bar Association committee meeting ever
held in that beautiful city.

A specific but comprehensive procedure for enforcement,
with punitive sanctions prescribed, was prepared. So far as I
know, it has not been adopted word for word in any state, but
most states, including Arkansas, have by Supreme Court rule,
or otherwise, established enforcement procedures which to
varying extents follow the 1978 subcommittee draft. The investigation and hearing procedures usually assure maximum
due process to accused judges, and the penalties imposed range
all the way from a slap on the wrist (reprimand) for minor in-
fractions, to suspension without pay and removal from office.

It might be difficult to prove that the conduct of today's
American judges has risen to ethical standards substantially
higher than those which prevailed a century or even a half
century ago, but it is certainly true that the standards are
clearer today, better known to the citizenry, to the bar, and to
the judges themselves, and more explicitly enforced.

An interesting sidelight connected with problems of judicial ethics developed in 1969, while we were working on the
new Code of Judicial Conduct. Justice Abe Fortas had recently resigned from the United States Supreme Court after it
was revealed that he had received large payments for services
rendered to certain law schools. It had been suggested that
these payments to him came indirectly from persons interested
in his work as a Supreme Court Justice. President Johnson's
nomination of him for the position of Chief Justice brought
these criticisms into the open, with the result that he not only
did not become Chief Justice but resigned as Associate Justice.

Justice William Brennan had served two weeks each summer for about ten years as a member of the faculty of the Appellate Judges Seminars at New York University Law School,
receiving payments covering little more than his expenses
each year. He felt the public reaction to the Fortas affair quite

keenly and late in May of 1969 he telephoned me that, though he had already agreed to serve during the summer of 1969 and had been assigned the topics on which he was to lead panel discussions, he was withdrawing from membership on the faculty. He simply concluded, so he told me, that the current public attitude required him to give up "every outside activity except my church. I will not give that up."

An equally interesting incident occurred with reference to Judge Warren E. Burger, then on the United States Court of Appeals for the District of Columbia. He was nominated by the new President to serve as Chief Justice. There was considerable opposition from certain quarters. I realized that since he had been on the Appellate Judges Seminar faculty questions might be raised concerning payments he had received in connection with that service while he was a judge on the Court of Appeals. I checked the records of payments to him, and phoned him to make sure that my records checked with his as to the amount he had received over the seven years that he had participated as a faculty member, after his student membership in the Seminar. The figures for the seven years were as follows:

1961—	$ 91.50	1966—	240.00
1962—	116.50	1967—	300.00
1964—	82.00	1968—	300.00
1965—	566.94		

They totaled $1,696.94, and the record showed that he had each year turned in a statement of expenses incurred reflecting these figures. He stated that he was quite willing for the facts to be known. I put a memo showing the figures in my pocket and carried it with me so that I could answer any inquiries that might come from investigators.

Sure enough, while I was in Little Rock on May 29, 1969,

presiding at the Constitutional Convention, I got a phone call from Drew Pearson of the Washington Merry-Go-Round asking about payments made to Burger. From Pearson's language it was evident that he was looking for something that would damage Burger's candidacy for the chief justiceship. I gave him the figures in detail, year by year. He seemed disappointed. He grasped at the total figure, however, and said, "Maybe I can make use of that."

I did not think it was fair to Judge Burger to create the impression that he had received nearly $1,700 improperly. I immediately got in touch with the local United Press reporter at Little Rock and gave her the same information, with a full explanation. She put it on the wires at once and it was published throughout the United States. There was nothing left upon which Drew Pearson could attack the Burger appointment. That was the end of that incident. And Chief Justice Burger, unlike Judge Brennan, has continued to serve as a faculty member, a few days nearly every summer, with the Appellate Judges Seminars, with reimbursement for his expenses only. His view is in keeping with what is now Canon 4 of the Code of Judicial Conduct, that "a judge is in a unique position to contribute to the improvement of the law, the legal system, and the administration of justice," and that it is in the public interest for him to pursue that opportunity.

War Relocation Authority (WRA)

One of the most controversial programs undertaken by the federal government during World War II was the evacuation of practically all persons of Japanese ancestry, both nationals of Japan and American citizens, about 110,000 men, women and children, from the mainland's west coast to relocation centers

scattered throughout the area west of the Mississippi River. *
This evacuation had been ordered by the Western Defense
Command of the United States Army. Much has been written
concerning the social and political wisdom, or unwisdom, of
the evacuation, its constitutionality, and the validity of the de-
tention that was involved in it and in the subsequent operation of the relocation centers. The majority decision of the
United States Supreme Court in *Korematsu v. United States*,
323 U.S. 214 (1944), sustaining the evacuation, has been severely criticized.

My part in the agency's work from 1942 through much of
1944 had to do not with the validity of the program but with
the operation of law, both civil and criminal, within the ten
relocation centers—two in Arkansas, two in Arizona, two in
California, and one each in Utah, Colorado, Wyoming, and
Idaho. My responsibility was for legal services and what might
be called "municipal government" within them, plus their relations with county and state authorities in the areas within
which the centers were located. We had, at each, a Caucasian
"project attorney" who, at most of the centers, was assisted by
evacuee lawyers who helped him with such routine matters as
making wills, probating decedents' estates, securing divorces,
and the like, as well as with more obviously governmental
tasks connected with maintenance of law and order.

Nearly all the immense amount of work involved in the day-
to-day operation of the centers—cooking, serving meals, policing, farming, maintenance of grounds, dozens of other jobs—
was done by the evacuees themselves. They were "employed"
for this work at $13, $16, or $19 per month. Evacuee law-
yers were paid the top rate of $19 a month. Like most of their

---

* Parts of this comment are copied from an article, Ferguson and Leflar, The Law
of the War Relocation Centers, 14 Geo. Washington L. Rev. 564 (1946). Ed Ferguson, one of the authors, was the principal attorney (Solicitor) for this wartime
agency, and I was Assistant Solicitor.

fellow-evacuees, they preferred to work rather than stay idle, despite the negligible pay.

Fully accredited schools were established for all the children at each center, with both Caucasian and evacuee teachers. They were on the whole good schools.

A principal purpose of the War Relocation Authority (as distinguished from the Western Defense Command) was to relocate the bulk of evacuees into useful jobs elsewhere in the nation. The Defense Command did not allow them to return to their west coast homes until after the war ended, but by that time nearly all the employable ones had left the camps to take jobs of one kind or another in the middle or eastern sections of the United States. Many of the young men had joined the nation's armed forces for service in the European theatre. By war's end a probable majority of the original 110,000 were no longer in the centers. The others left as soon as they could.

Within a year or two the war relocation centers became ghost towns, then reverted to farms and open land, but for three years they had been small cities of a special kind. It could never be said that they were normal American communities. The crude buildings and desolate surroundings, the barbed wire and the sentries, the resentments and suspicions, the clash of loyalties and cultures, and the all-pervading sense of insecurity were everywhere. The centers certainly were not desirable communities. Government controls sapped individual initiative; normal income opportunities were denied; frustrations developed; assimilation into the American culture was retarded at a time when, for others, it was being hastened.

About all that can be said for the program is that the Relocation Authority bent its major efforts toward resettlement of the evacuees throughout the United States as the only temporary solution to the problem. Management policies were shaped in such a way as to minimize the unhealthy aspects of institutional living as much as possible. The evacuees were not treated as prisoners of war, though some of them undoubtedly felt as though they were, at least until they were told to leave the centers and live on their own with jobs in Chicago, Cincinnati, or on a New Jersey vegetable farm like one they had been forced to abandon in California.

Public reaction to the operation of the ten centers was mixed. Many critics thought they should be operated as prisoner of war camps. Some politicians made a public issue of this, charging that we were "coddling the Japs." A Senatorial investigation ensued. I will never forget that I was assigned to go along with the investigating committee, headed by Senator A. B. (Happy) Chandler of Kentucky, which was directed to check up on the "coddling" at the centers. My job was to see that the facts were fairly presented to the committee. Senator Chandler, after the first one or two visits, helped me in this effort, though some other Senators, showing up only occasionally, persisted in talk about "aiding the enemy" and "anti-American bureaucrats." In the end the investigation fizzled out when the newspapers ceased to give space to reports of its hearings. If a final committee report to the Senate was ever made I did not see it.

The War Relocation Authority could at least take credit for moving sensibly into a bad situation and for the most part preventing maladjustment of a demoralized people. It was the Western Defense Command, supported in its decisions by the nation's top military authorities, that caused the American Japanese to be evacuated and detained as they were. The majority of American citizens at the time had no strong feelings about the rightness or wrongness of evacuation. They simply accepted what the military prescribed. Recognition of the program's wrongness, along with efforts to ameliorate what could not be terminated, was WRA policy. It was WRA policy long before it became American political policy, let alone military policy.

Uniform State Laws

Life in the United States would be simpler if there were one set of laws, and one only, to regulate most matters throughout the entire nation. Instead we have fifty sets of state laws plus District of Columbia law—51 different sets of laws, each governing transactions legally connected with its geographical area, along with federal law that overrides state and District laws on a variety of matters not always clearly defined. This multiplicity of laws inevitably gives rise to confusions. The conduct of a traveler from California to New York may be governed by a dozen different systems of law before his trip ends, perhaps in less time than a single day.

A century ago, or two centuries ago when our federalism was devised by the founding fathers, this multiplicity of laws created fewer problems than it does today. Travelers moved about, but less readily than today, and less swiftly. Commercial transactions did cross state lines then, but less often and on a smaller scale. The "states' rights" concept, designed to retain a maximum of legal authority over facts and happenings in their own locality, worked most easily in the days when facts and happenings as well as socioeconomic (political) attitudes toward them were more localized than they are now. Moralities were to some extent local too, and moralities often became part of the law.

Not that there is but one morality in America now, nor any commerce that does not cross state lines, nor political preferences for local laws as against federal ones. The states' rights slogan is still a potent one, not just for its persistent loudness but for good-sense reasons that frequently justify it. Law imposed from a distance may be cumbersome and expensive, even irrelevant and inappropriate. Homemade law can more accurately reflect community needs and standards. That is why we leave some kinds of regulation to municipal ordinances. Other areas of regulation are best left to legislation by larger units of government. On patently national and international matters national law is necessary. As long as the United States consists of states (which we can wish will be forever, though history denies the possibility) the structure of state government must be for each state to decide, however similar all of the fifty turn out in fact to be. There are other matters that are of necessity peculiar to one or only a few states: Alaska has some unique problems; a dozen oil-producing states and twenty coastal ones have problems different from those of Kentucky and Nebraska. Certainly there are problems special to Arkansas. Some of these in each state involve national concerns as well; some do not.

A great mass of American law relates to human, including corporate, activities and interests that are neither peculiar to a locality nor national in their effects. This mass of law constitutes the bulk of what lawyers advise clients to follow in their personal and business transactions or seek to apply while representing their clients in litigation. Some of it the clients are able to understand and apply without consulting their lawyers; some of it they may misapply. It is the law governing contracts, wills, the sale of goods (eggs, tractors, drugs, and a thousand other things), personal and property injuries, most crimes and punishments, titles to land and chattels, the organization and conduct of most but not all corporations, defamations, administration and distribution of estates, divorces and their consequences, employer-employee relationships, allocating space in condominiums, spitting on the sidewalk, and some hundreds of other important and less important matters. In the United States, the differing laws of the fifty states and the District of Columbia, occasionally modified by federal constitutional and statutory requirements, control all these matters.

Could these be equally well controlled by single national laws, so that the law would be the same in all the states? In most modern nations these matters are governed by national law. Our system is exceptional. Theirs is simpler. Ours makes more business for lawyers, and thus supports more lawyers and their satellites in proportion to total population than can find livelihoods in other lands. There is room for difference of opinion as to how great an advantage that is. Even among lawyers there are many who seek a better or less expensive system.

Enactment of uniform state laws can do much to lessen the multi-state confusion, while at the same time it preserves the historic states' rights tradition. Uniform laws are offered to the states, not forced upon them. No state enacts a uniform law save through the act of its own legislature. The state's own self-interest provides the principal pressure for enactment. Yet the result can be almost the same as a national law.

The independent sovereignty, or semi-sovereignty, of each of the fifty states is basic to our system of government. Apart from the limited authority conferred by the Constitution upon the federal nation, the individual states are self-governing, and make their own law. The great bulk of law within the United States is state and local law.

When people cross state lines or engage in business or other transactions across state lines, problems inevitably arise. They are conflict of laws problems. Which state's law governs their two-state or multi-state transactions? Could the conflicting laws of two or more states connected with a transaction be somehow coordinated? How could the parties know in advance what the governing law would be, and plan their transactions accordingly? What if they did not think at all about the potential conflict of laws when they engaged in their transactions?

From the beginning of our Republic, state lines were not like the boundaries of nations. They were not guarded. People traveled freely, without passports. We were at first thirteen then eventually fifty states, but one nation within which we traveled freely and engaged in business, both as individuals and corporations, where we pleased. Federal laws governing some aspects of interstate commerce were enacted from time to time, but they covered—or cover in 1984—only a small fraction of all the legal issues that arise in noncommercial transactions. As the years passed, more and more activities and interests of American citizens became less and less isolated within their home states. Citizens even changed their home states more often. The inconvenience inherent in differing state laws became constantly worse.

Yet there was no serious thought of doing away with state government and state law. The Constitution two centuries ago located the reservoir of governmental power in the several states. States' rights is a part of our established political theory, and we are not about to abandon it. Can state laws be adjusted so that we can live with the theory?

That is the major function of uniform state laws. When the first meeting of the National Conference of Commissioners on Uniform State Laws gathered at Saratoga, New York, in 1892, the problem was just being perceived by a few farsighted juristic thinkers and worriers. Their thoughts and worries were centered largely on business transactions that were beginning to be conducted on a national scale.

Their first major work was the Negotiable Instruments Law, promulgated in 1896 and subsequently adopted by the legislatures of every one of the states. This enabled the makers, endorsers, and holders of promissory notes, bonds, and other commercial paper to know what their rights and obligations on the papers were, whether in Arkansas, New York, California, or anywhere in between. Most of the other early uniform acts were similarly in the business area, since it was there that the vagaries of variant laws were most publicly noticeable. The Warehouse Receipts Act and the Sales of Goods Act were promulgated in 1906, the Stock Transfer Act in 1909, the two acts governing partnerships in 1914 and 1916, the Fraudulent Conveyances Act in 1918, the others affecting business matters in intervening years.

Not all uniform acts were in the business law area, however, even in the early years. The Desertion and Nonsupport Act, promulgated in 1910, dealt with obviously troublesome practical problems in the course of which two or more states might be involved in a single case. Its replacement, the Uniform Reciprocal Enforcement of Support Act (sometimes called the Skipping Pappy Law) prescribes procedures whereby two states—the state in which an abandoned spouse and children reside and the state where the "skipping" husband and father is found—can cooperate in compelling the latter to make support payments. It is interesting that this act or its equivalent became law in every state in the Union in the 1950s, more quickly than any other Uniform Act ever drafted. It has since been updated somewhat, but in its basic form it is law in every state today.

The most comprehensive act ever sponsored by the Commissioners on Uniform State Laws is the Uniform Commercial Code, commonly called the UCC, now law in every state except Louisiana which because of its French law background has adopted only parts of it. This Code revised and incorporated all the earlier commercial law acts and added provisions covering just about all other kinds of commercial transactions, including those by banks.

Work on the UCC was begun in the early 1940s, discontinued during the latter part of World War II, resumed in 1945, then offered for state adoption in 1952. Adoption was slow at first. Further research and redrafting occurred, and improvements in the Code were made in succeeding years. An improved draft came out in 1958. I recall that Joe Barrett, Ed Wright, and I appeared before a joint session of the Arkansas Senate and House of Representatives in January 1961, ad-

vocating its enactment in our state. Questions asked of us by
the legislators showed that few of them knew what it was all
about, but it was duly enacted nevertheless. There was confidence in the Uniform Laws organization, nearly everybody
who did understand it said we needed it, and the rest of the
states were rushing to adopt it. No state has repealed it. Later
amendments, updating particular UCC sections, have been
approved by the Conference of Commissioners from time to
time, and adopted by the legislatures of this and other states.
As a result, commercial law is substantially uniform throughout the United States, even though it is the law of more than
fifty different states, territories, and other units of American
government. In fact, it has also been accepted by the federal
courts as governing the federal government's business transactions that are not covered by other federal laws.

Nearly 100 different uniform acts on as many different legal
topics are available for state enactment. They deal with adoption of children, anatomical gifts, arbitration of private and
corporate disputes, attendance of out-of-state witnesses in lawsuits, child custody cases, class actions, common trust funds,
comparative fault in torts, condominiums, consumer credit and
sales practices, criminal extradition, disposition of unclaimed
property, eminent domain, rules of evidence, gifts to minors,
land transactions, the metric system, motor vehicle accident
reparation, planned communities, post-conviction procedure
in criminal cases, the probate of decedents' estates, securities
transactions, simultaneous deaths, and dozens of other problem areas in the law. More are promulgated each year. Some
have been enacted in nearly all the states, others in only a few
states, but all are available to all the states when the need for
uniformity regardless of state lines, as against persisting conflicts between differing state laws, comes to be more acutely
recognized.

I became one of the three Arkansas Commissioners on Uniform State Laws, whose members serve without pay, in 1945. My old college classmate, Joe Barrett of Jonesboro, had been named to one of the three places by Governor Ben Laney two years previously, then Joe persuaded the Governor to name Ed Wright (who later became President of the American Bar Association) and me to the other two places when they became vacant. Joe was from the beginning one of the most effective and respected Commissioners, and he served as President of the Conference in the 1950s, as did his son-in-law and law partner, Jack Deacon, also of Jonesboro, a good many years later.

My own work in the Uniform Laws Conference has been continuous and interesting (after twenty years and six gubernatorial appointments I was named a Life Member, so that I no longer needed to be reappointed). My first assignment was in 1946, as chairman of a committee to draft an act to simplify the enforcement of judgments already validly rendered in sister states, and therefore entitled under the Constitution to "full faith and credit" in every other state. The result was the Uniform Enforcement of Foreign Judgments Act, promulgated in 1948. Arkansas was the first state to enact it. Nearly all the states today employ either this act, its Uniform Laws successor, or some equivalent procedure facilitating the quick and inexpensive enforcement of final sister state judgments. Others that I have worked on include the Post-Conviction Procedure Act, the Unclaimed Property Acts, a Model Medical Examiners (autopsies) Act, a Survival and Death Act (torts law), and an act governing the effect of out-of-state statutes of limitations. The latter was promulgated in 1982. The variety of subjects upon which uniform acts are drafted assures a valuable kind of continuing legal education for every Commissioner.

There is one other Uniform Laws experience that I want to

mention. At one time I was named chairman of a committee on Uniform Interpretation of Uniform Laws. This was important because incorrect interpretation of uniform laws completely defeats the goal of uniformity. Someone arranged for me to speak to the Conference of Chief Justices, at their annual meeting, on my "uniformity of interpretation" topic. I was pleased by the opportunity, because the chief justices can do just about as much as anybody to prevent unsound statutory interpretations, and most of my distinguished auditors were quite sympathetic with their questions and incidental remarks. But there was one elderly C. J., from a state adjacent to Arkansas, who would have none of it. He spoke up several times, purporting to ask questions (as is the custom of appellate judges) but actually making flat statements. His view was that uniform laws, of which "thank God, my state has adopted very few," are essentially "communist in character," because they undermine the basic principle of "states' rights" which is central to the American way of life. I don't know for sure what this little incident, now nearly a quarter of a century past, tended to prove. At least it showed me that my legal analyses were not always convincing. Perhaps it also shows why it is often not easy to modernize either our law or our judicial system, though it is revealing that his state has, since his departure, enacted a considerable number of the uniform acts, including the Uniform Commercial Code.

I still think that uniform state laws, uniformly interpreted, constitute the best available means of preserving the traditional political concept of state's rights in the United States. Their enactment enables the states to retain sensible control over matters whose diversity among state laws would almost surely produce a popular demand for federal laws. I am convinced that my participation, now for nearly forty years, in the drafting and promulgation of uniform state laws has been a truly worthwhile activity. The legal areas within which uniform acts have up to now been made available to state legislatures, however, are just a beginning. It is impossible to foresee today all the areas in which America's society will ask that governing laws not change each time a state line is crossed.

The law of conflict of laws is a fascinating subject for legal study. It has been my favorite field in all the law. But to the ordinary citizen whose interests cross state lines, it may seem to be nothing but an unmitigated nuisance. Uniform state laws can mitigate this nuisance.

Arkansas Laws and Constitutions

My first active involvement in efforts to improve my home state's law and legal system began in the early 1930s. As with other such efforts, there was room for difference of opinion about whether "improve" was the right word.

CRIMINAL PROCEDURE   In 1934, at the annual meeting of the Arkansas Bar Association, Abe Collins of DeQueen as chairman of the Committee on Law and Law Reform presented a report pointing out many defects in the state's criminal procedures, specifying 21 areas in which changes were needed, and memorializing the Governor to name a citizens group to draft the needed changes. The Committee report was adopted by the Association. Later in the year Governor J. M. Futrell, complying with the Association's request, created an honorary body called the Arkansas Criminal Law Reform Commission, and named as its members Abe Collins, Circuit Judge W. J. Waggoner of Lonoke, W. G. Dinning of Helena, Judge B. E. Isbell of DeQueen and myself. My inclusion on the Commission was due to the influence of Marion Wasson, gubernatorial adviser and old Northwest Arkansas friend, who knew that Criminal Law was then one of my law school teaching subjects. When the Commission met, Collins was named chairman and I was named secretary.

After extensive study of the statutes of other states and of the American Law Institute's Model Code of Criminal Procedure, and much correspondence with experienced persons and groups outside of Arkansas, the Commission presented to the 1935 General Assembly a proposed constitutional amendment and two bills, one to regulate sentencing, punishment and executive clemency after conviction, the other to simplify judicial procedure in criminal trials generally. All three measures were introduced and public hearings were held on them, but the two legislative bills were cut to pieces and not considered on their merits. The constitutional amendment was submitted by the legislature for vote by the people, with two clauses: (1) permitting prosecutions to be initiated by informations signed by prosecuting attorneys as well as by grand jury indictment, and (2) authorizing the legislature to put prosecuting attorneys on a salary instead of a fee basis.

Though pleased by submission of the proposed constitutional amendment, we felt that our principal program had suffered decisive defeat in the legislature. We so reported to the 1935 meeting of the Arkansas Bar Association, which then committed itself by resolution to support an initiated act, to be drafted by the Commission, embodying as much of the original reform program as it deemed feasible.

The measure which thereafter was known as Initiated Act No. 3 of 1936 was then drawn up. For policy reasons, and to avoid excessive length, none of the bill to regulate sentencing, punishment and executive clemency was included, and only about three-fifths of the general procedure bill. The necessary signatures for initiation were secured (Governor Futrell helped by instructing State Highway Department employees to circulate the petitions for us) and a vigorous campaign was sponsored by the Commission to secure adoption of both the constitutional amendment and the act. In the November election both were approved by overwhelming majorities, and both became effective in January, 1937.

For the next several years, my concern with new law was largely limited to a series of articles prepared every two years for the Arkansas Press Association, for publication in the state's newspapers, "impartially" analyzing the referred and initiated acts and constitutional amendments that would appear on the state's biennial election ballot. Despite purported impartiality, it was inevitable that objectivity at times revealed either soundness or asininity in some of the measures discussed.

REVISION OF THE STATUTES   The next major job with reference to Arkansas law came with enactment by the legislature of Act 50 of 1945, creating an Arkansas Statute Revision Commission with the duty of preparing and publishing a new digest of the state's existing statutes. The Dean of the Law School and the Attorney General were made ex-officio members of the Statute Revision Commission, and three other members were appointed by the Supreme Court: Cecil R. Warner, Fort Smith; Charles W. Norton, Forrest City, and Paul Jones, Texarkana. At the first meeting of the Commission, I, then Dean of the Law School, was named Chairman. Under Act 50, the Commission was directed to select a "person, firm or corporation experienced in editing and publishing law books, to be known as the Digester of statutes" to do the editorial work on the Digest. The act provided that after the editorial work was completed a separate contract should be made on competitive bids for the manufacturing job. I wrote letters to all the well-known law book publishing houses in the United States, on the assumption that only such houses satisfied the statutory requirement. Replies were received from most of them though several, including the West Publishing Company, indicated that they would not be able to bid on the contract because they were already overloaded with work. Among the bids received, that of the Bobbs-Merrill Company was not only lower in price than any other, but also promised a more complete and thorough-going editorial job than did the bid of any other publisher. It was on this basis that the contract was let to that company.

In editing the statutes, Bobbs-Merrill undertook to go back to the original Acts of the General Assembly in each instance and to prepare its text from those Acts, thus eliminating errors which may have crept into the prior digests. Notes to the sections indicated such errors as were discovered. In preparing the annotations, they undertook to go back to the reported cases in each instance. As directed by the Commission, I took the responsibility for identifying and omitting many old statutes that were altogether obsolete or superseded, though not expressly repealed, by later enactments. The Commission also determined to abandon the old alphabetical arrangement of topics in the Digest, and to establish instead an arrangement based on related subject matter. The principal advantage of this was that each separate volume in the eight-volume Annotated Edition dealt with a single general field of law. Volume 1 included the Arkansas Constitution, previous State Constitutions, the Federal Constitution and other historical and preliminary matter. Volume 2 dealt with Government, including State, County, and Municipal, Improvement Districts, Public Officials and related matters. Volume 3 covered Courts and Civil Procedure, including Attorneys at Law. Criminal Law and Procedure was the main topic of Volume 4, though Intoxicating Liquors and the Fish and Game Laws were included in this volume. Volume 5 covered Property, Estates and Domestic Relations. Business, Commerce and Transportation was the general topic of Volume 6. Taxation and Public Welfare statutes made up the 7th volume, and the 8th volume consisted of the index, comparative tables and similar matter.

The Commission on June 14, 1947, made a final contract with the Bobbs-Merrill Company for manufacture of the Arkansas Statutes, 1947, in two editions, the Annotated Edition to appear in eight volumes totaling about 8,000 pages, and the Unannotated Edition in two volumes, totaling about 4,000 pages. This contract, let after competitive bidding, supplemented the earlier editorial contract. Fairly substantial savings to the State and increases in efficiency were attained by the fact that both contracts went to the same publisher. The Bobbs-Merrill contract was probably a better one than the state of Arkansas had any good reason to hope for. It enabled the state to secure the necessary copies of the Unannotated Edition for free distribution, offer the eight-volume Annotated Edition for public sale at $37.50 a set, and give to the state of Arkansas the right to purchase up to 500 copies of the Annotated Edition at a price of $34 a set.

The $37.50 price at which the eight-volume set was sold to the practicing bar was probably the lowest price for which any comparable set of books could be purchased anywhere in America in 1948. It certainly was far different from what such books cost today. I have ever since taken real pride in the negotiations which produced these very satisfactory contracts. They did not make any changes in Arkansas law, but they did make the state's law more readily accessible and perhaps even a bit more understandable.

A NEW STATE CONSTITUTION?   Informed citizens of Arkansas have for many years realized that the state's 1874 Constitution is in many respects obsolete and productive of inefficient government. Scores of amendments and amendments of amendments have been added to it. The need for comprehensive revision of the document has been publicly discussed throughout most of the present century.

The State has had five constitutions, dated 1836, 1861, 1864, 1868 and 1874. The first one, in 1836, was framed to meet the requirements for admission to statehood. It was more nearly modeled after the Constitution of the United States than were any of the later documents, and contained only about 9,100 words. (The United States Constitution of 1787 has 5,300.) The later constitutions of Arkansas were all much longer, the 1874 one originally having had 21,440 words, now increased by amendments to about 50,000.

The 1861 Constitution was designed primarily to take the state into the Confederacy, the 1864 one undertook to formalize federal military government during the latter part of the Civil War, and the 1868 document set up the framework for Reconstruction, or Carpetbag, government in Arkansas. The present 1874 document was framed largely as a reaction against the excesses of the Carpetbag regime, caused not by the 1868 Constitution itself but by the men who administered it. The legislature in 1917 called a constitutional convention without first submitting the matter to a vote of the people. The resulting convention, held in the midst of World War I, attracted little public attention, and its product was defeated 2–1 by a light vote in 1918.

After the abortive 1918 effort, there were few attempts for many years to update the Constitution, save by isolated amendments. Governor Ben Laney pointed to the need for a revised constitution during his administration in the 1940s, but the times were not propitious. Bills calling for a constitutional convention were introduced in successive sessions of the legislature in the early and middle 1960s, but none was passed.

Finally, in the 1967 session, a compromise proposal by Governor Rockefeller setting up a 30-member constitutional revision study commission was enacted. Ten members were appointed by the Governor, five by the Supreme Court, five by the Senate, five by the House of Representatives, and five by the Arkansas Bar Association. I was one of the Governor's appointees, and was then elected chairman of the group. This commission worked through the year 1967, produced a comprehensive study which analyzed the state's constitutional needs, and proposed that a constitutional convention be called. Bills designed to implement the commission's recommendations were enacted by the General Assembly. The new enactments authorized a vote at the 1968 general election on whether a constitutional convention should be held, and the election at the same time of 100 delegates to serve in the convention if the vote favored its being held.

The 1968 vote was 227,429 to 214,432 in favor of holding a convention, and the 100 delegates were elected from House of Representative districts. I was elected as a delegate from the Washington County district, and in January, 1969, at the organizational meeting in Little Rock, was elected president of the convention. By the end of August we completed a tentative draft of a new constitution and distributed it widely, to get the reaction of the people to its proposed provisions. Then in January, 1970, we met again and reviewed every part of the document, deleting, adding and altering parts of it in keeping with advice received and our own more matured thinking. At the November 1970 general election the new constitution was rejected by a fairly narrow 43–57 margin.

Advocates of constitutional reform were disappointed but not wholly discouraged. In 1971 the new governor, Dale Bumpers, looked for ways to salvage some of the constitutional revision effort, but the defeat was too recent. When Governor David Pryor took office in January, 1975, his first recommendation was "Arkansas needs and deserves a new constitution." He induced the 1975 legislature to enact a statute setting up a convention consisting of 35 delegates, 27 named by the governor and 8 by the two houses of the legislature, to meet promptly for 63 days only, with its product to be presented to the people at a special election in September. Significantly, the statute prescribed a "limited convention," excluding from its consideration twelve subject matter areas, such as reapportionment of legislative districts before 1982, judicial selection, and usury, most of which were so controversial that, as the 1970 experience showed, any change in preexistent law would produce negative votes against a new document.

The provision limiting matters to be considered turned out to be fatal. A lawsuit challenging its legality, and that of the convention itself, was filed at once, and was advanced for quick hearing by the state Supreme Court. That court on May 27 held by 4–3 vote, despite arguments by Attorney General Jim Guy Tucker and an *amicus curiae* brief in which I participated, that the 1874 constitution did not permit a limited convention. Thus Governor Pryor's well-planned effort died aborning.

Next, the question "Shall a constitutional convention be called?" was placed by the legislature on the November, 1976, general election ballot. The vote was a fairly clear "Yes." The 1977 legislature then authorized the election of 100 delegates, again by House of Representative districts, at the 1978 general election. I was again elected as a delegate from my Washington County district and at an organizational meeting in December I was elected president of the convention. Committees were appointed and began their research and preliminary drafting at once, so that when the convention met formally on the legislatively prescribed date of May 14, 1979, much of its groundwork was ready. Two months of continuous sessions produced a tentative document which was printed and distributed throughout the state for public discussion. In June of 1980 the convention reconvened and made changes based upon the intervening eleven months of public discussion. It was decided that the document should not be divided into separate parts for submission to the voters, but should be offered as a single proposal though with one exception: that the proposed methods for selecting appellate judges be voted on separately. Every one of the 100 delegates signed the document, thus providing unanimous approval of it. Yet its adoption was defeated at the general election in November. Why? Explanation must begin with the changes that would have been made had the new constitution been adopted.

Appellate judicial selection has already been mentioned. Alternative proposals were presented. One was for continued popular election of Supreme Court and Court of Appeals judges, as in the past, except that the election would be non-partisan rather than by political party. The other was for "merit selection," under which a high-level nominating commission would designate three nominees for each appellate judicial vacancy, the governor to appoint one of the three, the appointee then to be retained or voted out of office at the next general election no less than twelve months after the appointment. The electors were asked to vote for one or the other of these alternatives, neither of which would take effect unless the new constitution was adopted. The vote between the alternatives was inconclusive. I was disappointed. For more than forty years I have argued for a merit system of judicial selection, preferably modeled on the procedure established in Missouri a half century ago and now employed in several other states. It is a sad fact that the mass of voters seldom know much about the qualifications of judicial candidates, so that they vote almost blindly for unknown names on a ballot. I still believe that most voters realize that this is so, and that if a clear vote on merit selection of judges, adequately explained, were had in Arkansas, we would choose the more intelligent method of judicial selection, at least for the appellate level.

The proposed constitution would also have established an official body to maintain a constant check on judges and related officers with reference to criminal misconduct, failure to perform duties, habitual intemperance, physical or mental disability, and other facts justifying discipline or retirement. This provision is a needed corollary of substantial independence of the judiciary, and is in keeping with the Code of Judicial Conduct and recommendations for enforcement of the Code on which I had worked in American Bar Association committees in previous years.

The administrative inefficiency inherent in the 1874 system of two-year terms of office was dealt with by prescribing four-year terms for all state executive and county offices, but retention of popular democratic controls over state executives was assured by provision for recall elections on petition of a substantial percentage of state electors at any time after the executive had been in office for six months. Also, the offices of State Treasurer and State Auditor (who has few real auditing duties) would have been combined, and the office of State Land Commissioner would no longer be an elective one. Salary figures would have been taken out of the Constitution altogether, and an independent compensation commission would propose to the legislature salaries for all elective state offices, with the legislature free to accept or reduce the proposed figures but not to exceed them.

Changes in operation of the legislative branch would have been significant, but not numerous. Regular sessions could be held annually rather than biennially, thus cutting down on special sessions, though these would still be possible. Secret legislative sessions would be eliminated; all meetings would be open to the public. Deficit spending by the state was to be prohibited by a requirement that the legislature not allow any expenditure in excess of funds available in the fiscal year. The vote by which state taxes may be levied or increased would have been unified at two-thirds in each house of the legislature, replacing the old (and present) requirement of a three-fourths vote to increase income and certain other tax rates, whereas bare majority votes can levy or increase such newer taxes as the sales tax. A procedure was prescribed for enactment of laws providing for statewide uniformity in property tax assessments.

The allowable rate chargeable for interest on loans (usury) was a hot issue in 1980, as it still is. The 1874 Constitution set 10% as the top rate, and made both principal and interest forfeit if more than 10% was contracted for. Interest rates nationally were above 10%, yet there was vigorous opposition to any change in the Arkansas limit. The convention compromised by keeping the old provision but authorizing the legislature to increase the permissible rate by a two-thirds vote of each house. That probably satisfied neither side, just as neither side is satisfied now with results from the 1982 amendment which changed the usury rate.

Additions to the Bill of Rights produced considerable debate. "Gender" was added to "race" and other grounds regardless of which "the equal protection of the laws" was guaranteed. Freedom of speech was included, and a measure of access to all public meetings and records was made specific. Unreasonable invasions of privacy were prohibited. A broad assurance of "a clean and healthful environment" was given. The right to bear arms was expanded beyond "for their common defense" to include also "for hunting and recreational use, and for other lawful purposes." It was declared that any citizen taxpayer may sue to prevent illegal exactions or illegal expenditures of public funds.

Finally, the new document provided that the question of whether a new constitutional convention should be held would be submitted to the voters of the state at least once within each 20-year period. Avoidance of the kind of constitutional stagnation that Arkansas had suffered would thus be facilitated.

There, of course, were many other changes in the state's basic law, but these are the ones that produced most of the debate. Why, then, was the new constitution defeated?

Public lassitude and its companion ignorance were, in my

opinion, the principal reasons. A person who in a voting booth faces an issue about which he knows little or nothing and in which he has developed no interest will usually vote "No." Others almost automatically vote "No" against any proposed change in anything.

Like most of the 99 other delegates and perhaps 101 other persons, I gave talks around the state, wrote letters, ads and other publicity, and spent money in the campaign for adoption. Our efforts failed to reach most of the voters.

Beyond the indifference, there was active opposition. Most of it centered on some one or another specific provision in the document. Many voters opposed any change in the usury law, and the authorization to the legislature to make changes, even though only by two-thirds vote, induced opposition to the entire new constitution.

There were firm advocates of popular election of all public officials who voted "No" because of the judicial selection provisions and removal of a few officials from the elective process. A considerable number of voters opposed four-year terms largely for the same democratic reason, never realizing that the recall provision might actually add to popular electoral control over officeholders. Some thought the legislature should meet only once in ten years, not every year. Some thought that official salaries should be kept low and the way to do this was to retain the figures set by Amendment 56 in 1975, superseding amendment 37 of 1945, superseding Amendment 15 of 1927 which raised the governor's salary to $6,000 from the $4,000 set by the 1874 constitution.

Some objected to making it easier to raise income tax rates and harder to raise sales tax rates. The legislature had proposed a five-year program for statewide equalization of property tax assessments, placed on the same 1980 ballot and backed by substantial campaign funds. (It was adopted.) Sev-

eral of that measure's proponents feared that the new constitution's section prescribing uniformity in property tax assessments would take votes away from their act, and chose for that
reason to discourage support for the constitution.

Finally, the added clauses in the Bill of Rights produced surprising opposition. Inclusion of "gender" as a basis for equal
protection of the laws caused almost as much negative comment as if the word "sex" had been used. "Environment" as
something worthy of protection was attacked, with references
to disfavored characters such as "hippies" and "do-gooders."
And true believers in the private right to bear arms were apparently frightened by the words "for other lawful purposes"
added to their constitutional guaranty, presumably fearing that
purposes they regarded as "lawful" might ultimately become
unlawful. Whatever their reasoning, they constituted another
small group that opposed the constitution.

No one small bloc of single-issue voters could by itself en-
danger the reform effort. When their negative votes were all
combined, however, the number was large. Beyond that, nearly
all of them were active campaigners capable of securing many
thousands of negative vote promises from friends and acquain-
tances who had no clear views one way or the other about the
need for a modernized state constitution. The various single-
issue partisans, through their combined influence, could and
did do much to defeat the 1980 constitution.

As far as the foreseeable future is concerned, I am convinced that major improvements in the state's basic law should
be presented singly, as amendments to the old Constitution. In
that status, each on its own merits, the majority of voters can
be persuaded to favor them. Any presentation of them all together, at a general election, will almost surely fail again.
Whether that would be the result if the vote were at a special
election, with adoption of a new constitution the only issue on

the ballot so that only informed and interested citizens would take the trouble to go to the polls, is another question. That *might* succeed.

Black Law Students

The first black student admitted to a state university south of the Mason-Dixon Line since Reconstruction days was Silas Hunt, who became a student at the University of Arkansas Law School in February of 1948. Hunt died during the next year, partially by reason of battlefield injuries suffered during World War II. He was succeeded in the Law School in the fall of 1948 by Jackie L. Shropshire from Little Rock. Shropshire was graduated in due course in 1951 and became a prominent lawyer and political figure in Gary, Indiana. Three blacks entered the Law School in the fall of 1949, and all were graduated three years later. They were Wiley Branton, who later served as Dean of the Howard University Law School in Washington, D.C., then joined a leading Washington law firm; George Haley, brother of Alex Haley of *Roots* fame, now a highly regarded international lawyer in Washington; and Chris Mercer, a successful Pine Bluff, Arkansas, attorney. After that there were many blacks in the Law School. Separate records according to race have not been kept.

As Dean of the Law School after World War II and until 1954, I was much involved with these students, with their law school careers, and especially with the University's decision to admit them. Previously, blacks had been deliberately barred, as was the case at all the so-called "white" schools in the South. The new President of the University of Arkansas had in 1947 signed a minority report advocating continued segregation in higher education despite a national Presidential Commission majority report urging gradual integration in

Southern colleges. There was little active pressure for integration, even among blacks, in Arkansas at the time, but there was some.

It was clear to me that, under the Constitution, blacks were entitled to admission, particularly to law schools. If qualified plaintiffs filed lawsuits seeking admission they would win in the United States Supreme Court, though possibly not in the lower courts. I was, in 1946 and 1947, moved by various reasons to work toward admission of blacks to our law school, but the limited reasons I emphasized openly were that I did not want Arkansas to be subjected to the unpleasant national publicity and expense that would accompany such a lawsuit, and I did not want my name to go down in legal history as the losing defendant. These were reasons more readily acceptable than reasons of conscience to some local officials and citizens.

During 1946 and 1947 I talked about the problem with scores of Arkansans, especially newspaper editors, ministers of churches, members of the University's Board of Trustees, faculty members, and others who I thought might help or might actively oppose the change if they were not quieted in advance. With the black community, in much fuller conversations, I talked especially with two respected lawyers, Scipio A. Jones of Little Rock and Harold Flowers of Pine Bluff. They recognized both the novelty and the difficulties inherent in the project, and believed that public acceptance depended upon not trying to do too much too quickly, but they encouraged me to go ahead.

One of my principal concerns had to with Governor Ben Laney, then serving his second term. Laney's attitudes are illustrated by the later fact that in 1948 he was a leading activist in the new States' Rights party and could have been that party's nominee for President of the United States had he not wanted to seek another term as Governor of Arkansas. The party's nomination went instead to Strom Thurmond of South Carolina.

I learned that Laney planned to be at the Arlington Hotel in Hot Springs during the annual Arkansas Bar Association meeting there in June of 1947. Through lawyer William J. Smith, the Governor's executive secretary, I made an appointment to talk with him there about the Negro problem. Smith and a few other carefully selected political friends of the Governor were asked to be present, and all were briefed in advance on the topic to be discussed. The problem was explained in terms of the probability of a lawsuit and its inevitable result, plus the publicity damage to the state, the cost in state tax funds of the suggested, but almost surely unsuccessful, alternative of a separate Negro law school, and other realistic aspects of the situation. The Governor noted standard white supremacist objections, but his lawyer friends in the room agreed that law school integration could not be prevented. As the afternoon ended he turned to me and said, "If that's the way it is, go ahead when you think you have to. I don't like it, but I won't interfere, and I'll stand behind you." In February of 1948 he kept his word, publicly.

Expectably, most of the University's faculty, including law teachers, appeared to welcome the admission of blacks. The Board of Trustees, led by Chairman Herbert Thomas and long-time member Henry Yocum of El Dorado, knew that the time was right for action, and authorized what had to be done. Most of the state's newspapers approved, some with obvious reluctance. My mail was divided. A majority of letters favored what was being done, but negative reactions were more forcefully expressed. Some were vitriolic.

It was publicly asserted at the first that black students would be taught "on a segregated basis." This quieted much of the criticism. Silas Hunt understood this arrangement, and a separate "colored section" was scheduled for him, in a separate room where he also did his studying. It turned out that he never met a class altogether by himself; always there were other students who sought the advantage of sitting in a class with only four or five persons, one a studious black man, rather than in a much larger and less intensive group. Hunt's life was far from being an easy or a pleasant one, but he was studying law successfully at the University of Arkansas. Then in the summer he became fatally ill.

When Shropshire enrolled as the only black in the Law School that fall, there were 125 first-year law students. I posted a notice on the bulletin board that the class would be divided into two sections, one with 100 students, all white, the other with 25 including the black man and the first 24 to sign an attached sheet. In less than five minutes there were 24 signatures on the attached sheet. When the class met, Shropshire was assigned to a railed front corner seat, in typical railroad "colored section" fashion. The next morning the railing was gone, torn down during the night and hidden in the Dean's securely locked toilet. The black student continued, however, to sit in the same corner seat the rest of the year. Thus he was "segregated." The next year, on the same theory, he and the three new black first year students were asked to sit in the front rows in their several classes and to use a designated area in the law library reading room. After that year, from September 1950 on, they were told to sit where they pleased. At all times they cooperated, accepting the unpleasantness of what amounted to segregated seating, for the time being, because they knew that it was designed to lead, gradually but surely, to an increasingly greater integration with as little disruptive controversy as possible. The objective was that the new arrangement should achieve acceptance in the Arkansas social environment as it was then.

It is difficult in the 1980s for many well-meaning citizens, including younger blacks, to understand the restrictions that were imposed when integration first began in the South. There is a tendency to charge that we who arranged the restrictions a third of a century and more ago must have been, must even be now, racists of the worst kind. The sort of arrangements that we sponsored then would not be tolerated now, would not be demanded today even by avowed racists. It is difficult to defend ourselves against such charges. All we can say is that we were trying to do something that we were convinced was right but had not yet been done in any Southern university. Times and attitudes were different then. We did not know that we would succeed, and we did not want to fail. We did what we thought was most likely to lead to success.

Above all, it would be wrong to think of the black men who cooperated in those early arrangements as docile and submissive acceptors of things as they were. Silas Hunt was no "Uncle Tom." He was a brave and upright man, willing to put himself on the front line, to live a hard life when he could have had an easier one, to open up new opportunities for his people. That was true of his immediate successors as well. They knew what they were doing, and why they did it that way. It was not because they liked it, or wanted it done the same way in years to come. They were breaking new ground. Breaking new ground is always harder work than plowing well-tilled soil.

III The Nature and Function of Law

Law and People

Law certainly does not exist just for its own sake. Law of some kind is a prerequisite to orderly human society, and any body of law is justified (justifies itself) only as it serves the purposes of the society in which it prevails. Historically, there has been an almost infinite variety of societies on this earth, and every society, including our own, changes constantly as time passes, so that laws need to be changed to fit the changed conditions. There will, by reason of the nature of humanity, be differences of opinion as to what laws best serve the interests of a given society, and representatives of these interests will not always control the law-making process whether it be legislative, executive (the king, the church), or judicial in character. Nevertheless, despite disputes and uncertainties, the test of rightness in any law or body of law is the extent to which it fits and serves the needs and interests (real, sometimes imagined) of the society of the time and place.

Perhaps this almost self-evident philosophical truth is more visible to the mass of people and their law-writing agents in a democratic society, such as ours is supposed to be, than in some others. At any rate it is a test that affords us a fair opportunity to delve a little deeper into the nature of our own system of law and developments within it.

It has always seemed to me that the ideal model for a state, by which I mean a nation—a model perhaps never achieved by any modern state—is the old-fashioned American family, in which each member had a sense of responsibility for every other member, or at least the responsible ones had that sense of responsibility. Maintenance of discipline among those not trusted to discipline themselves, and obedience to standards fixed within the family for conduct both internal and toward outsiders, were basic characteristics.

The family system was not just for regulation and control; but imposed duties of protection and sustenance. The children of a brother or of a cousin who died prematurely were taken into the homes of those who survived. Widows and maiden aunts were cared for. Ne'er-do-wells were helped back onto their economic feet, perhaps more times than their sober kinsmen liked, but helped nevertheless. Even the black sheep who returned after a term in the penitentiary was encouraged to reestablish himself, sometimes in another community where he was not known. At least he was not kicked out and abandoned. Lots of the "good advice" that often accompanied the aid may not have been gladly received, but there was a better chance of its being followed than if advice alone were given. Furthermore, one who merely cadged on his more industrious relatives, when he could have been working and self-supporting, was apt to be told, in no uncertain terms, to go to work. A job might be found for him—with the ultimatum "Take it or else!"

Not every family was like that, and I fear that fewer are today than were in an earlier era. But many were, and some still are. The family took care of its own. Competent and ambitious members were assisted in their efforts to get ahead, and they in turn accepted the obligation to watch over less fortunate uncles and sisters and cousins.

Should not a state, in its full and best sense, have the same function for all its citizens as the old-fashioned family had for its own smaller but related group? Discipline and the maintenance of reasonable order within the group are basic to both. The complexities of good order in a modern state require infinitely more rules and regulation than are needed in the family, but the essential need is the same for both.

What of the comparison as to obligations owed to family members? The comparison is not one based solely upon legal duties existing between father, mother, and infant child in the family, or between government and members of its armed services. Rather, it raises questions of acceptance of moral duty, or social obligations voluntarily undertaken and turned into legal duties only as the state chooses through its law-making processes to recognize in itself the same breadth of social obligation to its citizens that an old-fashioned responsible family voluntarily undertook toward its members. In other words, the analogy if carried out leads us, in terms of government, to what is loosely called "the welfare state," though with the possibility of considerable variations in specific welfare programs and significant limitations upon them. Arguments for and against such programs are common nowadays, and the content of the arguments is well known. Voluntary undertaking of constantly increasing state responsibility, in the United States, goes back at least to FDR's New Deal days, perhaps further. Until recently it has been the political trend, which may be temporarily reversed in today's Ronald Reagan period.

The value of my "family analogy," now that I've written it down, appears doubtful to me. It may be descriptive merely, descriptive of a societal trend already long existent, for which arguments both pro and con are far more basic than any mere analogy can be.

Yet it seems to me that the analogy is sound, and that it explains a part of the very reason for a state's existence, and the very justification for the creation of states. States exist to perform the functions which society's complexities have placed beyond the power of smaller social units, such as the family, to perform. Another societal entity that might perform these functions could be the church. But if the church performed them for all people, the church would have become, or at least would seem to have become, the state.

The Great and Common Law

The great mass of law in the United States is judge-made law. This is our system of common law. That is true despite our much-praised separation of powers, under which the legislative branch is to make the laws, the judicial branch to decide disputes in accordance with the laws, and the executive branch to enforce the laws. All of us have known since we studied eighth grade civics that the three branches overlap.

In one almost meaningless sense the legislatures of the American states did, with theoretical thoroughness, perform the complete law-making task for their respective states in early statehood. This was by enactment of the so-called "reception statutes." The Arkansas statute is typical. It reads:

The common law of England, so far as the same is applicable and of a

general nature, and all statutes of the British Parliament in aid of or
to supply the defects of the common law made prior to the fourth
year of James the First (that are applicable to our own form of government), of a general nature and not local to that kingdom, and
not inconsistent with the Constitution and the laws of the United
States or the Constitution and laws of this State, shall be the rule of
decision in this State unless altered or repealed by the General Assembly of this State.

The fourth year of James I was 1607, which was the year of
settlement of Jamestown, in Virginia. Some states instead, for
their reception statutes, picked the year 1620 when the Pil-
grims landed at Plymouth Rock, and a few chose 1776, for an
obvious reason. It did not make much difference which year
they selected, because our American courts have paid little if
any attention to those late medieval laws of England. They are
obsolete today.

Yet we do inherit the common law from England, and that
common law contains within itself the legal system that governs us in our daily lives. The rules, principles, standards, doctrines, and policies which our courts apply are the substance of
this common law system, though few of them were known to
English courts in 1607. The point is that the common law is
greater than the rules that lie within it at any given time, because it is founded upon and has as its central feature a principle of growth, a capacity for meeting the needs of whatever
time and place it operates in.

All common law was new judge-made law in its beginnings,
and the mass of it today, a thousand times larger than it was in
1607, has been affected by legislation only in little spots and
corners. Legislatures deal typically with problems of government, taxation, education, and large issues affecting public
welfare. Neither the legislature of Arkansas nor that of any
other state undertakes to lay down rules to govern every private dispute.

The key to this, I suspect, is the necessity for the courts to decide all the cases that come before them. I am speaking mostly of our appellate courts, though the same necessities exist for trial courts. When a case is appealed to a state supreme court, it has to be affirmed, reversed, remanded with directions, or otherwise decided. A court cannot say that there is no law on this issue and therefore we can't decide the case. It cannot wait for the legislature to enact a law, two years or ten years hence. It must decide the case with reasonable promptness. And if the case involves difficult issues it must file a written opinion stating what it has decided and giving its reasons for the decision.

These opinions have the force of "law," and they serve as precedents for future decision. The doctrine of *stare decisis*, which is part of the common law, says that the rule and the reasons stated in the opinion bind the court—constitute the law—for future cases. We know, however, that no rule laid down by a court in 1607, or for that matter in 1907, or 1967, can give wise answers for all the issues that arise in 1984. By then there will be new problems that have never appeared before; additionally, some of the answers given in 1907, that were perfectly valid then, would be utterly inappropriate for what superficially appear to be the same problems in 1984. The doctrine of *stare decisis* is flexible enough to take care of most of these newer cases which are surrounded by 1984 circumstances, since older cases can often be distinguished on their facts. But sometimes old cases, even though sound for their times, eventually become so inappropriate that they simply have to be overruled. The doctrine of *stare decisis* has always recognized the possibility of overrulings.

It is with regard to overrulings that we observe one of the most fascinating jurisprudential controversies in the history of the common law. It has to do with whether judges "make" new law, or only "discover" it. Blackstone said that the perfect law had been there all along, perhaps from the beginning of time. Speaking of overruling, he said:

> But even in such cases the subsequent judges do not pretend to make a new law, but to vindicate the old one from misrepresentation. For if it be found that the former decision is manifestly absurd or unjust, it is declared not that such a sentence was *bad law*, but that it was *not law*; that is, that it is not the established custom of the realm . . . And hence it is that our lawyers are with justice so copious in their encomiums on the reason of common law; that they tell us, that the law is the perfection of reason. . . .

One of our fairly recent American presidents, the late Calvin Coolidge, spoke from the same era:

> Men do not make laws. They do but discover them. Laws must be justified by something more than the will of the majority. They must rest on the eternal foundation of righteousness. That state is most fortunate in its form of government which has the aptest instruments for the discovery of laws.

An earlier president, Theodore Roosevelt, did not agree. He said:

> The chief lawmakers in our country may be, and often are, the judges, because they are the final seat of authority. Every time they interpret contract, property, vested rights, due process of law, liberty, they necessarily enact into law parts of a system of social philosophy; and as such interpretation is fundamental, they give direction to all law-making. The decisions of the courts on economic and social questions depend upon their economic and social philosophy; and for the peaceful progress of our people during the twentieth century we shall owe most to those judges who hold to a twentieth century economic and social philosophy and not to a long outgrown philosophy, which was itself the product of primitive economic conditions.

The judges on the Chancery (equity) side of our judicial system never quite agreed with Blackstone (or Coolidge). Lord

Jessel, for example, almost a hundred years ago made a neat distinction:

> The rules of Courts of Equity are not, like the rules of the Common Law, supposed to have been established from time immemorial. It is perfectly well known that they have been established from time to time—altered, improved, and refined from time to time. In many cases we know the names of the Chancellors who invented them.

Jeremy Bentham, who was a realist, knew how the bulk of law was made, though he didn't much like it:

> It is the Judges that make the common law:—Do you know how they make it? Just as a man makes laws for his dog. When your dog does anything you want to break him of, you wait till he does it, and then beat him for it. That is the way you make laws for your dog; and this is the way the Judges make laws for you and me.

Bentham preferred legislation to common law, but he was unable to turn the tide against the already established Anglo-American system.

If the Blackstonian idea were sound, it would be as though the first cases decided by common law judges were seeds patterned within themselves to include all the law's future growth, as the acorn patterns the future growth of the oak. If that were true, all common law would have been known, or at least theoretically knowable, from the beginning, to one who understood the pattern set in the seed. No lawyer, no judge, no citizen yet has had such perfect understanding. Some may have thought they had it, but their colleagues have seldom agreed. If the seed pattern be complete, we have not trained ourselves to read it. We still do not know what the law will be for new claims and defenses that come up for the first time ten years from now.

It was Mr. Justice Holmes who said:

> It is revolting to have no better reason for a rule of law than that so it was laid down in the time of Henry IV. It is still more revolting if the

grounds upon which it was laid down have vanished long since, and the rule simply persists from blind imitation of the past.

He did not go as far as Thomas Jefferson, who once wrote to James Madison that "every constitution . . . , and every law, naturally expires at the end of nineteen years" (his 1789 idea of the length of a human generation) since each new generation should have the responsibility for its own government and laws. Though Americans today would not accept the ninteen-year period, and neither Jefferson nor Madison would accept it for such fundamentals as a bill of rights, nearly everyone today does recognize the practical necessity for constantly updating the common law.

Our common law started in the Middle Ages, from practically nothing. In its beginnings it dealt on the civil side with little more than assaults, batteries, and unpermitted entries upon the lands of others. The early common law of crimes was mostly concerned with the protection of interests of what we today call "the establishment." There was a long period when much new common law was lawyers' law, dealing with forms of action, pleading, and the like. Probably these preoccupations of the courts served the dominant interests of late medieval and early modern society, which was primarily concerned with maintaining things as they were, protection of the vested interests of landowners and royalty, with a minimum of change and any change that was achieved to come as slowly as possible.

But change did come, whether wanted or not. The merchant class came to be important, and law was needed to govern commercial transactions. When Lord Mansfield became Chief Justice of England, the common law courts knew nothing of business law. A wide variety of sales of goods, contracts, bills of lading, promissory notes, bills of exchange, and the like were employed by merchants, but their interpretation and enforcement depended upon the merchants' good faith and private sanctions rather than upon the law. Mansfield brought the law merchant, the customs of the merchants, into the law, made it part of the common law, with no help from Parliament. Also, during the same period, he created the common law of quasi-contract, derived partly from equity jurisprudence and partly from simple principles of ethics and morality.

What Mansfield's opinions brought into the common law of England was with little hesitation accepted by our judges as the common law of the American states as well. Yet it is notable that Mansfield was Chief Justice from 1756 to 1788, well past the dates fixed by most of our reception statutes for state adoption of England's common law. What happened was that the courts of England and of our states simply accepted as part of the common law a mass of materials whose time had come.

That is what common law courts have always done. The whole modern law of insurance, the law of corporations, the law of trusts, the law that governs new types of interests in land, oil and gas law, the law of aviation, the law of conflict of laws, and many other areas of today's law, have been created by our courts, with creation taking the form of judicial opinions, but with the demand for the new law coming from the extrajudicial society whose activities create a need for it. To use a physiological analogy, the whole society is the male-parent of new common law, and the judiciary is the mother. The semen that fathers the child is the felt need for new and better rules of law in any given area, and conception occurs when the felt need becomes urgent. The child is delivered in the form of judicial opinions. It must be noted, obviously, that conception does not always occur on the first try, and that the period of gestation is by no means the standard human one of nine months. Not even an analogy to the elephant's lengthy period of gestation seems appropriate here, and there are some courts that seem to produce as rapidly as rabbits.

Until quite recently caveat emptor was the rule of the marketplace, and the rule in the courts as well. It was a rule of dog eat dog, and even more of dog eat sheep. It is largely within my lifetime that the courts, motivated by a changing of social mores, have begun to develop the law of misrepresentation and products liability and to extend it to protect the mass of consumers under the prepackaged economy that increasingly prevails in our modern society. Thus partially eaten sheep are beginning to receive compensation for the dog bites that have been taken out of them, and the new rules may even restrain the dogs somewhat in their sheep-eating tendencies.

One major difficulty with judicial law-making in years gone by was the assumed necessity that it operate retroactively. That was not true of legislatively enacted statutes. As to them, the constitutional ex post facto prohibition applied. It is utterly unfair for a new statutory rule, becoming a law perhaps on March 1, 1985, to govern substantive transactions that occurred in 1976 or 1984, when the parties could not have known of the new statute and would instead have relied upon the old law that it superseded. Yet new judge-made rules were until recently always deemed to be retroactive. This was under the Blackstonian notion that the old rule, now replaced by a new judicial decision, had never been law at all, but was merely an erroneous misinterpretation of the true law, so that the new decision actually had been the law all along—just not yet "discovered."

New judge-made law could be just as hard on a citizen who had acted in reliance on an older judge-made rule as could an ex post facto legislative enactment, but the discovery theory caused it to be treated differently. An incidental result was that, because of this unfairness, courts were less willing to overrule old decisions even though they no longer represented good law.

It was in 1932 that the United States Supreme Court, in the

famous *Sunburst* case (287 U.S. 358), made it clear to state courts that they were not bound to render retroactive decisions. Since that time, nearly all American courts have approved procedures for prospective overruling. A new rule announced in a current decision, apart from being applied in the principal case, can be made applicable to cases tried thereafter only, or only to cases the facts of which occur thereafter, or only to transactions that take place after a named future date, or only after the adjournment of the next session of the legislature (if the court thinks that the subject matter is one that the legislature might wish to deal with now that the judicial decision has called attention to it.) If the new decision involves no overruling, the prospectivity issue does not arise. Most judicial decisions do not call for prospective treatment. The great majority of judicial decisions involve situations in which there has been no justifiable reliance by anyone on prior contrary law. In those cases the newly announced rule can be applied across the board, retroactively as well as prospectively. And the prospectivity technique can take care of the remaining small number of reliance cases.

Another difficulty with judicial law-making has been its typical incompleteness. The theory has long been that a court in deciding a case should confine itself to the narrow issue presented by that case and should not deal even with related matters. The analysis essential to the decision is called the *ratio decidendi*; anything beyond that is called *obiter dictum* and was supposed to be ignored. Actually, it often was not ignored, since lawyers and judges knew that it indicated what the writing judge thought the law should be, and that it might afford a fair hint as to how the next case would be decided. Nevertheless, law students for two centuries were taught that only the *ratio decidendi*, and not the dictum, in judicial opinions was worthy of study.

The difficulty lay in areas of the law (areas of human activity) in which fact situations might vary widely so that, to clarify the whole law to which a new judge-made rule applied, a number of incidental rules or sub-rules might be needed. This was the sort of thing that a well-planned statute could take care of, by successive sections in a single enactment. Too often, statutes are not well planned, so that courts have to fill in the statutory gaps, a piece at a time as the cases come up, by a sort of pseudo-statutory interpretation. That is a part of the problem. Whether the incompleteness is in a statute or in a new judge-made common law rule, the trouble is that the unanswered issues leave the citizenry in doubt. People can only guess at what the law is on related but not covered matters. To get the answers they have had to wait, like Jeremy Bentham's dog, until new cases present each unresolved question to the state's top appellate court. That may take years.

There is no doubt that legislatures ordinarily can do a better job than can common law courts in planning and organizing the details for large new areas of law. Legislatures can set up research committees, they can gather information from impartial as well as from adversary sources, they can secure the advice of experts who are able to foresee future developments in the area, and they can employ draftsmen who correlate and systematize the rules. No one would argue that the Commercial Code, or its equivalent, could have been as well promulgated by the courts. No one would argue that judicial law-making should take the place of all legislation. Much of law-making is without question the function of the legislative branch of government.

But, recognizing as we must that some part of the business of making law is for the common law courts, we are entitled to ask how can that part of the courts' function be best performed, and when. We know that new judge-made law, when it appears, will be set out in judicial opinions. How should those opinions be framed?

Some recent common law decisions appear to deal with this difficulty. The trend attaches a new importance to judicial dictum. Judges having future problems in mind, and trying to be helpful, include in their opinions statements affording guidance to solution of the impending problems. These statements are deliberate dicta, but they are useful. In the past these useful dicta have been offered almost apologetically, with restraint and hesitation. Today, judges are offering such statements more boldly, recognizing not just that they are not improper but that there may be a judicial obligation to make them. There are times when it is a part of the appellate judicial function to lay down rules of law to guide future conduct, beyond what is exactly necessary for decision of the very case before the court.

A recent Oklahoma case (*Kirkland v. General Motors Corp.*, 521 P. 2d 1353), affords an illustration. Strict liability for injuries caused by a defendant manufacturer's defective products was a legal doctrine whose time had come. Largely developed by judicial decision without much legislative direction, the doctrine had been accepted in most of the states, but acceptance was incomplete in Oklahoma. Then a Miss Kirkland sued General Motors for injuries suffered in the wreck of a new car. She alleged that defects in the car caused her injuries. The Oklahoma Supreme Court decision was in favor of General Motors, on the ground that Miss Kirkland's car wreck and resultant injuries were caused by her own fault. That was all that was necessary for the decision of the case. But the court went on and announced that strict liability for injuries caused by defective products would thereafter be the law of Oklahoma, and it defined in some detail the limits of the new rule. This was dictum pure and simple. But it was dictum fated to be followed, and from that time on, the bar of Oklahoma knew what the state's law was, as did automakers and other manufacturers as well as injured citizens. They were all better off than if the court had left them to guess at the law. A common law court had made another advance in appellate judicial performance, but it was an advance well within the spirit of the common law tradition.

Closely related is an old cliché, never with much truth in it, that is today being rejected on its merits. This was that, after a judge-made rule of law—good, bad, or indifferent—had been announced by decision at some earlier time, and the legislature over a period of years had not by new statute changed the rule (as of course it had the power to do), the legislative silence constituted an approval of the rule, a sort of tacit enactment of it, giving it a greater force than it originally possessed, and constituting an additional reason against reconsideration and overruling of even an unwise decision. That interpretation of "legislative silence" is unsound. State legislatures make no effort to keep up with the mass of judge-made common law. Their attention is mainly centered on matters having to do with the organization of government, taxation, regulation of utilities, crime and public morality, issues of whatever nature are currently exciting the public.

Judge-made rules controlling the rights of parties in private litigation often may not come to legislative attention unless some lawyer-legislator, unhappy because he has lost a case in court, seeks legislative reversal of his own prior defeat. Even that happens less often nowadays than it once did. The fact is that legislators deliberately leave most common law matters to the common law courts. Even if a bill designed to change a common law rule be introduced, most legislators will ignore it, not because they believe the rule should not be changed but rather because the mass of judge-made law should be left to the judges to handle. "It's their job, not ours," say busy legislators. Legislative silence may mean almost anything.

That these areas of common law difficulty, and others too, do exist, does not prove that the common law system is in trouble. Just the opposite! The areas of difficulty are being openly recognized, dealt with, and revised. The system's inherent capacity for growth, for devising new techniques that can eliminate old defects largely traceable to over-reliance on a special kind of formal logic, for adapting itself to meet the needs of the changing society, is what I emphasize. The common law has had its share of defects, and still has many, but they are not fatal. Rather, as good judges recognize them, they become the challenges that lead our courts onward to better law and the better legal system that our new times demand.

My wife's father, Charles J. Finger, once said to me that in his opinion law in our society has but one function, which is the maintenance of order. I think the statement is sound. It does not mean the same as "law-n'-order," pronounced as one word. Obviously, it means "good order," neither disorder nor too much order as in a society of robots. It means good order for our society, today's society, not just for some primitive society in medieval times, not for a pioneer society like that of early America, nor for a horse and buggy society such as that into which I was born, nor for a Russian or Chinese or even an English society. The needs are those of a social system alive and changing, not static but constantly developing, different from our society yesterday, different from Japan's or England's or Africa's today, and different from Utopia's both yesterday and tomorrow.

Order and liberty appear to be opposites. Maintenance of good order in society requires compliance with rules which limit an individual's conduct with reference to his fellows. A maximum of liberty for any individual would permit him to act as he pleases without regard to the interests of other human beings. That would be intolerable. Law is the source of rules that must be obeyed, and so is the enemy of complete freedom. Yet only through law can there be any real freedom in a populated society. The maintenance of order assures a preservation of most, but not of all freedoms. Preservation of a maximum of freedoms should be the ultimate objective of law. The orderliness compelled by law in society is not itself the objective, but is rather the means to optimum freedom, the end we seek. Good law must balance off mankind's wanted freedoms against each other, the choices to act as one wishes toward one's self, toward others, and toward all the world, against the unwanted consequences of freedoms exercised by others. This I suppose is what law is all about. It is not simple, nor is it the same in one generation as in the next. The catalog of mankind's wanted freedoms include some elemental ones that have been with us through the ages. But a changing society, and a more complex one, gives constant rise to new wants, new freedoms desired, and new conflicts between competing desires.

It is the genius of our common law system that wise judges administer not just old rules handed down from the past but are duty-bound to update the old rules, to make them fit current conditions. A decent "lag" is to be expected, since modern needs may be unclear and judges may have to wait until new trends have stabilized before they can know what new rules are called for. It is more likely that courts will condemn old practices only after they have been long deplored by ethical laymen, after higher standards have already come to be accepted by the better element among those who must live and work together or do business in the marketplace. The point is, though, that the system of the common law contemplates the need for change to assure good order in the society of the time and place, and provides for it by authorizing our lawmakers, the appellate judges, to modify and adjust the rules as changing times demand.

We know of course that our appellate judges in times past were not gods, though passage of years tends to give them that reputation. They were human beings, as you and I are and as today's appellate judges are. Most of them were honest, competent, and incorruptible, as are today's appellate judges. The occasional exception has had little influence upon the totality of the common law.

Codes of ethics were less rigorous in the "good old days," and public access to deliberately hidden facts was harder to come by then. That is another aspect in which the legal system continues to improve itself. The ethical standards for judges promulgated by the American Bar Association in 1924 were in many respects vague and ambiguous, but by 1972 were superseded by a new set of standards much more pointed and specific. The public keeps a closer watch on judges today than in times past, as it does on most public servants. This agrees with the fact that our law-making judges today tend to correlate their judicial decisions more closely with the interests and concerns of a public whose life is to be controlled by the law laid down in such decisions.

Common law has always reflected the dominant interests of society, but it may well be that appellate judges today need to keep in closer and more constant touch with life around them, in order to reflect those interests correctly, since life changes more rapidly today than ever before. In this connection, it is worth nothing that appellate judges, as well as other judges, recognize an obligation to increase their competence by continuing their formal education after going upon the bench. This, too, is a new development, attributable largely to current judicial recognition of the truly socioeconomic character of the appellate task.

One important effect of new socioeconomic conditions in America today is a substantial increase in the amount of litigation, in the number of cases filed in our trial courts and eventually in the number of cases appealed. The number of cases taken up to the Arkansas appellate courts in a year now is approximately three times as great as when I served on the Supreme Court a few short years ago. Throughout the United

States the same increase has occurred, in many states more rapidly than in Arkansas. Obviously a growing population does not by itself explain the additional caseload. The fact is that as a people we have become more litigious. We sue on causes of action that were not available to us a generation ago, for harms caused by pollution, for interferences with privacy, for injuries caused by defective products regardless of unproved negligence, and for discriminations that formerly went without remedy. All of this represents growth in the law, and most of us agree that it is good. We agree that a good system of law should serve the needs and interests of the society of the time and place, and that these new types of claims derive from the culture of America today.

The increasing number of appeals, however, calls for more appellate decisions, more opinions written, more reams of paper and gallons of ink consumed in the decisional process. That is not necessarily bad; it's what our appellate courts are for. But the multiplicity of opinions does dilute their value as precedent, especially when dozens and hundreds of them repeat standard rules and principles, merely applying them to slightly variant facts. Law library shelves bulge with each year's product of as many opinions as came out from all the common law courts in Christendom in an entire century. No lawyer and no judge can read, let alone master, all of them. Their very bulk could destroy the common law system of future decision based upon past precedent.

But here again the system is capable of adjusting. If publication of all opinions serves no useful purpose, not all opinions need be published. If a mass of duplicative opinions be useless as precedents, their citation as such can be barred. Opinions that add nothing to the substance of the law can be written for parties and their counsel, photocopied but not printed, and barred from subsequent citation. Decisions governed by clear precedent can be supported by three-line opinions citing the precedent, without further discussion, and without official publication since they add nothing to the law. Court rules establishing this procedure of limited publication and citation are being currently adopted in many states. Thus in another aspect the basic character of the common law system is being sustained by a judicial readiness to change nonessential details.

Some time ago a student asked me a searching question, one which he had obviously thought about before he asked it. I had previously identified in class discussion the judges who, from the era of my youth, had been regarded as the great jurists of that period—Holmes, Learned Hand, and Cardozo, and I had named the judges of my generation whom I regarded as being of the same high company—Chief Justice Roger Traynor of California, Justice and sometime Chief Justice Walter V. Schaefer of Illinois, and Chief Judge Henry Friendly of the Second Circuit, United States Court of Appeals. Then I had said that of all these I regarded Cardozo as the greatest master of the common law, the one who as Chief Judge of the New York Court of Appeals, before he went on the Supreme Court of the United States, contributed more than any other judge to sound understanding of our American law and legal system. I had singled him out as greatest among the great ones.

A few days later, in the corridor, came the question. The student, with others listening in, asked, "Was Cardozo really a great judge? We are told by Prosser that Judge Andrews' dissenting position in the 1928 *Palsgraf* case [248 N.Y. 339, 162 N.E. 99] is sounder than Cardozo's. His great 1916 case of *MacPherson v. Buick Motor Co.* [217 N.Y. 382, 111 N.E. 1050] is today merely a relic of the past, a way-stop from which we have departed as the modern law of products liability, based on warranty and strict liability, has taken over the field. Others say that contracts law has passed him by. You point out that his choice-of-law theory in Conflict of Laws is no longer followed.

Can a judge whose pronouncements are thus disregarded be as truly great as Cardozo's reputation would make him?"

The answer must be, of course, that Cardozo was a great judge! If greatness were to be measured only by asking whether a judge's statements of law were eternal in their verity, no judge dealing with the problems of his time would ever be great. Problems change and the law changes with them. True greatness in a judge rests in his ability to recognize issues that confront him in their context of time and place and to deal with them in such manner that his answers will be accepted and used in the law as bases for further growth.

Cardozo did not try to move forward in the law faster than the spirit of his time would sustain him. If he had, he would have failed. There were those who would have moved more slowly, or not at all, and some who would have moved more rapidly. He was considerably more innovative than the average judge of his time. But he was writing for his time, not for 1984 nor for the year 2000. His principles and approaches, his analysis of the nature and function of the judicial process, can guide our judges for generations yet to come. The guidance, though, is in his techniques and attitudes, his approach to the judicial process, not just the results in his cases.

Among lawyers and judges, it is not enough to announce results. The law is a learned profession, and it has its professional techniques. Logical reasoning based on legal principles, and particularly the doctrine of precedents, is central to those techniques. A judge who rejects the standard professional techniques, or who—worse—is clumsy and inept in employing them, will never gain the admiration of the bar, however much his results and conclusions are liked. The great judges are the ones who skillfully employ the traditional techniques, understanding that they do not lead automatically to the lazy repetition of similar results generation after generation but, rather, afford the opportunity for growth that is the very life of the common law.

Above all, the test for propriety of any judicial change in the law is the society's readiness for and probable approval of the change. Theoretically this is about the same as the test for legislative change in the law. Yet it requires a more delicate testing of, or guessing at, public attitudes, since legislators through their political contacts have readier means of measuring social pressures than judges have, and the pressures are likely to be more evident in legislative areas than in less political areas where judicial revision of the law is indicated. Nevertheless, judges can be and quite often are aware of major surges in social attitudes. They may even be more aware of them than legislators are, with respect to problems that regularly come before the courts and do not come before legislatures. Also, good judges who keep abreast of new thinking in the law may have better ideas about what new solutions should be than do most legislators.

Common law courts do make law, and they make it through their judicial opinions. Yet the sources of law, including new judge-made law, are for the most part neither the courts nor the judges themselves, but the society. The activities, interests, and ethical attitudes of the citizenry, especially among dominant groups, provide the real sources of the common law. This was true in the Middle Ages when the common law had its beginnings, it continued to be true as the common law grew and developed during intervening centuries, and it is true as the common law undergoes today the most rapid modernization in its entire history.

The common law system could not have survived through the centuries if it had been no more than a method of perpetuating its own past. It has survived and is healthy today because, in the hands of wise judges, it calls for growth, and builds on the past to meet the needs of the present and the future. The system will not tolerate hog-wild innovation, but without innovation, it will die—it would have died long ago. Legislatures can aid the courts in updating the law, but much of the ultimate responsibility rests upon our appellate courts, and specifically, upon the judges who sit on those courts.

No one discipline of human thought and study can be shown to be more important than the others. They stand together. It is law that binds them together. In our Anglo-American law, particularly as the system has grown and developed in these United States during the past two hundred years, it is the common law, the law that from its beginnings has been and still today is pronounced by our appellate judges, that is central to the system, not because the judges have pronounced it, but because their pronouncement reflects the needs and standards of American society as it grows and changes, always with solid ties to the past. It is living law. For us its life has spanned two hundred years—and more. But its present life is a continuing one, vigorous and healthy, rooted in the past but with its vision and its aspirations firmly fixed upon the present as the present constantly and inevitably moves into the future. It has a lasting permanence within itself, and an ever-changing, ever-growing adaptability suited for 1776, and 1976, and 1984, and for times only dreamed of, yet to come.

Adversary System

Every judge and every lawyer knows, and is quite ready to explain to anyone who will listen, that appellate courts deciding appealed cases serve, in our common law system, two related but separate functions. The first and most obvious one is to settle the controversy between the litigants, thus presumably achieving justice under the law. The law is found in constitutions, statutes, and in precedents—the prior decisions of the appellate courts. That is the common law system. The court's decisions in the same case in which it performs its function of achieving justice under the law for the immediate litigants becomes a precedent, laying down the rule of law for future cases. The appellate court's second function as it decides each single case is thus a law-making function. Precedents also provide authoritative interpretations of constitutions and statutes.

The "adversary system" is the accepted and descriptively correct name for the method by which litigated cases are presented to our courts, including appellate courts, for decision. Attorneys representing the interests, usually private interests, of the respective litigants, their clients, present to the court the assertedly competing precedents and other legal materials that purportedly sustain their respective positions, along with arguments that tend to explain and support the favorably cited precedents and tend to distinguish the opposing ones. Arguments and even precedents that may be relevant but are not helpful to either side may be ignored, never brought to the court's attention. They do not serve the function, probably the only function, in which the parties and their counsel are interested—getting the specific case favorably decided in keeping with their specific interests.

The adversary system is well designed to make courts aware of reasons, legal and otherwise, which support and oppose the claims of immediate parties to a lawsuit. Each party's purpose is normally to win, to enforce the claims or defenses he asserts. Litigants are not knights errant protecting interests other than their own, and the adversary system of presenting controversies to a court suits their purposes exactly. It is just right for serving the first and most evident function of appellate courts.

But what of the law-making function inherent in the doctrine that precedents constitute the law for the future? The adversary system creates private incentives that reasonably assure the presentation to a court of some of the considerations relevant to its law-making duties. Is it possible that still other considerations relevant to the public interest or to the interests of third persons different from those of the immediate litigants ought to be brought to the court's attention before it establishes precedents that constitute future law? Ought there to be some regular procedure by which relevant considerations not helpful to any current litigant will regularly be brought to a court's attention?

On a multi-judge appellate court, one or another of the several judges will probably think of concerns that employed counsel choose to ignore. That is one reason why appellate courts are multi-judge bodies. Also, if the court itself or some person or institution not a party to a pending cause recognizes that the case potentially involves interests different from those of the litigating parties, arrangements can be made for the filing of *amicus curiae* briefs, or for the presentation of oral argument by *amici curiae*. The original parties may not appreciate this, however, and there is no assurance that either the court or such third parties will know about the unargued considerations or move promptly to make arrangements for the added representation. In a few states the Attorney General's office is by statute given the duty of keeping up with all appealed cases and intervening, perhaps as *amicus curiae*, in any case in which a public or state interest appears. That solves the problem for those few states, at least if the lawyers assigned to this duty are diligent, but only for the limited class of cases in which there is a state interest.

There may be cases in which the two immediate parties to a lawsuit choose to ignore the interests of third persons who are not involved in the particular controversy yet whose nonidentical but similar interests may be affected by the precedent established in the current decision. Briefs and arguments do not call these unrepresented interests to the court's attention. If the judges do not on their own initiative identify and evaluate them, the resulting precedent may lay down unwise new law.

The adversary system does not perfectly serve the law-making function of the appellate judicial process. Ultimately, it is the judges' diligence and wisdom that must be relied upon to assure that the function is properly performed. They must think not only of the little sets of facts that the immediate cases present but of an undetermined number of sets of facts to which the precedent may in the future be applied. Judges may rely upon the writings of scholars not employed to represent the interests of litigants, but concerned rather with sound correlation of law with the socioeconomic and political needs of the community. These are the ones who today most conscientiously present to the courts the needs and concerns of society. Their work may be cited in briefs of counsel, or it may not, but wise judges avail themselves of it whether it is cited or not. And in their opinions good courts do cite it, or at least make use of it.

Statutory Construction

When we talk about problems of statutory construction, we are talking about cases in which there is a problem concerning the meaning or the effect of a statute. The judicial decisional process often involves the construction of statutes. * If we could simply employ the traditional idea—that courts do not make law, legislatures make law, and courts merely apply the law as the legislatures have laid it down—then our courts dealing with statutes would have an easy job. Except, of course, the

---

* Back in 1975 I was asked to talk at a Federal Appellate Judges Conference (U.S. Court of Appeals judges) at Washington, D.C. The topic assigned was the judicial interpretation of statutes. This is an area that troubles judges constantly, since statutory meanings are often unclear.

statutes are not clear. That's what the arguments are about. Three short excerpts from the writings of great jurists indicate the problem.

"When things are called by the same name," wrote Justice Cardozo, "it is easy for the mind to slide into an assumption that the verbal identity is accompanied in all its sequences by identity of meaning." *Lowden v. Northwestern Bank & Trust Co.*, 298 U.S. 160, 165 (1936).

Justice Holmes wrote, "A word is not a crystal, transparent and unchanged; it is the skin of a living thought and may vary greatly in color and content according to the circumstances and the time in which it is used." *Towne v. Eisner*, 245 U.S. 418, 425 (1917).

Judge Learned Hand: "It is one of the surest indexes of a mature and developed jurisprudence not to make a fortress out of the dictionary; but to remember that statutes always have some purpose or object to accomplish whose sympathetic and imaginative discovery is the surest guide to their meaning." *Cabell v. Markham*, 148 F.2d 737, 739 (1945).

Lawbooks and articles on statutes list three major approaches to statutory construction. One of them is commonly called "the literalness test." It calls for rigid adherence to the letter of the law as written regardless of consequences. We find courts or individual judges insisting that the judicial task is to accept the law as written, to take the words as they appear, look in the dictionary at what those words mean literally, and go on from there. Writers on statutory construction today generally condemn that approach, but it is still used.

A second approach, which is much talked of in the books, has been called "the golden rule approach." That makes it sound attractive. It rejects the principle of purely literal interpretation, and suggests that the words of the statutes should be given their plain and natural meaning unless manifest injustice or absurdity would result. The word "unless" is not very broad. It leaves out the possibility of considering the true purposes of the statute. The emphasis under the golden rule approach is on literalness unless extreme absurdity or injustice would result. That's better than literalness alone, but it doesn't carry us very far beyond it.

The third approach, sometimes called the modern approach, comes from Chief Justice Edward Coke's famous Heydon's case—the "mischief rule," to the effect that four things are to be looked for and considered in interpreting a statute. One, what was the older law before the making of the act? Second, what was the mischief and defect for which the previous law did not provide? Third, what remedy had the parliament resolved and appointed to "cure the disease of the Commonwealth?" And fourth, the true reason of the remedy. The office of judges is always to make such construction as shall suppress the mischief and advance the remedy, or in words more customary to this day, to advance the purpose of the statute.

I would like to think in terms of another approach—one that is not formally named, but I think it is representative of what judges in most courts do today. It might be called "the proper judicial function" or "sound law approach." I will give some illustrations.

Suppose that we have a statute enacted in 1880, or in 1910. How do we interpret that? If we look at a 1910 Webster's dictionary or law dictionary we will find that a given word is shown with a different meaning than in a 1980 dictionary. Do we interpret the 1910 statute in terms of the 1910 intent of the legislators? We talk about legislative intent as being the controlling fact. Should we interpret "legislative intent" in the light of a 1980 meaning for the 1910 words?

We know that the U.S. Supreme Court persistently does go back to legislative debates and legislative records to determine what legislators had in mind when they enacted a particular statute. But should the court be bound by what legislators said in 1910? Are we bound by the problems that they were thinking of in 1910 or, applying the statute in 1984, are we concerned with the different issues, the different social attitudes and the different wisdom that would characterize an initial consideration of the problem today? The literalness approach to the statute certainly would prevent us from using 1984 attitudes.

Suppose the 1910 statute used the word "obscene." Do we in the 1980s define obscenity as it was defined in 1910? The bastardy acts and other statutes affecting the status of illegitimate children, mostly enacted in the 1800s, are still on the books. Are they to be applied as they were a century ago? Are the protections of the due process clause of the Fourteenth Amendment and its implementing statutes, adopted just after the Civil War, to be interpreted only in the light of nineteenth century ideas as to what constituted "due process of law"? Does the "restraint of trade" proscribed by the antitrust laws refer only to reasonableness of business practices as conceived at the turn of the century? I could go on with illustrations of that sort at great length. The books are full of them.

We say frequently that in interpreting a statute we want to discover the *intent* of the legislature. It was Chief Justice Brian who said that the devil himself "knoweth not the mind of man." It is difficult to discover intent; and when you cannot discover with any certainty the state of mind of one man, the process of discovering the states of mind, the intent of 535 men who make up the federal Congress, becomes an extremely difficult matter. The United States Supreme Court has time and again referred back to legislative debates, to discussions in committee, and to other background sources. But if you have to work with state law few legislatures have transcripts of proceedings comparable to those that are available at the federal level. The problem of legislative intent as such involves as much possibility of being misled as almost anything one can get into. There are bits of legislative record that are devised peculiarly by legislators for the purpose of misleading judges. And much legislative discussion is designed primarily to persuade, to get votes pro or con, rather than to present impartial analysis.

There are some types of legislative record that I think are truly useful. If you have a record of what was said and done by the Commissioners on Uniform State Laws or by the members of the American Law Institute, you have a pretty authoritative and reliable key to legislative intent. But even there, provisions enacted or promulgated thirty years ago may not be applicable to current conditions, in the same way that they were applicable to conditions prevailing in the commercial world of 1955. True, the Commissioners on Uniform State Laws try to keep things of that sort up to date, but they sometimes don't quite do it, and amendments are not always enacted in every state.

An equally common difficulty with legislative intent as a guide to statutory interpretation is that often there simply was no legislative intent with reference to the problem that has now arisen. The legislators just did not realize that the problem inhered in their enactment. Even the wisest lawmakers cannot think of everything in advance.

This situation was well set forth in 1941 by one of my old law school teachers, Zechariah Chafee, who came from Rhode Island. In "The Disorderly Conduct of Words," 41 Colum. L. Rev. 381, 400, he wrote:

> Years ago I drafted an intestacy act for the Rhode Island Bar Association. . . . I explained the bill to the legislature, which enacted it. . . . Later the Rhode Island Supreme Court had to decide whether the words "real estate" in the statute included a peculiar interest in

land. Both sides wrote to me to learn my intention. . . . I [wrote] that I had never thought of this point before, but that I now considered the interest to be "real estate" within the act. Both lawyers offered to read my letter to the court, which very properly refused to listen to it. So the intention of the only person who had given prolonged thought to the bill was ignored, and in fact he had no intention on this point. The court decided the case . . . and said that [its] construction was "not inconsistent with the manifest intent" of the legislature. . . . "When the judges are professing to declare what the legislature meant, they are in truth legislating to fill up *casus omissi*". . . .

Let me repeat a story about Robert Browning. Toward the close of his life he received a letter from Professor Hiram Corson of Cornell, asking whether one of his early obscure poems meant what Corson supposed it did. Browning replied: "I didn't mean that when I wrote it, but I mean it now."

My fourth approach to the interpretation of statutes in terms of "the proper judicial function" or "the sound law approach," does not leave the judge as free as a bird in terms of his interpretation of the statute. He has got to start with the words of the statute. But, assuming that there is argument about the meaning of words in any statute, what I am suggesting is, and what I think the recent history of judicial interpretation of statutes bears out, is that a sound law approach is what we are attempting to use today; that is, sound in terms of the current demands of society relating to the particular area of law to which the statute refers.

That this approach has at least received some specific judicial recognition is shown by a restatement of it in the dissenting opinion in *Croker v. Boeing Co.*, 662 Fed. 2d 975, 999 (3d Cir. 1981). Most courts, however, employ it *sub silentio* while they purport to discover "legislative intent" by nominal reliance upon the traditional approaches and so-called canons of construction.

Constitutional Interpretation

What do I think of the death sentence in criminal law? Should it be eliminated?

An argument has been made that killing (death) is "cruel and unusual punishment" prohibited by the Bill of Rights (Eighth Amendment) in the U.S. Constitution. That argument is a worrisome one. The death penalty may be cruel; perhaps most punishments are cruel, and it is difficult to believe that death is any more cruel than life imprisonment. The infliction of death as punishment was certainly not unusual in the United States when the Bill of Rights was adopted in 1791, if that is the time from which we attach meaning to the constitutional language. If we define this language as of today, it is hard to say whether or not the death penalty is now "unusual," let alone whether it is "cruel *and* unusual."

Such a technical analysis of the question is, of course, not characteristic of current debate on it, even though the debate is normally classified as one of constitutionality. The actual content of the debate is most often sociological: What rule best serves and represents the interests of today's society, concerned as it is with humane crime prevention and control? Some citizens, perhaps a minority, would include a comparison of taxpayer costs: Does it cost less to execute a prisoner than to feed and house him (or her) for the period of a life sentence?

When I was on the Arkansas Supreme Court, more than thirty years ago, the matter of death sentences worried me, though the question of constitutionality was not yet seriously presented. Death sentences were definitely not "unusual" then. I am not particulary proud now of the way I then resolved my problem. I made up my mind that if it should fall my lot, by rotation of assigned cases, to write the court's opinion affirming a death sentence, I would accept a personal responsibility for the decision by compelling myself to be present at and witness the execution. Fortunately, I was not assigned a death penalty case during the year and a half that I served on the Court. That would not have had anything to do, in any event, with the problem of constitutional interpretation.

That problem is even more regularly presented by the "due process of law" and "equal protection of the laws" clauses of the Fourteenth Amendment. This amendment, adopted in 1868 in the aftermath of the Civil War, was designed to ensure to newly enfranchised black persons the same legal rights of life, liberty, property, and the law's protections as are accorded by state laws to white persons. Now, joined up as the Fourteenth is with the Fifth Amendment (1791), it is established as the guarantor of an almost unlimited body of rights, many of which had never been identified in terms of constitutional law in 1791 or 1868. There is little difference in legal or general public opinion today concerning the propriety of this expanded application of constitutional language. The only current debate is as to whether this or that still newer area should now be brought within the old constitutional guaranties.

Appellate Judicial Opinions

The writing of opinions is probably not an appellate judge's most important work, but it is the work which, more often than not, has most to do with his public reputation. He has to take it seriously, and usually he does.

The court's tentative decision has been made before he starts to write. He is aware of the views expressed in conference by his fellow judges. He knows that his assignment is to write an opinion for the whole court, or its majority, and not just for himself, though he does not want to dissent from his own opinion. He is entitled to employ his own writing style and his own jurisprudential concepts, but he needs to refer to divergent concurring reasons expressed by other judges so that they will not find it necessary to write separate opinions.

The writing judge knows that if his case is a difficult one his colleagues are relying on him to do the further research and analysis that may raise doubts about the tentative decision to which he agreed. He is free to talk with his colleagues about his opinion as he writes it. Often he will not, because writing is a one-person job. The writing should be done as soon as possible after the conference, while the writer can still remember what the other judges' views were. He may choose to check with other judges as he writes to make sure that he understands their views, perhaps to the extent of showing them drafts of relevant paragraphs and asking, "Does this adequately take account of your views on that point?" A draft can be revised before it is seen by all the judges. The fact that the writing judge puts his name on the opinion does not relieve the court as an entity of its responsibility, nor does it relieve the writing judge of his duty to make this opinion the court's collective statement. No piece of writing can become a court's opinion until it has been formally approved by the members of the court as a group, or by the required majority. Normally this approval will come at an opinion conference held shortly before opinions are due to be released.

It has been said that appellate judges are, by the very nature of their work, professional writers. Yet few of them have gained acclaim, even among members of the bar, for their performance of that part of the judicial task. There has been a considerable volume of writing about opinion-writing, and most of it has been critical.

Dean Wigmore's comments are among those most quoted. Writing early in the century, in the first edition of his great treatise on the law of evidence, he listed six major shortcomings in the bulk of the many thousands of opinions he had read. Five of the shortcomings had to do with content and form. First was the failure to exhibit knowledge of and reliance upon broad legal principles as distinguished from narrow rules. Others comprised disregard of controlling precedents, overemphasis on techniques and technicalities, undue bondage to the servitude of precedent, and over-consideration of every point of law raised in the briefs. The sixth, probably not in point here though once a common basis for criticism, was the one-man opinion, not truly representative of the court as a whole. Mercifully, he did not dwell upon the too-frequent clumsiness of legalistic style and even grammar that more ordinary critics have often observed.

Should judicial opinions set forth the courts' real reasons for their decisions? Or does the nature of the law and of the judicial process call for a discreet non-reference to some kinds of considerations that actually induce courts to decide as they do? Are the prevailing arguments that judges present to each other in the decision conference, before they vote on a case, the same as the reasons that are set out in the subsequent opinions? Should they be?

Karl Llewellyn tells of an experiment he conducted when he was collecting material for his great book, *The Common Law Tradition: Deciding Appeals*. He asked a number of his friends, law professors newly become appellate judges, to "make notes on how your cases get decided, how it happens," and to let him study the notes. Llewellyn was concerned with what factors affected results either in decision conferences or later, if minds were changed then. The findings would have made an interesting chapter in his book, but not one of the judges provided the requested information.

I was one of those he asked, when I was appointed to the Arkansas Supreme Court in 1949. My promise to Llewellyn was from the first a hesitant one. I checked with the other, and older, judges on the court as to whether I should, and one exploded in anger. I was lectured on the confidential nature of the conference, and there were implicit references to something like the sacred secrets of an ancient priesthood of justice. At any rate I desisted, and thus became merely another of those who did not furnish Llewellyn with tangible evidence of what he already knew.

Judge Jerome Frank said that "opinions . . . disclose but little of how judges come to their conclusions. The opinions are often ex post facto; they are *censored expositions*." The failure of judicial opinions to set out the real reasons for a court's decisions is seldom deliberate cover-up. A good result (or a bad one) may be based more on judicial intuition, on a judge's sense of what fits in with his standards and ideals, than on thorough analysis. Briefs filed by counsel may have done no more than argue by analogy or otherwise from opposing precedents. An opinion becomes a poor one when the judge has not thought through the problem and has not identified the real reasons that support his decision. He has not been dishonest, but his writing does not reflect the completeness and clarity essential to thoroughgoing integrity in judicial opinions, if not in judges.

Failure to state these real reasons can occur in opinions that break new ground as well as in those that retain old law. An opinion that breaks new ground is more honest if it sets out that fact clearly, and does not pretend that it is merely applying settled law. Lawyers and other judges can be misled by that pretense. The hidden fact may not emerge, or may emerge incompletely. Similarly, reasons that truly supported a rule a half-century ago may no longer support it, though other relevant reasons do. In such a case, it is not enough to cite the precedent; the currently good reason also should be given. Nor is it ever enough to say simply that "public policy" justifies the result. There are a thousand different public policies of variant strengths that might be asserted. The specific policy should be identified and its relevancy made clear. Simply stated, neither precedent nor policy genuinely justifies a result except as the precedent's or the policy's own basis affords the justification.

Justice Cardozo is praised as one of the few judges in his time who was willing (and able?) to explain explicitly the application of social and economic values to the processes of judicial decision-making. Yet these explanations appeared almost exclusively in his great books, *The Nature of the Judicial Process* and *The Growth of the Law*. These set out the real reasons for his court's great decisions far more clearly than his opinions did.

It must be remembered that Cardozo wrote his common law opinions more than a half-century ago, and that often he wrote not just for himself, but for the majority of a seven-judge court. Neither his times nor his colleagues left him free to bare in official opinions the nonlegalistic reasons that motivated both him and them in their wise decisions. The tradition was that judicial decisions must be grounded on "legal" considerations altogether, and Cardozo could not completely escape from that tradition. Perhaps he did not really wish to escape from it. He recognized a practical necessity for tying forward-looking opinions into the precedential past in order to make them acceptable to other judges, the bar, and to a tradition-minded public.

Even Justice Holmes employed different writing styles for his opinions than for his other writings. In *The Common Law*, he insisted that "the life of the law has not been logic; it has been experience," based upon "the felt necessities of the time, the prevalent moral and political theories, [and] intuitions of public policy. . . ." He repeated the same idea more than once in his later writing. Yet in his opinions he wrote largely in terms of precedents and legal principles and the analogies that could be derived from them. Even the aphorisms with which he star-studded some of his opinions were only incidental to his legal

analysis. He believed in real reasons, but chose not to parade them.

Roger J. Traynor of California is often named as one of
America's great common law judges of the most recent generation. Some of his opinions have been cited and re-cited hundreds of times. Perhaps the one most frequently referred to is
his concurrence in *Escola v. Coca Cola Bottling Co.* The case
involved a simple set of facts. A bottle of Coca Cola exploded
in the hand of a waitress. She sued the bottler. In the absence
of specific evidence as to what caused the bottle to explode,
the majority of the Supreme Court of California fell back
on the Latin magic of *res ipsa loquitur*, enabling the plaintiff to
establish defendant's negligence as the cause without producing actual evidence of that negligence. Traynor's concurring
opinion was more honest and realistic:

> The manufacturer's negligence should no longer be singled out as the
> basis of a plaintiff's right to recover. . . . It should now be recog-
> nized that a manufacturer incurs an absolute liability when an article
> that he has placed on the market, knowing that it is to be used with-
> out inspection, proves to have a defect that causes injury to human
> beings. . . . Even if there is no negligence. . . , public policy de-
> mands that responsibility be fixed wherever it will most effectively
> reduce the hazards to life and health inherent to defective products
> that reach the market. . . . The risk of injury can be insured by the
> manufacturer and distributed among the public as a cost of doing
> business.

This brief analysis stated, in 1944, the reasons which forty
years later sustain the law of products liability. Scores of books
and law review articles have said the same thing at much
greater length, but this short opinion, giving real reasons
rather than traditionally artificial legalistic ones for a result
that all the judges favored, was the judicial parent of a mass of
modern law.

Traynor's devotion to the giving of real reasons in his opinions was consistently secondary, however, to his devotion to good craftsmanship in dealing with the traditional materials of the law. Not only did he seek results that made good social and economic sense, but he also sought to disassociate his own predilections from them by showing how the results fitted neatly into the regular framework of the law.

Every reader of the Illinois Supreme Court Reports for the last third of a century knows that the opinions written by Justice Walter V. Schaefer achieved both clarity and understandable good sense. Those two qualities complemented each other. Beyond that, they identified relevant facts of modern life as they related to issues raised in his cases and dealt with them in realistic fashion. It is not difficult to understand why the late Adlai Stevenson once remarked that, of all he was able to do during his years as Governor of Illinois, the one official act that he was sure would yield long-time benefit to the state was his appointment of Wally Schaefer to the Supreme Court.

The history of the common law records the names of only a few truly great judges, and it is notable that all of them were men who saw their cases, even routine ones, as opportunities to examine the relation of law to the needs and practices of the society which they served. Lord Mansfield in his time saw that traders were operating largely outside the law because the medieval common law had been developed without them. He remedied this deficiency by bringing the law merchant into the common law. Similarly, he saw principles based on good conscience developing imperfectly on the equity side, and he created the beginnings of quasi-contract on the law side. John Marshall in developing constitutional law looked primarily to the needs of the new nation as he went beyond what he found in books to lay down principles that would stabilize and guide the nation's growth. Chief Justice Doe of New Hampshire saw law as the servant of the people, not their unthinking master,

and sought to bring into it the common sense that characterized his people's Spartan, yet enlightened, way of life. Cardozo
took cases that other judges might have disposed of with easy
reliance on old precedent, and made great cases out of them.
They carried the law forward, away from outmoded limitations, to positions more commensurate with the changed conditions of a burgeoning economy. So it has always been with
the score or so of American judges to whom history has accorded the topmost rank. They have all been men of vision
and broad understanding, men willing and able to see, in their
cases, more than the pettily important features of a single
dispute.

Yet they were all more than men of vision. They were expert
craftsmen. Vision and understanding alone cannot achieve results that make for greatness. The great judge must have the
facility of a great lawyer in dealing with the materials of
the law. He cannot create new law out of whole cloth, but
must labor within the framework that the law provides, and
his opinions must fit the precedential pattern of the common
law. He cannot innovate from scratch. If he did, his opinions
would not be acceptable either to his colleagues on the bench
or to members of the bar and, being unacceptable to them,
would be by their advice scorned by the citizenry as well.

Law, even more than other disciplines, is effective only so
far as there is popular acceptance of it. Judges, and particularly
elected judges, are aware of that fact and, to varying extents,
are governed by it. If they believe that the public's conception
of law is a Blackstonian one, they may write to that view without themselves accepting it. Whether this aids law's effectiveness in the latter part of the twentieth century is increasingly doubtful. Today's citizenry possesses some measure of
sophistication, and the unsophisticated rarely read judicial
opinions. Non-lawyers who do read them are usually interested more in results and the societal justification for them

the virtue be at least latent in them. Ethical decency, perhaps even ethical superiority, is generally agreed to be a proper end of law, and should therefore be aimed at by opinions that make law.

The most immediate function of an opinion is to explain to parties and their counsel what is being done with their case. The law-making aspect of the common law appellate judicial process does not outweigh the dispute-deciding aspects of it, even though the latter is sometimes overshadowed. Actually, the theory is that the dispute-deciding part is the court's main job, and that the law-making part is a consequence of the decision of the dispute. At least this is the traditional way in which our common law has developed. The dispute must be decided and the adversary procedure is supposed to assure that there is inquiry into all facets of the problem. Whether this breadth of inquiry is achieved or not, the case is decided, reasons are given for the decision, and the parties or their counsel read the reasons.

One of the major functions of any system of law is to assure its own acceptance in the society it governs, and this is part of the job of each judicial opinion. Law that is rejected by the people it undertakes to control, or that is received by them with doubts and misgivings, often is not good law, and may not even be accepted as law at all. To a great extent the validity of law for a people depends on their confidence in it. There is more mystery, more lack of accurate public information about appellate courts than about any other agency in our democratic government. Some see this as largely the doing of judges themselves who, by wearing robes and keeping silent about their work, set themselves apart as a sort of priestly cult. Others point out that robes and judicial silences have their own justification, unconnected with public mystification and sense of legerdemain. Regardless of whose fault it is, the public, including even the bar, remains woefully uninformed.

Using current jargon, our appellate courts' public relations are bad. Perhaps explicit interpretation of the courts by their own judges, speaking and writing to appropriate public groups, is needed; seldom will there be harm in this, and judicial exposition need not achieve the lucidity of Cardozo to justify itself. Whatever makes for better understanding is good. But it remains true that opinions are the principal vehicle for judicial communication.

Do judicial opinions have a function with reference to their own authors? Pride of authorship is by no means always an evil. When it builds a protective fence around poor writing and preserves it at the law's expense it is wrong. When it preserves minor defects that would have been easily eliminated, it is unfortunate. When it induces a judge to forego the advantages of group criticism it is all bad. The poorest opinions are apt to be written by judges who take no pride in them, who regard the preparation of them as mere chores. Pride in work well done is a proper incident of good craftsmanship in any field of work, including law. This pride can drive a judge to hard work and meticulous effort. I will even say that one proper function of good judicial opinions is to give a sense of satisfaction, of work well done, to their authors.

Is there any guidance available to new members of appellate courts on how to write their opinions in order to achieve literary quality, sound professional craftsmanship, and in general the ends that good appellate opinions are supposed to serve? Must new judges always work these things out for themselves? Too often it seems that they must, or think they must.

Older judges are usually willing to give advice, some sound and some unsound. Too often they do not truly know their own virtues, and misdescribe them. Or they praise what they are accustomed to, confusing the familiar with the good. The advice is apt to put emphasis on little techniques and lofty ideals, neglecting the central problem of how best to see that the appellate court's total job in our society is well performed.

It would almost be taken for granted that new judges would be told to read Cardozo and the few others among our great opinion writers who have undertaken to analyze themselves and their work in print, unless it were assumed they had already commenced such reading when they began the contemplation of judicial careers. Strangely, this advice is often not given and such reading often not done. There is no body of writing in English that is closer to the appellate judge's job than that which comes loosely under the head of jurisprudence. Yet works with this word in their titles have little more popularity among appellate judges than among practicing lawyers. Nor are many judges aware of the available literature on the nature and function of the judicial process.

The greatest difficulty that an appellate judge faces in developing himself as an effective opinion writer is that he may receive no real criticism of his writing for months or years. Unlike ordinary editors or publishers, state reporters and the West Publishing Company never refuse to print opinions, nor do they even edit them. A judge's writing is published whether good or not. Almost no one except law review editors and losing litigants criticize his work, and even these critics usually dwell only on the correctness of his legal analyses rather than on the quality of his presentation. It is no wonder that most appellate judges tend to become self-satisfied with their opinion writing. No one ever tells them that there is something wrong with it, or encourages them to improve it. They are never compelled to analyze their work, or to read analyses of it by their peers, in terms of whether their opinions are truly performing the functions that judicial opinions are supposed to perform.

The purposes served by judicial opinions may properly be

identified with the functions of appellate courts in our legal system. These could be thought of as the functions of a magic priesthood, and some remnant of this thought undoubtedly remains with us. Our sane intelligence rejects the thought, but it persists. Judicial opinions are the voices of our courts, and they serve many purposes of government itself, though not all. Opinions are the public voice of appellate courts, and so represent the judiciary to the public. But they are not voices merely. They are what courts do, not just what they say, and provide the substance of judicial action, not just news releases about what courts have done, though they have that function too.

It is certain that judges can improve their opinion writing by conscious attention to the question "Who am I writing for, and to what ends?" It is equally certain that opinion readers can improve their understanding of what they read if they bear in mind the purposes that the opinion is intended to serve. The very act of thinking about the judicial process tends to improve the thinker's judicial product, just as it improves also the non-judicial thinker's understanding of the product.

It would seem that the opinion writing process has in the past been too much taken for granted, and that we will all benefit from more thinking and talking and writing and arguing about it. Whether conscious and deliberate reexamination of the functions of judicial opinions will yield any new insights, the reexamination will at least make us more aware of old insights, and that added awareness will by itself usefully serve the total functions of the judicial process in our society.

Trial by Jury or by Chancery Judge

Arkansas is one of the very few American states that still retain the old English system of separate courts of Law and Equity. Our Circuit Courts have general "law" jurisdiction, including criminal law, and sit with juries. Equity jurisdiction is vested in Chancery Courts, presided over by Chancellors who hear "equity" cases without juries. In most other states one court handles both law and equity cases, the same judge presiding over both but using juries only in cases on the law side. The constitutional guaranty of the right to trial by jury has never applied to equity cases.

Approximately a half-century ago I wrote an article under the title Equitable Prevention of Public Wrongs, published in 14 Texas Law Review 427 (1936). In it I discussed the extent to which criminal activities may in effect be prosecuted in equity courts sitting without a jury, with possible sanctions that are essentially penal in character. The jurisdictional situation is not appreciably different in the 1980s, though we have grown more accustomed to it. The following comments are taken from that 1936 article, with footnotes omitted.

It is traditional for courts of equity to state that they have nothing to do with the enforcement of criminal law, that their sole concern is with the protection of civil and property rights, and that those who fear crime must seek relief in courts of law or elsewhere. At the same time, it is equally usual for chancery judges to declare that when civil and property rights require protection, equity will undertake to protect them against imminent dangers, including the danger of crime. It is said that the criminal aspects of a threatened injury operate neither to create nor to destroy equity's interest in a case.

The fact is that equity courts frequently do issue injunctions against the doing of acts which are crimes, either because such acts also involve interferences with property or civil rights or are deemed public nuisances. Vigorous objections to the use of the injunction as a means of enforcing the criminal law have been expressed, the objections being just as strenuous in reference to cases in which protectible private or public property interests are clearly discernible as toward cases in which such interests are to be found only by following tenuous paths of economic-legalistic logic.

Such objections are apt to include some reference to the Court of the Star Chamber in England, where the need for quick justice administered by a strong hand characterized the troublous period in which the Star Chamber enforced the criminal law, and to the gradual return of more peaceful and

law-abiding times during which the harsh and sometimes unjust rule of the Court of Star Chamber became so unnecessary
and unpopular that it was abolished. The inference is that
though these be somewhat troublous times in our own land,
the prevalence of unbridled crime has not reached a point at
which its control demands employment of the quick justice of
courts sitting without juries.

Objections urged against the operation of criminal equity
have been vigorous and numerous. It is contended that summary punishment for contempts arising out of disobedience to
injunctions restraining criminal acts is violative of the trial by
jury and due process of law guaranties contained in state and
federal constitutions. A ready answer to this, of course, is that
the punishment imposed is not for the crime itself, but rather
for the contempt of court which is involved in flouting an order to do or not to do particular acts. Still, a defendant who
has been enjoined from operating a saloon in violation of the
criminal law, then sentenced to a term in jail for violation of
the injunction, is apt to think that he is in jail on account
of the alleged commission of a crime, and he knows that he
has not had a jury trial. The conclusion drawn by a nonlegal
mind is almost irresistible—there is punishment for crime
without trial by jury.

If the only question was whether decisions by judges sitting
without juries are more apt to be unfair and unjust than the
verdicts of juries, the matter might be dismissed quickly. There
is no evidence to indicate that juries are more accurate or
more unprejudiced than judges sitting alone. The whole history of equity courts, and certainly current practice in them,
indicates that the public generally and litigants particularly
are at least as well satisfied with the intelligence and integrity
of equity judges trying equity cases as with the same qualities
in common law juries trying criminal cases. Possibly the peculiar nature of equity jurisdiction presents to the chancellors

types of cases more suited to one-man trial than are criminal cases generally, but equity cases are on the whole no less complicated than penal trials, and there may also be certain types of criminal cases which are peculiarly suited to one-man trial. It must be admitted that trial by jury is a very slow, costly, and cumbersome process, which in modern times is becoming increasingly unfitted to care for the huge mass of business, both civil and criminal, that accumulates in law courts, and that the tendency today is to dispense with jury trial in a great number of criminal cases, either by voluntary waiver of the right to trial by jury, or by the extra-judicial method of allowing prosecuting attorneys to bargain for pleas of guilty, to enter *nolle prosequis* in cases where guilt is doubtful, and to select for trial only a comparatively small proportion of the cases which come before them, the selection being usually based on the prosecutor's guess as to the likelihood of conviction. If all criminal cases be considered, the percentage of them which terminate in jury verdicts of conviction or acquittal is amazingly small. Trial by jury in criminal cases is in practice a kind of last resort, rather than the usual thing.

The question is not merely whether judges alone are more or less honest, efficient, and wise than juries. Difficulties arising out of mass psychology and the effects of deeply rooted popular traditions and beliefs must be faced. The criminal jury is not merely a practical piece of machinery, or even a constitutional guaranty; it is in America well-nigh a sacred institution, held in popular esteem high above considerations of mere practicality.

If it is recognized that the function of a judicial system is not only to administer justice in the controversies which come before it but also to present to the people generally an exemplary and confidence-inspiring appearance of ideal administration of justice that will induce non-controversial obedience to the law, it becomes apparent that both individual litigants and the interested public must feel satisfied that the judicial system is operating with fairness and certainty. In America, it is undoubtedly true that the prevalent faith in the institution of trial by jury is to some degree responsible for such popular satisfaction as exists with the criminal court system. To the extent that equity, by eliminating jury trials in essentially criminal cases, destroys this popular satisfaction in the conduct of the judicial system, equity is harmful. It seems possible, however, that the public may not associate this assumed semisacredness of the jury with all types of cases that technically turn upon violation of the criminal law, and there may be some cases in which advantage can be taken of the efficient operation of criminal equity without suffering any material loss of popular confidence in the integrity of the general system for enforcement of the criminal law.

It is familiar legal language that equity acts to protect property rights only, and not personal rights. This language has been much cited as a reason against the granting of injunctions to restrain tortious or criminal acts, but courts actually granting injunctions have always had a ready answer to the argument—they can discover property interests to be protected in almost any case. The discovered property right in many instances may seem a flimsy one, but at least it is no flimsier than the reasons for the requirement of a property right as a condition to equity's action. No reasons except historical ones are today advanced to support the rule, and even these are much more honored by evasion than by observance. A legal system having its reason for existence in the need for relief from the inadequacies of an older and more formal body of law, yet at the same time giving such relief only to property and not to persons and interests of personality, would be absurd, more absurd than equity in fact is. An ancient method of growth in the law is by means of fictions which, appearing to comply with old and rigid rules in the law, yet actually evade them, thus after a fashion achieving justice in the name of injustice. This time-honored process is repeating itself in equity, in the courts' easy discovery of semi-fictional property interests satisfying the formal requirement.

Another explanation of equity's activity in restraining criminal conduct is in terms of the jurisdiction to restrain public nuisances, it being stated that an injunction will issue against any particular criminal act which is also a public nuisance. This explanation in turn leads to the criticism that sometimes equity courts go outside the orthodox concept of public nuisance in granting injunctions, wherefore it is concluded that criminal equity is extending itself too far. Both the explanation and the criticism take it for granted that the concept "public nuisance" really has a definite meaning and content based upon fundamental principles of some sort. Search for the fundamental principles fails altogether to discover them. Actually, Thayer's classic "'nuisance' is a good word to beg a question with" is revealing. The public nuisance formula is a statement of result rather than of reason for the result; a given situation or activity is enjoined because it is deemed so harmful to the health, morals, property, or general welfare of a large enough section of the public that its continued existence ought to be terminated specifically, and not because it has in years gone by been technically classified as a public nuisance. Both by judicial decision and by legislative fiat, new situations are constantly being brought within the scope of equity's restraining powers, and generally they are called public nuisances. This formal denomination comes as a kind of afterthought; it is obvious that the only real problem seriously considered either by court or legislature is the efficacy and social desirability of the quick remedy.

Probably the most usual, certainly the most all-embracing, statement of the basis of equity jurisdiction generally is that equity acts when and because legal remedies are inadequate.

This inadequacy is spelled out, in one way or another, in every area in which courts of equity afford their specific relief.

Are legal remedies actually inadequate for some or all crimes? The criminal law undertakes to provide punishment for all crimes but, as with other legal remedies, this is relief after the event. The respect in which equity rises superior to the inadequacies of law is that it gives specific rather than merely substituted relief. In terms of criminal equity, this amounts to saying that injunctions are preventive, whereas the remedies afforded by the criminal law are merely punitive. Criminal law in most jurisdictions still relies upon orthodox punishments such as death or fine and imprisonment as the standard means of dealing with crime and criminals. These are assumed to have the preventive effect of frightening evildoers from their contemplated misdeeds, and of course they prevent certain crimes from being committed by a punished individual during the period of his enforced separation from society. Nevertheless, the prevention aimed at both by orthodox criminal procedure and by its modern adjuncts is of antisocial conduct generally, rather than of particular immediately threatened criminal acts, whereas equity's preventive efforts are directed toward particular imminent injuries. If there is inadequacy of legal remedy in the equity sense, it must be an inability of the regular criminal procedure to prevent impending specific harms.

A bond to keep the peace may sometimes be an effective deterrent to threatened criminal acts. It is in nearly all American states governed by statutes, and is practically limited to activities involving breaches of the peace. Generally a magistrate determines whether a defendant will be required to give bond, though a few states permit appeal from the magistrate to a regular court, and a very few statutes allow the accused to have a jury trial on the issue of whether a bond shall be required. Imprisonment for failure to give bond is commonly provided for. Forfeiture of bond occurs in almost all states only if subsequent conviction by a jury for an offense covered by the bond is upheld, rather than by mere determination by a judge that an offense has been committed. If the use of peace bonds were more common, and if statutes controlling them permitted their application to a greater variety of offenses, they might well be deemed to serve the same purposes as injunctions against criminal acts. The fact is, however, that the comparatively small group of cases in which bonds to keep the peace are permitted are cases in which criminal equity seldom intervenes. In practice the two areas do not much overlap.

Preventive justice as such seems to have small place in criminal law. But equity does not discover inadequacy of legal remedy from the mere absence of preventive agencies on the law side; rather, the question in equity is whether forms of relief available at law are on their face adequate, and usually they are. It is enough if a standard legal remedy be even theoretically available. The remedy is said to be adequate for what it theoretically does, even though in practice it may accomplish nothing. Such are the cases in which, due to political influence, corruption, private interests, public sympathy and the like, prosecuting attorneys fail to prosecute, juries refuse to convict, or nominal punishments permit regular recurrence or continuance of the crime as if for an occasionally payable license fee.

Actually these are the cases for which the legal remedy is in fact inadequate, simply because the legal remedy is on the books only, and is not applied. Despite textbook insistence that equity is not concerned with legal inadequacies in this sense, it is believed that examination of the cases in which equity has acted by issuing injunctions against criminal acts will reveal that in nearly all of them inadequate enforcement of technically adequate laws is an underlying fact.

This fact serves to minimize the importance of one criticism sometimes directed at the criminal injunction. It is said that after an injunction has issued, the legal situation remains the same as when the act was merely prohibited or commanded by the already existent common law rule or statute, the injunction being no more than a duplicating command repeating in more personal fashion an already applicable rule of law, therefore adding nothing either to the law or to the parties' obligation to obey the law. Theoretically this is true, as far as the substantive criminal law is concerned. But the problem is not merely one of substantive law; it is a problem of law enforcement, and the issuance of the injunction sets in motion a swift and powerful punitive machinery which, in some types of cases at least, has been found to be more effective as a deterrent of crime than are the orthodox criminal procedures.

The truth seems to be that a great part of the objection to so-called "government by injunction" is really directed against interference of any sort whatever with the conditions or activities enjoined, rather than against the manner of the interference. The majority of writers who have opposed equity's activity within this area have been interested in labor disputes or related cases, in which injunctions were given restraining the conduct of strikes, picketing, boycotts, so-called criminal syndicalism, and public meetings generally. Injunctions against liquor nuisances have in the past claimed some adverse attention, but are almost everywhere accepted today as a normal part of the regular legal-equitable scheme of things, along with changing ideas of what constitutes a liquor nuisance. The injunctions objected to have enforced laws which public sentiment, or at least large segments of it, opposed. The objection was that criminal equity operated too efficiently; if violations of these laws were left to the regular criminal courts, they would pass unpunished, either because of the slow, cumbersome, and inefficient machinery of criminal courts not motivated by the urge of popular approval, or because the sympathy of juries would prevent convictions despite breaches of the substantive law.

On the other hand, little objection has been made to the operation of the injunctive process in the enforcement of criminal laws strongly supported by public opinion. If injunctions were granted only against the commission of crimes dangerous to the public health, violations of election laws, maintenance of brothels, breaches of the usury laws by small loan sharks, violations of building ordinances and zoning laws, interferences with government property, including waste of natural resources, the *ultra vires* acts of corporations harmful to the public, transgression of laws against monopoly, restraint of trade and other unfair business practices, and violations of the blue sky laws, the outcry against "government by injunction" would probably never be heard except from a few individuals who would inevitably protest interference with their own antisocial activities by whatever procedure. Insofar as disapproval of criminal equity is attributable to its securing results by way of enforcement of the law in situations where such results are not desired by the objectors, the disapproval seems scarcely valid. If the laws being enforced are bad laws, repeal rather than non-enforcement seems proper.

The area of criminal law enforcement in which the weapons of equity were first regularly used in America was in preventing the maintenance of premises whose purposes were deemed harmful to public morality. Cases falling within the area were readily susceptible to the designation "public nuisance," either legislative or judicial, and themselves doubtless contributed to the notion that criminal equity was limited to cases within the public nuisance concept. A notably common feature of these cases is their political-moral aspect. They involve activities of a type considered reprehensible by the sedately orthodox group which dominates the social and political life of many communities, especially in rural districts and non-cosmopolitan cities, while other economically influential or professionally political elements either secretly condone or tacitly favor and foster them. The usual situation tends to be one in which there is a strong public demand for rigid enforcement of the law voiced by one powerful group in the community, whose demand is being thwarted, perhaps through undercover machinations, by another group less numerous but almost equally powerful. This thwarting is rendered easier in the regular criminal courts by the complicated procedures of indictment and jury trial which offer opportunities for personal prejudices against the law to make themselves effectively felt.

A variant of this situation occurs when a "liberal" local area exists within and is governed by laws enacted by a larger "conservative" political unit. Regular criminal procedure lends itself readily to a sort of local self-determination which results in actual nullification of particular criminal laws within the local enforcing district. In these situations, the numerically and vocally dominant faction in the law-making jurisdiction is apt to demand some more efficient enforcing machinery for the laws thus being flouted. Criminal equity is an obvious answer to the demand.

Injunctions have frequently been granted against the unlicensed practice of such professions as law, medicine, and dentistry. In granting these injunctions, courts generally go carefully through the process of spelling out a property interest in duly licensed members of the same profession, to be protected, but the whole tenor of their opinions makes it clear that the interest primarily considered is protection of a gullible public against the quackeries and incompetencies of unlicensed practitioners. The sense in which the term "public nuisance" is also used in these cases serves merely to stress that fact. A well-known case in which the Kansas court enjoined the violation of the usury laws on a widespread scale by small loan sharks, (128 Kans. 772, 280 Pac.906, 66 A.L.R. 1072), mentions the public nuisance concept only casually in connection with an emphasized public need for a more efficient protection of wage earners against these illegal activities than could be given by the criminal courts. In these cases, situations were presented in which criminal prosecutions after the event would result in small punishments having little preventive effect, leaving the general public to be subjected to serious injury not only during the period of pending prosecution but afterward as well. The real reason for use of the injunctive process was a practical one since it was the only available means by which the antisocial activity could be effectively curbed.

The maintenance of premises in a condition dangerous to public health was treated rather early as a public nuisance and therefore enjoined, but numerous new types of health-threatening activities, including many unconnected with the use of particular premises, are restrained at the suit of the state. Preservation of public health is better achieved by preventive action than by substituted relief in the form of punishment after the event.

It seems that the greatest possibilities for future usefulness of criminal equity lie in the field of business crimes. Typical of these are violations of the modern blue sky laws. Criminal prosecutions have always been useful in combating fraudulent sales of bogus stocks, but their usefulness has been practically limited to cases of outright confidence men the crooked arithmetic of whose gold-brick schemes could readily be made evident to jurors. The more permanently plausible "investment plans" of semi-reputable security dealers and shoestring wildcatters in the business world do larger harm to the estates of widows and orphans, and to the savings accounts of the gullible, but criminal convictions can rarely be secured against these promoters. When public policy concludes that such promotions are socially unprofitable and should cease, the problem becomes one of effective legal machinery for that purpose. A blue sky commission may issue an order forbidding the sale of certain securities, but if the prospect of criminal conviction for its violation is dim and remote, that threat alone may not assure obedience. For that reason, blue sky statutes often contain some express provision for resort to the injunctive process. This is true both of the Federal Securities Act of 1933 and the Securities Exchange Act of 1934, as well as of many state enactments. For cases in which the commission's order is being disregarded, modern practice makes the injunction a principal weapon for enforcement.

The suitability of equity procedure for prevention of business crimes has been recognized in many other situations. It was early employed by the anti-trust laws, both federal and state, and in practice injunctions constitute for the national government a major device for compelling observance of these laws. There are state cases in which combinations in restraint of trade or other unfair business practices have been enjoined though there were no statutory provisions for such procedure. The enforcement of modern public utility laws has to a large extent been by means of injunctions. The Interstate Commerce Act provided for their use, as do most of the state enactments. The increasing variety of activities which in recent years has come to be regarded as falling within the public utility concept, and therefore subject to regulation, has correspondingly increased the variety of such activities enjoined. Enforcement of modern banking and insurance laws by injunction is also frequently provided for by state enactments.

Are there any common features of the criminal injunction cases distinguishing them from criminal acts to which the injunctive process has not been applied? For the most part, the cases appear to involve criminal acts against which the threat of punishment after the event will not have a very strong deterrent effect. With some of them, this is because the criminal punishment is small and unimportant to the offender compared with profits to be gained from the criminal act. This circumstance may be accompanied by the fact that the act is a recurrent or continuing one, necessitating successive petty prosecutions if the regular criminal procedure is to be followed. Frequently they are acts for which it is difficult to get jury convictions, either because local juries are prejudiced against the enforcement of the particular law involved, or the factual situations are too complicated for an ordinary jury to grasp, or the social philosophy which moved the legislature to create the crime is not sufficiently self-evident to move the jury's punitive conscience to a conviction even in the face of open violation of the law.

Genuinely serious difficulties are inherent in the last-mentioned possibility. The obtuseness of juries to a judge's technical instructions on the law is traditional. The social immorality of the act charged in business crime cases may not appear to the juror's mind except after careful explanation, and some juries tend not to return verdicts of guilty unless they are convinced of the moral wrongness of the defendant's acts. In their arguments to juries, defense attorneys pleading on behalf of guilty defendants may be relied upon to deny any essential wickedness in their conduct, and to extol a rugged individualism which that conduct exemplifies. One further feature of these cases is that they usually involve a sort of criminal act against which the threat or the fact of summary punishment for contempt is apt to be fairly effective as a deterrent. This is especially true for violations of zoning laws, unlicensed practice in the professions, and of the business crimes. A violator of these laws might be willing to pay even a substantial fine in order to continue the violation, but he will rarely be willing to go to jail for it.

Assuming that these are fairly common characteristics of cases which have fallen within the scope of criminal equity, wherein lies the superior efficacy of the injunction, compared with regular criminal remedies? Its advantages may be summarized briefly:

1. The summary nature of proceedings for contempt, and the resulting speed possible in dealing with law violators. Crowded dockets and the slow process of jury trial prevent many criminal cases in which no "bargain plea" is entered, from ever being tried. A greater number of cases can be handled with less congestion by fewer equity judges.

2. The direct and personal nature of the order issued, and the reasonable certainty of arraignment for violation of the command, both by reason of the judge's already aroused personal interest in the case, and of the non-necessity for indictment by grand jury or other preliminary proceedings.

3. Elimination of the influence of popular prejudice against punishment for particular types of criminal acts, to the extent that such prejudice represented in jurors' attitudes prevents convictions despite clear violations of the law.

4. Better analysis of complicated sets of facts, often difficult for juries to understand.

5. More intelligent appreciation of the purpose and spirit of the governing law, particularly when it deals with acts made criminal because of their disordering social or economic effect.

Perhaps this summary may in turn be abridged by saying that the advantages of criminal equity are a measure of relief against the disadvantages of trial by jury. By the same token they involve a relinquishment of other advantages which inhere in trial by jury. For the great mass of criminal cases, there cannot be serious doubt that the old form of procedure will in its essential features be continued, changes in minor detail sufficing to suit it to current needs.

Inadequacy of legal remedy is the standard generalized basis for equity jurisdiction, but the sense in which the word inadequacy is used must be determined before it has any useful meaning as a guide to concrete results. If it is used in the sense of a complete absence of relevant remedies in the criminal courts, then it explains nothing, for most, if not all areas of criminal equity would exist outside the explanation and in spite of it. Actually, the cases show that equity courts do consider the adequacy of available criminal remedies when they are asked to enjoin criminal acts, and that the sense in which that adequacy is measured is by whether the criminal remedy, admittedly on the law books, is or will be practically efficient in achieving reasonable enforcement of the law.

That does not mean that equity now does or ever will intervene in all types of criminal cases in which the regular criminal courts are inefficient and ineffective; rather it means that it will never intervene except in such cases. The suitability of equity procedure to the preventive ends aimed at, and assurance to defendants of fair opportunity to be heard on both law and evidence, will always be prerequisites to equity jurisdiction. But its growth, whether by statutory extension or by judicial decision, will almost inevitably be guided by the concept of legal inadequacy defined in this fashion.

No Task for the Short-Winded

When Chief Justice Arthur T. Vanderbilt used the expression from which the title of these remarks is drawn, * he was thinking about the seventeen long years during which he labored with the New Jersey State Constitution Revision Commission and the New Jersey Constitutional Convention to update that state's obsolete judicial system. Because he was not short-winded, success ultimately crowned his New Jersey efforts. At

*This item consists of excerpts from my address to the American Judicature Society at its annual meeting in Chicago some years ago. The entire text appears in 54 Judicature 366.

the same time, and in years that followed, he labored to improve judicial administration throughout the United States. So have many others. Success has not always crowned these efforts. Perhaps this has been because too many of us are short of wind, and short of effort. I like to think, however, that more often it is because we are still in the midst of the effort, and that we have wind enough and energy enough to keep working at it as long as we live, and then to hand the baton on to fresh new runners whose wind, we hope, will be better than our own. Perhaps among them will be some whose power and influence will equal those of Vanderbilt himself. The breadth of the effort that lies ahead of us is what I want to dwell upon. It is broader, I fear, than some of us like to admit that it is.

All of us agree that much of the law's shortcomings lies in our administration of it. If our courts were more efficient, or if all our courts were as efficient as our best ones are, a good deal of public dissatisfaction with law and lawyers would cease. We know pretty well what improvements in administration could be made to achieve the increased efficiency that we need, though many of our brothers are slow to accept them. Methods of judicial selection with less petty politics in them, but without turning the selection of judges over to lawyers alone, are first in importance.

Competent judges exercising the rule-making power can eliminate many wastes and weaknesses in judicial administration more speedily and soundly than can legislators through legislative rule-making. Pre-trial hearings, discovery procedures, planned assignment of cases and courtrooms to achieve maximum use of time and space available, minimization of waste of jurors' time, careful calendaring, simplification of pleadings, intelligent use of special verdicts, businesslike procedures for the handling of routine cases, modernization of evidence rules, sensible arrangements for sifting of cases to be heard on appeal, realistic internal operating procedures within appellate courts, limitation on publication of appellate opinions to those which add something to the understanding of the law, all these and more are areas in which administration of the law in the courts can be measurably improved by means of wide conferral of rule-making power upon the courts and wise exercise of the power conferred.

However wisely conceived the law may be, it is not really good law for any given time and place in society unless the citizenry thinks well of it. That is one reason why we dwell so much upon judicial administration. That is where the public sees the law's faults. But all of us know that the law's faults often lie deeper, and that faults in administration are sometimes surface manifestations of defects that lie within the body of the law itself, within the substantive as well as the procedural law. The task that lies ahead of us, no task for the short-winded, is to better the whole body of law. We must recognize that a good legal system which the public properly expects of us is not merely law efficiently administered but *good* law, law appropriate to its time and place, efficiently administered.

Obsolete and anachronistic laws efficiently administered are likely to be worse for society than if they were inefficiently administered. One saving grace of our legal system is that our courts, when dealing with impractical law that has ceased to fit the times, can lay the impractical rules gently to one side, or reinterpret them, so that their impracticality will not too much disturb the sensible operation of society. Thus in the field of accident law, the old fellow-servant rule and the assumption of the risk rule once applied to employees have almost completely fallen by the wayside.

The whole mass of negligence law, especially as it is represented by automobile accident cases, affords even a better illustration of how the law by a sort of inefficiency can remake itself well enough to get by for an added generation or two. No one would argue that automobile accident liabilities today are much like what legal theory pretends that they are. Civil liability for automobile accidents is governed largely by liability insurance fleshed out over a framework of old negligence rules. Had it not been for the development of liability insurance into the tremendous business that it is in America now, automobile accident law would already have abandoned its traditional form. Something else would have to be worked out. The economic ingenuity of the insurance industry temporarily solved the problem, largely outside the law, and the courts by a kind of tacit indirection accommodated themselves to this temporary solution.

Temporary solutions, however, do not last forever. The law must somehow provide a better answer for the automobile accident problem than is afforded by the old common law of negligence, regardless of the partially new form that has been given to it by private enterprise on the part of the insurance industry. The presence of powerful vested interests which seek to retain the present system as long as they can, and to drain as many dollars in private profit from it as they can before its inevitable demise, constitutes the principal barrier to current reform. These vested interests, coupled with the influence of inertia, make the task of reform in this area of the law a slow and difficult one, yet it is a task which must be undertaken and performed if we are to achieve that betterment of the whole body of the law, both substantive and procedural, which the public rightly expects of us.

It is easy to say, and many among us have been accustomed to saying, that the sort of improvements in law that I have just been referring to are the task of the legislatures and not of the courts. This assertion seems to carry with it an inference that they are not the responsibility of individual lawyers, or of the mass of members of the bar, either. When judges and lawyers, and law teachers too, speak of improvements as being legislative matters, they somehow seem to shuck off any concern with them. It is as though the legislature, and legislative law-making, existed in some strange and altogether separate realm where lawyers never travel, or upon whose product lawyers never have any effect.

Of course we do not take this view consistently. On other occasions we discuss freely our efforts to secure the enactment of beneficent legislation, and the misguided efforts of others among us to defeat legislation which we regard as good. We know that legislation is lawyer's business, and is part and parcel of judicial business too.

Since courts and legislatures are partners in the lawmaking task, and since it is the job of the rest of us to assist them in that task, we need constantly to concern ourselves with ways in which we can help. One of the most useful is by aiding and encouraging legislatures to enact well thought out statutes covering particular areas of the law that would otherwise have to be dealt with bit by bit in the courts. The Commercial Code is a classic example of successful effort along this line, but over a score of other uniform acts and other available legislative proposals are comparable in merit. They range from comprehensive codes such as the Uniform Consumer Credit Code and the Uniform Marriage and Divorce Act to drafts covering narrower topics such as the public defender system and jury selection. Any single state legislature, (like the Congress of the United States,) can by thorough research, comprehensive hearings and careful drafting come up with well thought out statutes. We can help our legislatures do those kinds of research and drafting jobs.

There is no question that, in large and complex areas, legislatures can do a better lawmaking job than courts can do. Legislatures have the opportunity, with the aid of drafting bureaus, study commissions, and the like, or by adopting uniform acts, to give us carefully planned enactments which foresee and prescribe the rules and procedures for all the variations that are apt to arise. Such careful preplanning produces better new law and correspondingly better guidance for trial judges, lawyers and citizens than can an appellate court that has to decide one narrow question at a time, then wait for litigation to present in unanticipated form some other aspect of the problem. There is no assurance that oncoming questions will reach a court in any logical order, nor that related matters that ought to be considered together will even be mentioned by counsel who are more interested in winning their cases than in the sound development of the whole body of the law. Important questions may not receive authoritative answers for years or decades after a basic rule is judicially announced. New rules of law that are laid down gradually leave everyone confused during the continuing period while the court is taking up first one and then another isolated aspect of the problem.

The great difficulty is that our legislatures too often have not done the sort of comprehensive jobs that theoretically they can do in enacting new laws to govern private rights and civil litigation. Too often they have, in slapdash fashion, promulgated laws as incompletely planned as those that appellate courts are compelled to announce when they decide individual cases. When legislatures enact poorly planned statutes the result is that the courts are left to work out the details by the same gradual one-case-at-a-time process to which, when it takes this form, we attach the fancy name of "statutory interpretation." The law that is ultimately established is judge-made after all.

The point of my remarks is that as lawyers and judges we should be more conscious of the lawmaking process, in both the legislative and judicial branches, and should participate in it more openly and deliberately. Good judicial administration involves *what* the courts decide as well as *how* they decide it. The two aspects of judicial functioning can be separated for purposes of academic analysis, and they have to be separated for the purpose of remedying specific faults, but in the larger view they are inseparable. The performance of our entire legal system is what we have to be concerned with, and that covers what happens in legislatures as well as in courts, and in police stations, in prisons, in parole offices, and even in private homes.

We need to concentrate upon achieving a legal system that is good not just for this year but for the year 2000, which is almost upon us. Prisons as schools for crime, the drug culture that is superimposing itself upon the already established liquor and cigarette culture in our society, the megalopolis, ecologic values, crowded dockets and trial delay, the historic sanctity of the jury system and its corresponding inefficiency—these and many others are problem areas that we do not deal with adequately today. Perhaps it all comes down to the complaint of today's youth, tomorrow's middle-aged citizenry, about the law's "relevancy." Is it possible that much of today's law and procedure is more relevant to yesterday's problems than to today's? What about the problems of the year 2000 which today's youth are justifiably concerned about because they will be here then, when most of us won't?

A critical reexamination of judicial administration in America calls for a critical reexamination of our entire legal system. Above all, it calls for a reevaluation which will break away from the vested interests within the legal profession and the establishment that it largely serves. The law does not exist just for lawyers, though there are some of us who seem to think that it does. The law is for all the people, and the lawyers are only its ministers. As the law's ministers we have the professional responsibility, more than anyone else has, of seeing to it that our law and its administration are good enough to keep a civilized society operating not only in 1984, and through the year 2000, which is the day after tomorrow, but even during years beyond 2000.

We must emphasize the fact that in many respects our system of law and justice is not as good as it should be, and may be even less so 25 years from now. It is our task to identify problem areas and try to do something about them. In performing that task we will be met with bitter opposition by many of our brother members in the bar. Paraphrasing Arthur Vanderbilt, it is certain that this is no task for the short-winded.

IV The Law of Torts

Tort Law Objectives

A large area of our law that most people think of or worry about occasionally governs injuries to persons and property. Technically it is called the law of "torts," and sometimes "accident law," though it includes intentionally inflicted harms as well as unintended ones. Much of it deals with injuries caused by what has traditionally been called the "negligence" of defendants or the combined "negligences" of both parties. It includes wrongful deaths, bodily injuries, takings of and interferences with all kinds of property, harms to reputation (libel, slander), and just about any other kind of harm-producing act or event that can ever be the subject of human complaint and that may be chargeable to other human beings or their creatures as defendants in lawsuits. Tort law, however, is separate from criminal law. The punitive effect upon the tortfeasor, of requiring him to pay damages to the injured person, is generally regarded as secondary, though it is not disregarded. The principal purpose of tort law is to compensate the injured person, usually by an award of money, for the harm suffered, or not to compensate him. When, and to what extent?

To answer that question, American legislatures have enacted thousands of statutes; American appellate courts have handed down hundreds of thousands of judicial opinions more or less authoritatively interpreting the statutes or establishing common law principles to govern situations not covered by the statutes; legal scholars have written a library of books and ten thousand articles in law reviews explaining and re-explaining and de-explaining and mis-explaining everything in every which way.

I began teaching the torts course in 1927, and have taught it ever since. It constitutes a controversial legal area in which lawyers tend to take sides permanently. Personal injury lawyers either represent plaintiffs who seek recovery for their injuries, or represent defendants. Their clients are all on one side or the other. Defense counsel usually represent insurance companies, since most prospective tort defendants today carry liability insurance. My teaching necessarily tries to present both sides, but with appropriate emphasis on the general public interest.

In my book *Appellate Judicial Opinions* (West Publ. Co., 1974), at page 16, I summarize what I believe to be the underlying objectives of tort law, both historically and sociologically, as follows:

1. A punitive objective, closely allied to traditional ideas of morality which have been manifested in criminal law: the punishment of bad actors for their bad acts.

2. A deterrence objective, the law being designed either to produce fear of sanctions, thus deterring tortious activity, or otherwise to make such activity so obviously disadvantageous

that people will not engage in it. Under this head "accident prevention" is what the law seeks.

3. A distribution-of-losses objective, calling for a system that will reasonably compensate those who suffer injuries and that will impose the cost of compensation equitably upon those who should reasonably and without undue hardship bear that cost.

4. A negative objective, of not unduly discouraging socially desirable enterprise and activity by imposing upon them financial or regulatory burdens that will stifle or substantially inhibit them.

The four objectives are not mutually exclusive. They coexist, and in some instances all four may serve to explain and justify some single rule of tort law. There will be difference of opinion, however, as to the soundness of one or another of the objectives, depending upon the critic's legal philosophy, his ideas about the correct functions of law—specifically, tort law—in our society.

This summary does not give us a specific answer as to what the law of torts should be in any particular area or on any particular problem. It affords an approach to tort issues, not a formula for solving them. It is relevant to legislative law-making, but it is equally relevant as an approach to the judicial law-making process under our system of the common law.

If a common law court has before it an issue on which there are prior local precedents, this summary of tort law objectives can help the court decide if the old rule should be modified and updated. If there are no local precedents but conflicting rules in other states, the summary can help guide the court to a sound choice among the possibilities.

Tort Law Questions

At a meeting of torts law teachers in Chicago, I handed out a set of questions upon which a seminar-type discussion was then conducted. I have handed out most of the same questions at the Appellate Judges Seminar sessions nearly every year. The questions were current ones in the late 1950s, and to varying extents are still current today in the sense that courts still have to answer them in cases presently filed, and law school students in torts classes still have to worry about them.

Legislatures have provided the courts with answers, usually partial answers, for some of the questions. Most of the questions have been incompletely, or only tentatively, answered in the state courts, so that they are still pending there. Other similar questions can readily be asked, and often are. To the extent that state courts have already answered the questions, either definitely or tentatively, they and other states remain interested in the reasons that produced the answers. Few if any of the answers so far given are truly final. The ultimate query is whether the answers that the courts, and occasionally the legislatures, come up with will be soundly based upon the true objectives of torts law.

Fifteen of the questions, still relevant more than a quarter of a century after they were first asked, are as follows:

1. There is a tendency by some writers in torts law to take the traditional definition of "negligence" out of negligence law. I'm referring to the term "negligence without fault" or "negligence in name only." What is the significance of these wordings?

2. What has been done with the *res ipsa loquitur* doctrine (the accident speaks for itself and indicates negligence, therefore liability) in the last 25 years—aviation cases, multiple defendant cases, malpractice, exploding bottle cases, etc.? Has it been used to achieve substantive changes in tort law, or is it merely an evidential rule?

3. How do you explain the recent run of common law decisions doing away with the tort immunity of charitable corpora-

tions? What about conditioning liability on whether the particular charitable organization carries liability insurance?

4. Is the trend toward abolishing intra-family immunities in tort explainable as another illustration of the same forces and reasons that operate in the charitable corporation cases; or are there some different considerations involved? Has householder's liability insurance had anything to do with it?

5. Why has governmental immunity in tort not been generally eliminated among the states? Why was the immunity of lesser governmental units narrowed by judicial action whereas the larger governmental units (states and nation) waited for legislation?

6. Does the increase of scientific knowledge and the greater reliability of scientific evidence promise to affect tort law substantially? (Illustrations: prenatal injuries, mental-nervous injuries, allergies, use of scientific and pseudo-scientific demonstrative evidence, expert testimony, etc.) What about atomic radiation injuries?

7. What is happening to the common law defense of contributory negligence? Is it fading out of the law? Is the same thing happening to voluntary assumption of risk? What does this imply in terms of the underlying theory of tort law and accident compensation? Is comparative negligence a common law doctrine? Or can it be made the law only by legislative enactment of a new statute?

8. Should adoption of a contribution between joint tortfeasors rule of law normally accompany the adoption of comparative negligence? And vice versa?

9. Where do the "guest statutes" (limiting recovery by automobile guests against their hosts for injuries caused by hosts' negligences) of many of the states fit into this picture? What induced their enactment? May we expect the remaining states to enact them? Will the "guest statutes" eventually be repealed?

10. Is compulsory automobile liability insurance in its vari-

ous forms properly to be regarded as an aspect of current accident law? What about so-called "no-fault automobile accident" statutes enacted in some states? What effect does the development of the liability insurance business in America generally have upon our system of accident law?

11. What is happening with reference to so-called "products liability"? Relation of warranty to negligence? Comparative justification for applying warranty theories to food products and to automobiles? Identify the competing interests which take opposing views concerning expansion of "products liability," and the logic underlying the respective positions.

12. Is the traditional legal concept of "strict liability" (liability without fault) expanding? To what extent do courts consciously apply it? Unconsciously?

13. Are damage verdicts rising, and are courts going along with the increasing awards? Will the trend continue, or be abated or reversed? Is this trend pricing liability insurance out of reach of the mass of surgeons?

14. What will the law school torts course consist of 25 years from now? What will be in the casebooks? How differently will it be taught?

15. Are you ready to make a three-minute statement (guess) as to how the accident law of 25 years from now will differ from today's?

Negligence in Name Only *

Sir Henry Maine in the last century concluded that legal history showed a continuing progress, from ancient times to

---

*The greater part of this comment was written in 1952. For a fuller version of it, with footnotes, see 27 New York Univ. L. Rev. 564. Its current relevance lies in the extent to which it suggests the directions of growth in torts law during the subsequent third of a century, and hereafter.

modern, ". . . from Status to Contract." Once much of the law governing enforceable legal rights, including those which we today call tort rights, was personal, growing out of the status of the persons involved—master and slave, master and apprentice or servant, husband and wife or other familial status, and the like. In some places there was one law for merchants, another for artisans, another for nobles and clergy. The law that was modern to Maine began breaking away from that; most persons were legally free to make contracts that the law respected. They could make binding contracts about almost anything they pleased, and the law would even read into their casual transactions contracts which they often did not know they were making. The trend stated by Maine's famous generalization was perhaps best illustrated by contracts of employment. An employer's hiring of a particular workman might be a quick and casual event, but the common law of the 1800s conceived it as an elaborate contract agreed to in all its details by both parties, including certain voluntary assumptions of risk, acceptance of the fellow-servant rule, and various other limitations on liability that were actually a part of the substantive law of the times. The legal philosophy exemplified by Maine's generalization discovered consensual undertakings to these effects in the fact of employment, and many courts used the same contractual theory as justification for judicial determinations of employer non-liability to aggrieved or injured employees. The employee's agreement in such cases was, of course, unreal and fictional, but the results were in accord with the fiction.

Corollary to and philosophically a part of the movement "from Status to Contract" was the progress from legal liability for all harmful acts to liability for fault only, in the law of torts. The basic idea in our earliest law of torts was that if a person committed an act which injured another he ought to pay for it, even if the act was an innocent one. Gradually this was replaced by the idea that there should be liability only if a harm-productive act was intentionally or negligently done. Thus liability ensued only from free-willing, or voluntary, conduct by a person who knew or should have known the nature of his act and, doing it voluntarily, might be deemed to have intended its legal consequences. The shift from an old liability regardless of fault to the newer liability for fault only (or for the consequences of what the law deemed to be fault) was like the shift that Maine noted, basing results on the free will of the parties as discovered from voluntary agreements or voluntary conduct the legal consequences of which were presumably known to the participants when they acted.

Simultaneously the concept of contributory negligence and related plaintiff-faults as a bar to an injured person's recovery were being developed, they likewise being grounded on the theory that man is a responsible creature, able to make his own legal bed and then lie in it. At any rate, fault (which most frequently took the form of negligence) in defendants was said to be the basis for tort liability, and fault in plaintiffs barred them from relief. When there was fault on both sides the law left the loss to lie where it fell.

No one was much troubled by the fact that the legal test for negligence shortly came to be an objective one—what an ordinary prudent man would have done in the same or similar circumstances—and not the subjective one of whether the allegedly negligent person had done the best he could according to his own understanding and capacities. The test was applied by leaving it up to a jury to decide whether the individual had satisfied the objective standard which the jurors necessarily formulated in their minds. In a given case, the sub-par actor may have done the best that he humanly could, yet be found guilty of negligence; in another, a superior man may have fallen far short of the care and judgment which he personally could have exercised, yet not be guilty of negligence, because his mean conduct still satisfied an external jury standard of what an ordinary man would have done. Personal fault had little to do with the test for negligence, but the word "fault" could still be used as a loose synonym for negligence, and for theory's sake it was.

True, there were still some fragmentary areas of the law in which so-called absolute liability, or "liability without fault," was recognized, but these were thought of as anomalies, relics of a less enlightened legal age so unimportant in the "modern" law of the late 1800s that they were regarded practically as museum pieces. Best known of these were the liability imposed for damage caused by escaping fire, and that imposed for the trespasses of animals or harms inflicted by dangerous animals. Then there was the disturbing case of *Rylands v. Fletcher* (1868) in which the House of Lords held that a defendant who kept a dangerous substance (in this case a reservoir of water) on his premises should be liable for damage caused by its escape even though he was not negligent in permitting it to escape. Today the doctrine of *Rylands v. Fletcher* is that "one who maintains a dangerous thing, or engages in an activity which involves a high degree of risk of harm to others in spite of all reasonable care, is strictly liable for the harm which it causes." England has followed the doctrine consistently, with uncertainty only as to what things or activities are so dangerous in their nature as to render it applicable. But in the United States, where philosophical notions of free enterprise and free volition were perhaps more firmly entrenched than in England, it was strongly urged that absolute liability was a legal throwback to a less civilized age in which men were not as free as they are in America, and that liability without fault was a concept alien to our society and its institutions. Others took less violent views, and contended that there was a place for the doctrine in the American scheme of things. The American Law Institute in its Restatement of Torts agreed, defining the doctrine

in terms of "ultrahazardous activities." Increasing acceptance
of the doctrine has been steady, though certainly not spec-
tacular, during the half-century just passed.

In 1951, Professor Albert A. Ehrenzweig of California wrote
a book entitled *Negligence Without Fault.* The title meant what
it said, that fault and negligence are not necessarily related
concepts, and that liability-producing negligence should often
be discoverable—in fact is often discovered—when there is
no real "lack of due care under the circumstances" in the defendant. The Ehrenzweig work not only analyzed the past and
present of negligence law, but undertook to look into its future. The book pointed out some of the many situations in
which a defendant may under the law be held liable in damages *for negligence* even though it had not been proved that he
in fact failed to conduct himself as would an ordinary prudent
man under the same or similar circumstances, and some of the
other situations (such as those covered by workmen's compensation laws) in which the law has completely abandoned negligence as the test of liability for injuries. He discussed the relative importance of what he called "the Siamese-twin functions"
of tort law—the "admonitory function"—which by punishing
"fault" is designed to discourage faulty conduct, and the "compensation function" which aims at making injured persons
whole again, partly for their own sakes and partly so that they
will not become impoverished burdens on society, and concluded that the main interest of modern law, despite talk about
fault as a prerequisite to liability, is the compensation function. His thesis was that "fault" as the standard basis for tort
liability had become fictional and meaningless, and that negligence can be redefined in terms of risks arising out of typical
activities of enterprises which ought to pay for injuries that
they typically cause—"liability without reference to moral
fault for harms which flow from typical risks of the enterprise."
He believed that the courts had already gone most of the way,

by means of fictions, presumptions, rules of agency, variations on proximateness in causation, and a score of other devices, to the honest redefinition that he advocated, but he believed that they should discard the devices, be honest about it, and say in so many words that liability is and will be imposed for "negligence without fault" discoverable whenever the "typicality" test is satisfied.

A 1951 article by Charles O. Gregory of Virginia, entitled "Trespass to Negligence to Absolute Liability" (37 Va. L. Rev. 359), told the same historical story in more popularly readable style, traced the wriggling and writhing of American courts which often (not always) tried to give compensation when the total of social considerations justified it, but at the same time tried to avoid recognition of the "foreign ideology" of absolute liability, and tried to frame their opinions in traditional language sanctifying the concept of fault as the source of nearly all torts. He concluded that common honesty demands either a rephrasing of the common law, or a frank resort to legislation to reframe the law in terms of new and sense-making theory.

Fleming James, who taught torts at Yale, wrote a series of articles which emphasized principally the impact of liability insurance on the law relating to negligence. He started off with a basic assumption that "the principal job of tort law today" is to deal with the "human losses" suffered by accident victims in our industrial society. He rejected the admonitory half of Ehrenzweig's "Siamese-twin functions" of the law of torts by showing that deterrence of dangerous conduct is far more often effected by other factors than by fear of the law, and pointed out that in one way or another the compensation function is the one primarily served by our accident law in its practical operation. He asserted that some system of social insurance would serve this compensatory function most efficiently but that, being unwilling to adopt social insurance as such, our courts and legislatures have instead cooperated with the insurance companies to satisfy society's needs by fitting a rough and incomplete equivalent of the body of social insurance into the slack skin of the common law of negligence, with standard statutory appendages. The inevitable inference was that "the expressed doctrines of tort law" are obsolete: "They are horse and buggy rules in an age of machinery; and they might well have gone to the scrap heap some time ago had not the tremendous growth of liability insurance and the progressive ingenuity of the companies made it possible to get some of the benefits of social insurance under—or perhaps in spite of—the legal rules." Some more realistic system of tort law, he believed, must be in the offing, and the misshapen carcass of the old law was merely being tolerated for the time being, until our legislators and judges acquired the insight and courage to fashion from Insurance's ready rib a new and more perfect body adapted to the functions which modern society demands that it serve.

An article by Wolfgang Friedmann, (63 Harv. L. Rev. 241) later on the Columbia University Law School faculty, filled in the picture. It starts by quoting Oliver Wendell Holmes' 1881 statement in *The Common Law*, beginning: "The State might conceivably make itself a mutual insurance company against accidents, and distribute the burden of its citizens' mishaps among all its members," after which Holmes examined the possibilities briefly, and said: "Universal insurance, if desired, can be better and more cheaply accomplished by private enterprise." Friedmann traced the infusion of the insurance concept into tort law in the preceding half-century or so, as manifested in the fields of manufacturers' liability for harms inflicted by their products and other areas of current development in tort law. He found that it was a major motivating factor underlying most of the changes in law which, during the period dealt with, achieved greater rights for persons injured in what are often called industrial accidents. His conclusions present openly a point of view not often stated in so many words:

> . . . The main function of the law of tort is the reasonable adjust-
> ment of economic risks in a capitalist . . . society and not the ex-
> pression of certain absolute moral principles. . . . It follows from this
> recognition of the law of tort as a set of rules designed to distribute
> economic harm according to changing principles of public policy
> that the law of tort should be clearly dissociated conceptually from
> the law of crime . . . it seems clear that the part of the law of tort
> with which we are concerned here is itself concerned not with states
> of mind but with standards of conduct . . . that part of the law of
> tort which concerns us here has steadily moved closer towards a so-
> cial insurance principle, although the two have not yet merged. . . .
> Even if there is still some substance theoretically in the difference
> between "strict" and "negligence" liability in common law, from the
> broader angle of the adjustment of social harm the difference in
> a given modern situation is of subordinate significance . . . the
> coupling of tort liability with standards of conduct, and with negli-
> gence in particular, is not without practical significance (in its deter-
> rent value toward discouraging dangerous practices). . . . Thus,
> although the day may come when compensatory functions of the
> law of tort are assumed entirely by state insurance—as Holmes en-
> visaged—the enforcement of standards of conduct need not become
> entirely a matter of penal law, the "accountancy" principle of social-
> ized enterprise may demand not the abandonment, but the strength-
> ening of the principle of fault.

This series of summaries and quotations from previous writing invites analysis by the reviewer. A good place to start is
with the common law doctrine of absolute liability—*Rylands
v. Fletcher* and its American aftermath.

The reasoning that sustains these cases has, in its recognition of law as social engineering, gone far beyond the reasons
originally given by the early courts that decided the animal
and fire cases, or even *Rylands v. Fletcher* itself. The earliest
cases merely said that one who committed an act or engaged
in an activity which caused harm ought to pay for the harm.
No social or philosophical considerations more complex than
simple causation were involved. Modern reasoning, in terms

of imposing liability upon the sponsor of an enterprise who by undertaking it incurs the social responsibility for managing it in such a way that losses due to harms suffered by innocent persons can be passed on to the whole group which benefits from the enterprise, perhaps amounts to no more than fancy language repeating the simpler rule. Were it not for intervening history the original simple rule might have sufficed. But the dogma of "fault" as sole basis of liability—the corollary of Sir Henry Maine's "Status to Contract" generalization of free human will as it was conceived of in the nineteenth century—did intervene, and became embedded in the concept which was called negligence. By many courts in this period it was thought of as the sole *rational* basis for tort liability; strict liability persisted only through the strength of the doctrine of precedents, a doctrine respectable enough in the law but still not one that would justify application of an old rule to distinguishable new sets of facts when reason (personified by the "fault" dogma) pointed in a different direction.

But strict liability did persist, because precedent dies hard. The modern reasoning gradually came to the attention of judges, and some were convinced that respectability of new enterprise reasoning, added to the respectability of old-time precedent, would justify application of the strict liability rule to some new sets of facts. They agreed that some types of activity, such as blasting with dynamite to open up new highways, were so dangerous that ordinary care, or even extraordinary care, could not with any assurance guard innocent persons from harm, yet these activities were so necessary, or desirable, in a civilized society, or at least in our society, that they should not be prohibited. They were not nuisances, in the sense that a nuisance was a noisome thing to be suppressed by abatement. They were "good" enterprises; our technology had merely failed to invent safety devices to control them adequately.

An enterpriser who satisfied society's demands by undertaking a dangerous activity could not be blamed for failing to employ uninvented safety devices, therefore negligence could not easily be charged to him. For example, the storage of blasting powder was essential to economic progress. Still, innocent passersby had their legs and heads blown off when powder magazines uncontrollably exploded, while contractors and the world generally benefited from lower construction costs as long as the passerby's loss was not charged to the construction industry. That seemed unreasonable, and some courts became willing to apply the *Rylands v. Fletcher* idea to such cases. They concluded generally that if an activity was so ultrahazardous that normal precautions could not guard against injuries from it, and at the same time it was not so common an activity that people were accustomed to its risks in everyday life, absolute liability would be imposed for injuries caused by it.

Manufacturers and dealers who maintain powder magazines, and those who conduct other similarly dangerous enterprises, can take out liability insurance, or can as self-insurers pay off claims filed against them, and can then pass on to the consumer this added cost of operation. In that manner, the dangerous activity can pay its own way. If it is worthy enough so the law will not abate it, it is by the same token worthy enough for its beneficiaries to pay what it costs not only for its mechanical operation but for incidental harms to innocent third persons as well. One who wants to operate a powder magazine would not be allowed to take the land on which to build the magazine without paying for it; neither has he any better moral or economic right to take a passerby's leg. Both costs are normally foreseeable incidents to the operation of the dangerous business, and should be included in the total costs from which the sale price of the product or service is calculated. Several American courts concluded that there was a place in American law for so-called liability without fault, against defendants engaged in ultrahazardous activities.

The arguments of Ehrenzweig, Gregory, James, Friedmann *et al.*, however, were that the theory should be vastly extended in its coverage. They sought to discover the true functions that a good law of torts should serve in American society and, without too much change either in the principles or the mechanics of the law as we knew it, to see if those functions would not be better and more efficiently served by a theory in which something other than fault was the basic factor.

Admittedly the function of tort law stressed by the "fault" concept was deterrence. A judgment for damages against a tortfeasor served to punish him and warn others. In that sense it was a kind of adjunct to the criminal law designed to induce vindictive or careless people to abide by the standards of conduct prescribed by law. Similarly, if an injured plaintiff was at fault (contributorily negligent, for example) recovery was barred and the same punitive and exemplary effects were presumably achieved. Compensation to innocent injured persons often ensued, but insofar as "fault" was the test of the right to compensation the compensation served a secondary purpose.

The fact is that a certain spate of "accidents" is inevitable, and reduction of their number in a society which conducts itself as ours does can be and is influenced more by other pressures or programs than by the law of torts. This does not mean the standards of conduct laid down by the law of torts are unimportant. Of course they are important; most people try to live up to them, when they know what the standards are. When a rule is laid down inflexibly (stopping at red traffic lights for instance,) it is generally known and obeyed. But when the relevant rule says that an auto driver or an occupier of commercial premises should use due care under the circumstances he needs some other guide than the rule of law to determine what his conduct should be in any particular situation. He might find a guide in the language of an appellate decision affirming a jury verdict on a somewhat similar set of facts occurring some years previously in another part of the state, but again he might not. Besides, he doesn't have a copy of the opinion before him at the moment, and it may be couched in the sort of well-considered judicial phraseology that needs to be studied carefully in order to be understood. And we have never encouraged truck drivers to study judicial opinions anyway. We know very well that conduct is controlled by the individual's own judgment concerning what will prevent unpleasant injury to himself and his neighbor, and this judgment will be conditioned by the experience and training in safety practices to which he has been subjected.

A liability insurance company may have based a person's insurance premiums, or those of his employer, on his accident record or may have initiated a safety propaganda campaign as a means toward reducing the accident rate. Specific courses of conduct for particular emergencies may have been suggested and mastered. Public safety programs may have had an impressive effect. The individual may have had other experiences, either as a participant in or observer of accidents, or may have read or talked about them, and found that these afforded guidance to him in the particular instance. Simple self-preservation, plus the preservation of one's own property, or (in the case of an employee) conducting one's self so as not to lose one's job, seem to be the major motives behind carefulness, and motives arising out of this or that judicial interpretation of the law of negligence will seldom be identifiable. Some rules of law undoubtedly do deter negligent conduct sometimes, but it is foolish to suppose that the law of negligence in general has much of that effect.

The accident rate in factories, on highways, among users of manufactured goods, among visitors on business premises, and in practically every situation in which substantial numbers of so-called injuries by negligence occur, can be reduced if intelligent efforts are directed specifically to the actual causes of accidents. Still, until human and machine perfection are simultaneously achieved, there will continue to be accidents and injuries, just as there have always been. Some of them can be attributed to negligence (as discovered in court after the event); others will be called "pure accidents" in which no negligence can be spelled out. In either event there will be losses caused not just by the unfortunate individuals who happened to be immediate participants in them, but by the enterprise or activity out of which the various incidents developed. The enterprise or activity responsible for an accident may be the operation of a factory or a trucking business or a powder magazine, it may be the driving of two among ten million pleasure automobiles on Sunday highways, it may be a construction job for a new skyscraper or a new dam, it may be the manufacture and sale of a defective household appliance, or it may be anything. Accidents happen and injuries are suffered in all of them. These harms are a part of the price of progress, or the price of whatever it is that is being done when the harm occurs.

We know that harms will be inflicted; they are so certain that it has become a matter of statistics, with the averages in some activities currently going up, and in others going down. The "injury cost" of operation varies from one industry to another, from one field of enterprise or activity to another, and from one operator to another even in the same field. Usually society says that the enterprise is worthwhile and ought to be continued despite the harms it inflicts; this is proved by the fact that no laws are enacted to ban it. At the most society usually does no more than enact safety laws requiring changes in modes of operation so as to reduce injuries suffered. Infrequently, harms are successfully reduced by eliminating the activity altogether. Society usually is willing to suffer the harms as part of the total cost of operating an activity which seems worth continuing. Society is willing to suffer the harms but, under the law, out of whose pockets?

1. When technical negligence was spelled out, the sponsor of the activity paid for the harms, and if he had liability insurance or was wealthy enough to be his own insurer he treated it as a cost of normal operation, spread out on a sort of amortized basis over the whole field of the operation and, if it was commercial, he passed it on as part of the price to the ultimate consumers for whose benefit the whole operation was conducted. 2. When contributory negligence barred recovery, the injured person paid it, even though he was no beneficiary in any sense of the activity from which his injury accrued, or if his pocket was empty then public or private charity paid for that part of the loss which was most urgent, like funerals and major hospitalization, leaving the rest of the loss to society as a whole in the form of an incompetent or less competent human being. 3. When it was impossible to prove negligence in anybody, and negligence was a prerequisite to liability, the result has been identical to that when an injured person is barred by contributory negligence.

In the last two situations, society and the injured person join to subsidize the activity that produced the loss. They pay the bill; those who benefit from the activity need not pay for the broken body or the property destroyed which was part of the outlay that brought their increased profit or enjoyment. The effect of the law was to take much from a few, and something from all, in order that a special group might pay less. That is the nature of subsidy, and subsidy is no uncommon thing in our economy, but the question remains whether any particular system of subsidies, or this system, is justified today.

The system may have been justified when America's industries were newly building in the 1800s, and the bodies and goods of little men were deemed a small price to pay for a commercial growth that brooked no hampering. The apparent fact

that American society's main concern was that this growth occur as fully and as quickly as the capitalists of the time could
build it is no proof that the system remains viable today. It may
well be that now each industry, each enterprise and each activity should pay its own way, save possibly some special few—
infant industries perhaps, or activities like churches or chari-
ties to which the law may give unique immunities. It is hard to
see why a subsidy or exemption from payment of any normal
cost should presently be granted to any industry, or even to an
activity such as driving for pleasure in automobiles. If rules of
law can be devised that will require each activity to bear the
burden of its own costs, the public policy that underlies both
our legal and our economic systems will be better served.

Actually our law has, in the last century, not been as callous
as the preceding paragraphs by their emphasis on theory have
indicated. Just as the objective (not subjective) standard of
ordinary care that defines negligence was a departure from any
true idea of personal fault, so there are numerous rules of law
which, as part of the law of negligence, manage in one way or
another to impose liability not only without fault but without
negligence as far as defendants are concerned. They are really
rules of absolute liability disguised in the language of fictional
fault and fictional negligence.

Most far-reaching of these is *respondeat superior*. The principal is held for his agent's negligent act (and the negligent
agent commonly not held at all) even though the principal
was guilty of no lack of due care whatever in either selection
or supervision of his agent. The reason behind *respondeat superior* is easy to perceive. It is that the principal, or employer,
sponsors the activity out of which the negligence arose, and is
thus the one who derives benefit from it. The injured person
probably can collect nothing from the employee who did the
harmful act. Between the innocent bystander who is injured

and the employer whose enterprise produced the injury it is fairer that the employer bear the loss. This sounds like the explanation of an absolute liability rule, and that in fact is what it is, merely stated, properly enough, in the form of a rule of agency rather than of torts because it is applied in agency situations. *Qui facit per alium facit per se* is only another way of saying the same thing, by stating the result without giving the reason for it, in a torts case. Some judges and writers today will still say that liability by *respondeat superior* is based on fault, but it certainly is not based on the defendant's fault. Neither is the statutory liability that is established in many states on any owner of a car in favor of anyone injured by a negligently operated car while driven by any person with the owner's consent. Both of these are "enterprise liabilities" pure and simple. They hold the economically responsible person (who incidentally has the deeper purse, or should have if he undertakes the car-owning enterprise) even though he is guilty of no lack of due care and there is no agency relationship between him and the negligent driver.

Extralegally, the fact of widespread liability insurance has had more effect than any of these rules of law toward securing general payment of claims for injury regardless of technical negligence. It is true that in trials of negligence cases, some states still formally preclude mention before the jury of the presence of insurance. Even assuming this rule of silence about insurance to be effective, which today it is not, the fact remains that the great mass of claims against insured persons are settled out of court and not by formal trial. Research cited by Professor James shows that "*some* payment is made in about 85 percent of motor vehicle accident cases involving personal injury or death, where there is insurance," (57 Yale L. Jour. 549, 566) yet it is scarcely arguable that negligence in defendants could be legally proved in that proportion of cases.

James concluded that where claims are small, particularly where they have a "nuisance value" (as most claims do), the common practice among insurance companies (who are of course the real defendants in such cases) is to settle for some reasonable sum rather than litigate. Ordinarily only the larger claims are fought to the limit. While this is primarily a matter of negotiation and bargaining, rather than law, it nevertheless represents what happens in actual cases, and therefore constitutes the "law in action" even though it is not in the lawbooks. The practical effect is that, "so far as the making of *some* payment goes, there is a closer approach to absolute liability in practice than in theory." Probably more than 90 percent of tort claims that reach the point of either negotiation and settlement or litigation have a background of liability insurance. Insofar as the fact of insurance furnishes new guides or standards for settlement, even though they are bargaining standards of the marketplace rather than rules of law applicable in the courtroom, our technical law of negligence is in fact being superseded.

The social policy that underlies a free enterprise system is that each enterprise should pay its own way. Indirect subsidization of any activity at the expense of society generally is as much a violation of this social policy as is direct subsidization out of the public treasury.

It is increasingly apparent that our civilization demands some system whereby the loss from those tort harms loosely termed accidental injuries will not fall altogether on the unfortunate individual who suffers them. A sympathizing society should insist that in one way or another the burden be at least partially shifted. Society might socialistically retain the burden for itself in cases where real fault cannot be pinned on some financially responsible person. That approach was the standard one in the last century, and still is for many cases, with the public treasury paying more and more of the costs through welfare grants. But it has already been rejected by the law for many situations; for them the approach now is that the one who sponsors an enterprise or activity should pay for the harm it produces. For the balance, our law has the choice between the same alternatives: the burden can be imposed on the states or the nation, in the form of public social insurance; or the idea of sponsor liability can be extended to the rest of the field, as it already has been under workmen's compensation acts and numerous other statutory enactments and common law rules.

Contributory and Comparative Negligence

The manner in which American courts and legislatures work together, and supplement each other in the making of state law, is illustrated by recent developments in the law governing contributory negligence.

Under the common law contributory negligence rule, a person injured by the combined negligences of himself and another could recover no damages from the other negligent party, regardless of the proportions of their two faults. Even though the injured person's fault was only five percent and the other's 95 percent, recovery was barred. Though lawyers frequently think of the contributory negligence rule as going back to the very beginnings of the common law, it is fairly new as legal doctrines go. The first reported cases stating it were decided in England after American independence was achieved. By 1900 the rule had reached full growth in both English and American courts, but today it is shrunken and diminishing. There are many situations now in which an injured plaintiff can on one newly developed legal theory or another recover compensation despite his own contributory negligence.

The principal one of these new approaches is so-called comparative negligence. As the name implies, the negligences of plaintiffs and defendants are compared, and some recovery calculated on the proportions, or percentages, of the negligences may be allowed. Several different methods of calculation are employed in different jurisdictions. One method allows a plaintiff to recover only if his negligence is "slight" and the defendant's "gross" (Nebraska, South Dakota). Others have allowed recovery if the plaintiff's negligence is "less than" the defendant's (Arkansas), or "not greater than" the defendant's (Wisconsin). A "pure" form of comparative negligence, advocated by the great torts scholar Dean William L. Prosser, allows proportional recovery regardless of whose negligence is greater, so that a 75 percent claimant can recover for 25 percent of his injury from a 25 percent defendant (California and other states). There are several other substantial differences between the newly adopted comparative negligence rules in various states.

One current controversy presents the question whether comparative negligence may be initiated in a state by the state's courts, or should be inaugurated in the place of contributory negligence only by a legislatively enacted statute.

No one today denies that appellate courts have a creative function, but argument persists as to how extensive the function is. It is clear that the scope of the function depends initially upon what type of appellate court is involved. An intermediate appellate court, which takes its law from a higher court in its own jurisdiction, is ordinarily not in a position to make new law and make it stick. The Appellate Court for the Second District of Illinois, which first decided that a rule of comparative negligence should replace the rigid rule of contributory negligence in that state (*Maki v. Frelk*, 85 Ill. App. 2d 439, 229 N.E.2d 284) did so only after it had been directed by the Supreme Court of Illinois to consider that very question. What the intermediate court did was to set up a case for subsequent review by the higher court at the latter's request.

In *Maki v. Frelk* a majority of the Illinois Supreme Court in 1968 declined to take advantage of the opportunity for which it had previously asked. Why? The reasoning in the majority opinion went no further than to say "that such a far-reaching change, if desirable, should be made by the legislature rather than by the court . . . and the legislative branch is manifestly in a better position than is this court to consider the numerous problems involved." The common report in Illinois was that members of the court were frightened by the complexity of a good comparative negligence system and were unwilling to promulgate a new rule of law that would require the many subordinate adjudications to be added then or later, that would inevitably be necessary before a workable system of comparative negligence could be made fully operative. Finally, however, thirteen years later, the Illinois Supreme Court reversed itself and, without waiting any longer for the legislature to act, adopted "pure" comparative negligence (*Alvis v. Riber*, 82 Ill. 2d 1, 421 N.E.2d 886). Details were left to be worked out in future cases.

One of the commonest characteristics of judicial overrulings in the tort field (and in other fields as well) has been that they involved clear-cut and uncomplicated issues, matters that could be answered one way or the other, without any necessity for considering incidental problems and elaborate judicial implementation. For example, when judges changed the old common law to permit recovery for prenatal injuries, they did not need to worry about companion problems or about procedure. The change in the law was complete within itself. There was no felt need even for use of the *Sunburst* technique to make the overruling a prospective one. The establishment of products liability was equally unitary and complete within itself, as was recognition of the right of privacy. The same was true when intrafamily immunities were eliminated. For elimination of charitable immunities, prospective overruling to give charitable associations time to take out liability insurance took care of the only incidental problem that raised serious difficulties. None of these were problems that the overruling court itself had to answer in order to make the new law a workable one. How do these innovations compare with the initiation of a system of comparative negligence?

In contrast, a judicial pronouncement merely promulgating comparative negligence would be baldly incomplete, because it would leave so many relevant questions unanswered:

1. Should injured persons recover only in cases in which their negligence is less or no greater than that of the other party, as in Arkansas and Wisconsin, or in every case in which the negligences can be apportioned, as under the Prosser "pure" form which is the law in most English-speaking states outside the United States?

2. Should the comparison of negligences be in terms of percentages, as in most jurisdictions, or in terms of "slight" and "gross," as in others?

3. If the comparison is to be in terms of percentages, should they be percentages of causal responsibility for the injury, or percentages of fault (relative badness)?

4. If both parties are injured, should each be allowed to recover from the other, with a setoff? Or, recognizing that recoveries usually are from insurance companies, should each injured party be entitled to his full comparative recovery from the other's insurer, without setoff, on the theory that a liability policy covers actual liabilities regardless of separable rights in others?

5. What about the multi-defendant case in which, for example, an injured plaintiff is responsible for 20 percent of the negligence, D for 45 percent, E for 25 percent and F for 10 percent? May the plaintiff recover from all or which of the others? And how much?

6. If comparative negligence, permitting recovery by a negligent injured person, is established, do not logic and equal

fairness require that a rule of contribution between joint tort-feasors be established as part of the same system?

7. If comparative negligence is put into effect, should the last clear chance doctrine, if any, previously accepted in the jurisdiction and allowing full recovery against a negligent defendant who had a "last clear chance" to prevent the injury, be abandoned or retained?

8. Should the rule, followed in some states, allowing full recovery for willful and wanton misconduct despite the injured person's contributory negligence be retained, or does comparative negligence take its place?

9. What about assumption of the risk? Should that defense be regarded as something completely embodied in contributory negligence? If not, what part of it still remains as a separate defense?

10. Should special verdicts or answers to interrogatories be required to set out the total value of injury suffered and the specific percentages of negligence charged to each party, so that a court can double check the jury's damage calculations, or should the jury be left free to return a damages verdict without supporting figures?

The list of problems that are peculiar to the initiation of comparative negligence is awesome; one cannot be surprised that the 1968 Illinois court was frightened by it. The list seems to call for the enactment of a comprehensive statute, with sections and subsections carefully worked out in advance by a legislative drafting committee aided by an advisory commission.

Is that the way our American systems of comparative negligence have come into the law? It seems not.

Almost every comparative negligence statute enacted in any state of the United States has been short and simple, leaving unanswered most of the companion problems that a one-line ukase: "Let there be comparative negligence," would inevitably present. Every one of these statutes had to be fleshed out in its working details, by the courts. The Wisconsin statute enacted in 1931 was one of the first, and the Wisconsin Supreme Court through the years handed down at least a score of decisions interpreting and implementing it. That court ultimately, by dictum clearly fated to be followed, announced prospective answers to a number of additional questions that it knew would arise eventually. Other top state courts are having the same experience. Puerto Rico's is the most vaguely and broadly worded of all the comparative negligence statutes in the United States: "Concurrent imprudence of the party aggrieved does not exempt from liability, but entails a reduction of the indemnity." I spent an interesting and pleasant week in Puerto Rico explaining to bar and law school groups the numerous problems that would arise under this statute and suggesting possible answers to them. Judicial interpretation has necessarily provided the answers to the questions left unanswered by this statute.

If the various legislatures had foresightedly thought about all the problems that would arise under their enactments and had included in the enactments reasonable answers to the problems, so correlated as to afford a logical and consistent system of law and administration, their approach would clearly have been superior. Legislatures have the opportunity, with the aid of drafting bureaus, study commissions and the like, to come up with carefully planned statutes which foresee and prescribe the rules and procedures for all the variations that are apt to arise under their enactments. Such careful preplanning can produce better new law and correspondingly better guidance for trial judges, lawyers, and citizens who have to comply with and administer the new law, than can the one-shot pronouncements of an appellate court that has to decide one narrow question at a time, then wait for litigation to present, in unanticipated form, the next aspect of the problem that it will have to pass upon. There is no assurance that oncoming questions will reach the court in any logical order, nor that related matters which ought to be considered together will even be mentioned by counsel when such matters do not bear directly upon the outcome of the immediate litigation. Important questions may not receive authoritative answers for years or decades after the basic rule is promulgated, and in the meantime lawyers and trial judges may simply bypass the problem because they cannot know the answer to it. Yet the whole body of the common law came into being in that fashion, and the legislatively created systems of comparative negligence in the United States have had the same sort of gradualist history. The reason for this is that the legislatures, in their slapdash fashion, have promulgated laws as incompletely planned as those that the courts would have been compelled, by the nature of the judicial process, to promulgate had they been doing the same job. The details of the job have been left for the courts to work out anyway.

The key facts seem to be that legislatures in the United States either took few steps in previous years toward establishing comparative negligence, or planned it incompletely when they did establish it. It must be assumed that for the late twentieth century the apportionment of losses between negligent parties is fairer than, and preferable to, the old harsh rule of contributory negligence. The change is one that ought to be made, somehow. Why did some legislatures not take care of the matter sooner?

The explanation probably lies in the nature of legislatures and legislative action. Comparative negligence involves a type of social progress to which no potent social action group is politically committed. The organized liability insurers are, for their own reasons, generally against it; the plaintiffs' bar is lukewarm about it; and the general public, except for the minority involved in accident lawsuits, hardly knows what the problem is. Legislatures are seldom alert to social needs that are not backed up by political pressures. Social needs with no potent lobby behind them, particularly if there is an active lobby against them, ordinarily do not receive much favorable attention in state legislatures. They are the sort of thing that courts have to take care of.

With reference to the sort of private problems that are normally settled by litigation, courts are more social-minded than legislators, since their attention is constantly called to the social problems which make up the standard grist of their daily work. They know about these problems and, if the judges are forward-looking and intellectually alive, they know something of what the answers should be. The courts are not equipped to foresee and to fore-answer all the questions that might possibly arise as well as a legislature theoretically is, but they can foresee more of them than the ordinary legislator can.

In nine states—Alaska, California, Florida, Illinois, Iowa, Michigan, Missouri, New Mexico, and West Virginia—in which the legislatures had not enacted comparative negligence statutes of any kind, the state supreme courts have in recent years overruled old contributory negligence cases and held that comparative negligence is now part of the common law of their states. Most of them adopted it in the "pure," or Prosser, form. In all nine, dozens of questions remained to be answered. In that respect the nine courts faced the same problems they would have faced had the same new rule been laid down by typical legislation. In the meantime they had at least answered the question whether it is permissible for courts to overrule long settled, judge-made common law of a fairly complex nature, and set up new common law in its stead. They did it.

Comparative Negligence in Arkansas

The history of comparative negligence law in Arkansas is unique among the American states. The first enactment, not unique among midwestern states, came in 1919. It provided that:

In all suits against railroads for personal injury, property damage or death caused by the running of trains . . . contributory negligence shall not prevent a recovery where the negligence of the person so injured, damaged or killed is of less degree than the negligence of [employees] of the railroad . . . ; provided that . . . the amount of the recovery shall be diminished in proportion to such contributory negligence. (Ark. Stats. § 73-1004).

Since comparison of the negligences presented a question of fact for the jury, plaintiffs could in most cases rely upon the finder of facts to conclude that the railroad's negligence was the greater and to fix an award of damages at whatever figure was deemed fair. No special verdict naming the percentages of negligence or the total damage suffered was required. Plaintiffs usually recovered.

The next enactment came in 1955. Dean William L. Prosser had visited the Law School at Fayetteville in the fall of 1954, and talked about comparative negligence, emphasizing the desirability of the "pure" form as prescribed by a model act which he had drafted. This called for recovery by injured persons regardless of whose negligence was lesser or greater, though only in the proportion of a defendant's negligence. An injured plaintiff responsible for 75 percent of the total negligence could recover 25 percent against a defendant responsible for that proportion of the total. Some members of the legislature who heard Dean Prosser's talk introduced his draft as a bill in the 1955 legislative session. It passed and in due course became law.

The state was ready for comparative negligence, and the liability insurance companies realized this, but they did not like the Prosser "pure" form of it. They and the defense bar undertook a campaign against the new law. They dwelt upon a horrible (though hypothetical) example of what it might do. The supposed case involved a highway collision between little P's ordinary auto and D's big truck. P's negligence was 25 percent, D's 75 percent. Both vehicles were damaged—P's little car

$4,000 worth, D's big truck $40,000 worth. Under "pure" comparative negligence each had a claim against the other. P's was for a puny $3,000, 75 percent of his total damage. D's 25 percent was $10,000. Thus poor P in the end would have had to pay D $7,000, despite his lesser fault.

Even the plaintiffs' bar pretended to be appalled. The campaign was successful. At the 1957 session of the legislature the "pure" act was repealed and a "less than" law was enacted in its place. Under it, as under the old railroad statute, injured but negligent claimants can get proportional recoveries from negligent defendants only if the fact-finder determines that the claimant's negligence was "of less degree than" that of the defendant or defendants. Again, no special verdict identifying the parties' percentages of negligence or the total damages suffered was specifically required. Subsequent revisions of the statute (now Ark. Stats. §§ 27-1763-1765) by the 1961, 1973, and 1975 legislatures have not changed the law's essential character. It is still a "less than" statute.

Contribution Between Joint Tortfeasors

The common law rule precluding contribution between joint tortfeasors was closely related, in social and legal philosophy, to the common law of contributory negligence.

If two or more persons, acting in concert, or merely concurrently, by their negligences cause a single injury to another person (P), their liability to him is "joint and several." It may be supposed that two autoists collide at an intersection, a not unusual set of facts. The negligence of A was in entering the intersection against the stoplight. The negligence of B was in speeding, so that he could not stop in time to avoid hitting A's car. Their collision injured a nearby pedestrian, P. A and B are, in relation to P, joint tortfeasors. P's "joint and several" claim against them enables him to sue and recover in full against either or both of them. P chooses to sue B, gets a judgment for his entire injury (say $20,000) against B, and proceeds by levy of execution to collect the full amount of the judgment from B. P has no further rights against either A or B. May B secure partial reimbursement (contribution) from A? The common law answer was "No."

Why not? A and B were joint tortfeasors, approximately equal in fault. Why should they not have to bear the loss equally? Because the law took a "hands off" attitude toward all claimants whose claims were based upon transactions or events in which the claimant was himself a faulty participant. The equity doctrine demanded that one seeking relief must come into court with clean hands. The courts denied all relief to any knowing party to an illegal contract. A person whose negligence contributed to his own injury could recover nothing from another whose negligence contributed equally or even more to the injury. All of these doctrines and rules illustrated a sort of self-righteous judicial attitude of refusing to sully the law's purity by affording relief to wrongdoers, even unintentional and merely negligent ones, under any circumstances.

Not all jurists agreed with this sanctimonious attitude. Admiralty courts regularly allowed both contribution between joint tortfeasors and partial recovery by contributorily negligent plaintiffs. It was known that the "no contribution" rule sometimes had a kind of corrupting effect. When P had a joint and several claim worth about $20,000 against joint tortfeasors A and B, one of the tortfeasors (A) might secretly approach P and offer him $2,500 in cash if he would sue B only, or levy execution on B's assets only, as P could. P might be tempted to accept the undercover offer, since he could recover the full $20,000 from B, and have the clandestine $2,500 extra. This undoubtedly happened at times.

Some exceptions to the "no contribution" rule were developed in common law courts. One of these went far enough to compare the faults of joint tortfeasors (were they *in pari delicto?*) allowing recovery by the one least at fault against the one most at fault—indemnity by the "passive" or "secondary" against the "active" or "primary" tortfeasor. The supreme courts in three states—Wisconsin, Pennsylvania, and Minnesota—rejected the old rule altogether and specifically allowed contribution between negligent, though not between intentional, tortfeasors. These courts were for the most part moved by the obvious injustice, as between two tortfeasors, of one bearing the whole loss while the other went free, when one was neither more blameworthy nor more free of blame than the other, the incidence of the burden being determined by the accident of the recovering plaintiff's levy of execution, or even by collusion between the recovering plaintiff and the other tortfeasor.

It is satisfying to note that, as the years passed, legislatures in more and more states enacted statutes providing for some measure of contribution between joint tortfeasors. In 1939 the National Conference of Commissioners on Uniform State Laws promulgated a uniform act, now twice updated, authorizing contribution, limiting it appropriately, and prescribing legal procedures for enforcing it. Today, contribution between joint tortfeasors is allowed to different extents and under variant procedures in most, but not yet in all, of the American states.

Defamation

One of my longtime interests, and part of the subject matter of the law school course on torts which I have taught since 1927, is the law of defamation—libel and slander. The law in this area has been and to a large extent still is one of the most haphazard and inefficient segments of our entire American legal system. It is a mass of late medieval English remedies combined almost accidentally with bits of precedent handed down by one state court or another and never coordinated into a coherent body of law. It just grew, like Topsy. It has never been made clear just what purposes the law of libel and slander should serve in our society, or how the law should be framed in order to effectuate whatever purposes might be allocated to it.

A number of recent United States Supreme Court cases based on the First Amendment to the Constitution of the United States, which guarantees freedom of speech and of the press, have modernized a few parts of the law of defamation, but have touched on far less than all of it. It is evident that there must be some connection between the Bill of Rights assurance of speech and press freedom and the contradictory imposition of legal liabilities, by the law of libel and slander, upon persons who have spoken or written too freely about their fellows. But it is difficult to fit them together.

The historical sources of our law of defamation, prior to the middle of the seventeenth century, were in the English ecclesiastical courts where the prime objective was punishment of sin for the good of the soul of the sinner, rather than compensation to an injured person. Money damages were not awarded to complaining parties. Instead, a combination of penance and public acknowledgement was ordered against defamers.

In due time the law of defamation in England was taken over by the king's courts. Its development came first in the Court of the Star Chamber and had to do primarily with libel as a crime. Reports from that period show that suits were largely brought to protect the interests of great men of the realm, who had the ear of the court. In libel prosecutions before the Star Chamber, truth was no defense. It was said that "the greater the truth the greater was the libel." The idea was that libel and the closely related crime of unlicensed printing were being punished, primarily because of the harm to reputations of the great personages about whom objectionable statements were published. Such personages were apt to be harmed most by damaging statements that could not be proved to be false, and the Star Chamber was most apt to punish for true statements. Spoken defamation (slander) was not a crime during this period, and later became so in the United States only by statute.

In this country all states have made libel a crime, and several states make slander a crime. Truth was, in early days, not necessarily a defense even in this country, though the United States Supreme Court ultimately decided that truth should be an absolute defense.

About 30 years ago I made an effort to discover what function the criminal law of defamation actually serves in the United States. To do this I checked all the reports to identify every criminal defamation case that had been brought before any American appellate court during the 36-year period from 1920 to 1955, inclusive. I found that there were only 110 of these criminal cases in all of the federal and state court reports. Of this total, 91 charged libel and the remaining 19 slander. Of the 110, 58 (more than half) were reported in the ten-year period 1920–29, 34 appeared in the 12 years from 1930 through 1941, and only 18 came in the 14 years through 1955. This shows a steady decrease in such cases. I also went back to 1897, not to study the earlier cases but to ascertain their number. Of these there were 98 in the ten-year period from 1897 through 1906, and 93 reported between 1907 and 1916. I did not check World War I years because they may not have been representative. It was evident that reliance upon criminal prosecutions for defamation was steadily decreasing.

In studying the 110 cases from 1920 through 1955, I noted that 44 evolved from or were part of political controversies. Most common among the political cases were those in which prosecutions were filed against an unsuccessful political candidate or his supporters for statements made during a campaign, now ended, concerning his now successful opponent. An obvious interpretation of those cases is that "winners" were trying to get even with obnoxious "losers" who had previously opposed them.

Ten of the cases were so-called "group libels" usually involving attacks on religious or racial groups such as Jews, Negroes or Catholics. Another 44 cases involved essentially private quarrels, such as statements connected with related litigation, family fights, business and professional disputes, labor disputes, quarrels within immigrant groups, church fights, stories in militant or sensational newspapers, and plain gossip. Eight of the cases could be classified as aspersions on female chastity.

A conclusion is evident that the criminal law of defamation had ceased to serve important or useful social purposes, and criminal cases were brought to serve essentially private interests. If an effective and socially desirable civil remedy for private injuries suffered by defamation were available, it could serve all the purposes that underlaid nearly all the reported criminal proceedings in the field. "Group libel" cases constitute the sole possible exeption to that conclusion, and they generally rest upon special statutes enacted in only a few states.

The difficulty is that the traditional private civil remedy for defamation is an award of damages. The vagaries of calculation appear more haphazard in the amounts of jury awards for defamation than in almost any other field of the law, running from six cents to millions of dollars. Factors such as the obnoxiousness of the defamer's behavior, his wealth, or the defamed plaintiff's wealth, often unrelated to the actual damage suffered by the plaintiff, appear to motivate a jury's calculations.

The theory is that if the plaintiff wins an award, regardless of the amount awarded, his reputation has been cleared. That is, however, not always the popular effect of six-cent or one dollar awards. A once famous case was that in which the first Henry Ford, automobile manufacturer, sued a newspaper in 1919 for libel, and won the case. The jury awarded him six cents, possibly on the theory that he did not need any more money. Almost every newspaper in the country then proceeded to make fun of the award, saying that it proved that Henry Ford's reputation was worth only six cents.

What a plaintiff principally needs in a private defamation case is vindication, an authoritative determination that a nasty statement made concerning him was actually false. He also needs to be reimbursed for any damages actually suffered, but in many cases the actual damage is difficult to determine and less important than the vindication. An award of damages alone, regardless of amount, does not relate directly to the principal function that should be served by the law of defamation.

About 40 years ago I learned of a remedy for defamation that had, at an earlier time, been enforced in justice of the peace courts in Madison County, Arkansas. It was called the "lie bill," and was said to be a common form of action in rural areas. Legend has it that the "lie bill" remedy was available in the last century in justice of the peace courts throughout Arkansas. A half dozen lawyers from different parts of the state have since told me that they have heard old-timers speak of it. It may have come from the rural areas in North Carolina and Tennessee whose people moved to Arkansas in the state's early days. The procedure was that a defendant who had allegedly defamed a plaintiff was required to appear before the justice of the peace court, which heard evidence as to whether he had made the statement as alleged, and whether it was true or false. If it was proved that he made the statement and that it was false, there was a judicial declaration to that effect and the defendant was required to sign an admission of falsity. It seems to me that this was very nearly the ideal procedure for dealing with defamation cases. It gave specific, not substituted, relief.

When I first heard of the "lie bill" I wondered whether it was no more than an old wives' tale, a bit of typically vivid imagination from the hill country. But reports of it came from too many scattered counties. Finally, one of my former students, Judge James W. Chestnutt of Hot Springs, undertook some research and discovered actual records of the use of the lie bill in justice of the peace courts in his district. Copies of orders issued in two lie bill cases are illustrated. It appears that fair justice was achieved in Montgomery County.

Assuming appropriate remedies, both civil and criminal, the question remains as to how the imposition of legal liabilities upon speakers or writers of defamatory words can be correlated with the Constitution's guaranty against laws "abridging the freedom of speech, or of the press." An absolute right to publish what one may thereafter be criminally punished or forced to pay civil damages for publishing, is obviously illusory in its absoluteness. Laws dealing with libel and slander, obscenity and blasphemy, contempt of court, treason, deceit and false advertising, among others, impose substantial limitations upon speech and publication in our society. I attempted in 1962 to evaluate these competing "rights," in an article in 15 Vanderbilt Law Review 1073 under the title *The Free-ness of Free Speech.*

Mr. Justice Hugo L. Black of the United States Supreme Court often stated that it was his belief that the words "Congress shall make no law . . . abridging the freedom of speech, or of the press" mean exactly what they say, that there must be no congressional legislation whatever in the proscribed area. There would be nothing truly earthshaking about this if it affected only what Congress may do. It would operate primarily to preserve states' rights, leaving the states free to do by their law what the federal Congress was barred from doing. But today the due process clause of the Fourteenth Amendment incorporates much of the Bill of Rights as a limitation upon state power also. Mr. Justice Black also said:

The First Amendment was made applicable to the states by the Fourteenth. I do not hesitate, so far as my own view is concerned, as to what should be and what I hope will sometime be the constitutional doctrine that just as it was not intended to authorize damage suits for mere words as distinguished from conduct as far as the federal government is concerned, the same rule should apply to the states. (37 N.Y.U. L. Rev. 549, 558).

Since the due process clause declares that "No state shall deprive any person of . . ." and not merely that "No state *legislature* shall . . . ," its prohibition is against all state action, including action by state courts under authority of judge-made law, and not merely against state legislative enactments. Mr. Justice Black was telling us that in his opinion all law—not just all legislative enactments—*all law* imposing legal sanctions upon freedom of speech and freedom of the press ought to be held unconstitutional today—or tomorrow. The right to freedom of speech and of the press, he thought, is an "absolute" one.

When asked about someone who shouts "fire" in a crowded theatre, Mr. Justice Black pointed out that this involved not only the speaking of a word but conduct that was disorderly. The point which correlates the shout of "fire" with the shouter's conduct, classifying it as disorderly conduct or breach of the peace, suggests that the lawfulness of using words is to be determined by the circumstances under which they are used including the time, place and manner of their use. To this the traditional law agrees; it has always made a difference whether particular words were spoken in a public speech, or in a play, or by a hermit alone in the desert. Speech is seldom in a social vacuum, and when it is it raises few legal problems. It is the surrounding circumstances that give rise to our problems.

A word or group of words is not only part of the totality of conduct that accompanies enunciation; the very fact of enunciation is conduct. The speaking of words is an act, as much the product of a deliberate, or thoughtless, engagement upon

Montgomery County Justice Docket, Leverne Township, page 26:

"SLANDER"

"This is to certify that the Slandreth Talk that was Reported on Miss Mattie Clemenz During the month of August 1896 or any other time During her Life Was Provin to this community and to the corts satisfaction to all Be Falts Being Prosicuted By the Parrents of the Miss Mattie Clemenz

Givin under my hand this Oct the 22 1896

N. E. Robinson, J.P."

Montgomery County Justice Docket, Parks Township, page 27:

"State of Ark County of Montgomery

I Allan Rainwater do solemnly swear that the reports that I told certain parties, on about the 10th March, 1902, Vis Jessie Davis, R. A. Davis and Will Arnold concerning James Putman about the cow stealing, is false. J.A. Rainwater.

Subscribed and sworn to before me this the 28 day of Feb. 1903.

I. W. Tweedle J.P."

a course of conduct as is the swinging of a fist or the exertion of pressure on the gas pedal of a motor car. Some of our most troublesome interferences with free speech by legal authority have been supported by a pretence that it was not the speaking but the tendency to produce public disturbance, or an unli-censed assembly, or a blaring loudspeaker, that was penalized.

Few will deny that these and like grounds for silencing speakers are sometimes legitimate, even though they actually prevent the effective conveying of messages deemed urgent by those who would convey them. The dissenter's inevitable sav-ing clause was illustrated by Justice Black himself in *Kovacs v. Cooper*, 336 U.S. 77, at 104:

I am aware that the "blare" of this new method of carrying ideas is susceptible of abuse and may under certain circumstances constitute an intolerable nuisance. . . . A city ordinance that reasonably re-stricts the volume of sound, or the hours during which an amplifier may be used, does not, in my mind, infringe the constitutionally protected area of free speech.

The difficulty is in deciding which is more important—the speaking as free speech, or as an interference with public or-der. Once we accept this as a matter for decision, one that can be decided either way, we recognize that free speech is not an absolute under the particular circumstances.

There are some kinds of utterances, both oral and written, that the free speech guaranty was never designed to protect. It was not intended to protect perjuries. This cannot be because perjuries are not speech; they are speech. It cannot be because the perjurer has no real interest in conveying the ideas con-tained in his perjured speech; usually he does have. The same is true of fraudulent speech. The guaranty leaves the law free to penalize fraud, and the law does so by criminally punishing the crime of obtaining property by false pretences, by allowing tort recovery for deceit, by awarding equitable relief in a num-ber of forms, and by administrative remedies. The law has made a start toward imposing sanctions against false advertising, and interference with free speech is not successfully urged today as an objection to laws regulating the free use of misleading language in, for instance, the registration of securities offered for sale to the public. The misbranding of food and drugs is merely another form of the use of words, yet it is punishable. It is easy to say that speech such as this, perjured or fraudulent, serves no public interest that is worth protecting, and that the private interests it serves are evil. But private interest and public interest shade into each other. In a free enterprise society many major concerns are promoted by private interests, often for private gain, and differences of opinion can exist not only concerning values but asserted facts as well. There can be instances in which laws against false swearing and other lying may be used to stifle truth or social doctrine. And laws against false advertising could be employed to discourage economic advances in a society organized as ours is.

What about punishment for contempt of court, or for contempt of any organ of government? Almost any contempt voices an expression of opinion or point of view, normally directed toward a public agency. That on its face is the sort of expression with which the free speech guaranty is genuinely concerned. It is true that contemptuous utterances in the courtroom directly affect the administration of justice, which is a matter of vast social concern. Yet the law of contempt is a powerful tool for silencing dissent at the time and place that it could be most meaningful. Here, the law deliberately puts the values inherent in free speech into second place, behind the values inherent in the free and untrammelled administration of justice.

There are situations in which the exercise of free speech may lawfully be limited or controlled because circumstances would make the speech unfairly potent in the very areas in which it is most important that free speech be maintained. Illustrations include lobbying before legislative bodies, political activity by presumably impartial government employees, electioneering within a certain distance from the polls during elections, and publications by employers or unions constituting an "unfair labor practice" within the provisions of the National Labor Relations Act. For these situations the constitutional guaranty becomes something like one of "free and equal speech" or "freedom only for equal speech."

The whole mass of common law defamation cases had its beginnings well before the First Amendment, let alone the Fourteenth, was written, and has developed almost without judicial reference to freedom of speech as a constitutional limitation upon them. Relevant also are the obscenity cases and the subversive publication cases in which free speech issues definitely were mentioned and in which the "clear and present danger" test or some variant of it emerged as a supposedly authoritative limitation upon the constitutional guaranty. The present state of the law was not what Mr. Justice Black was talking about, however. He knew the present state of the law concerning the "defamation family" as well as anyone, but he believed it was wrong, that it improperly disregarded the constitutional guaranty. What the cases prove is that others hold views contrary to his, and that there are at least *some* circumstances in which the First Amendment does not preclude legal sanctions against the exercise of completely free speech.

It can quite properly be pointed out that laws designed to achieve orderliness in, therefore maximum enjoyment of, the free speaking that the Constitution guarantees are not really interferences with free speech but are rather, in a sophisticated and realistic sense, further protections of it. They are like the rules of order in a parliamentary body, providing that only one person may speak at a time so that each may ultimately be heard in turn. A speech-regulating law that has for its purpose the more complete effectuation of the totality of relevant speech is by its nature not just a permissible abridgement of the right of speech. It can fairly be called no abridgement at all. It affirmatively aids the constitutional guaranty.

Not many of the law's limitations on free speech are of that protective sort. Most limitations are designed to prevent or penalize the kinds of speech with which they deal, not to facilitate them. They are based on the asserted lack of social value inherent in the kind of speech that they proscribe, on the legislative or judicial determination (not always clearly correct) that the social badness in the speech substantially outweighs whatever good it has in it, either intrinsically or as free expression. The orderliness they help to achieve is the general orderliness in society that regulatory law as a whole seeks to achieve; it is not just an orderliness in freedom of speech as such.

Absolute freedom of speech is an ideal not yet realized in human society. No state organized by mankind has been willing to permit the completely free and untrammelled communication of every idea that might emerge through the lips or pens of those who seek for one reason or another to affect their fellows by the use of words. There is much room for difference of opinion about how far the law in practice should depart from the philosophical ideal of absolute freedom. Probably the degree of variation from the ideal depends upon how firmly the law-giving state is established as a civilized and democratic legal entity. The less firmly it is established in that desirable condition, the more likely it is to try to prevent the free expression of ideas.

Before we give up on Justice Black's "means what it says" approach, it is fair to suggest that the Constitution's words may not actually say that there must be no interference whatever with completely free speech and press. The words are "no law . . . abridging the freedom of speech, or of the press. . . ." The framers did not say no law "respecting" freedom of speech, "or prohibiting the free exercise thereof"—words used in the same amendment with regard to laws about religion. They said no law "*abridging* the freedom of speech," thus identifying "the" freedom of speech as an existent concept, that is, one existent in the social and legal mores of the time, and declaring that there should be no law "abridging," that is, curtailing, diminishing, narrowing or shortening the content of this concept as it then existed. This is very different from the comprehensive language used in the part of the amendment that deals with religion, but it is the same language employed in the rest of the amendment with respect to (abridging) "the right" of assembly and of petition, both already existent concepts in Anglo-American law. The amendment does not forbid "prohibiting the free exercise of" speech; it forbids "abridging the freedom of speech." The great difficulty with such an interpretation is that it might tie us now and forever to the meager guaranties of free speech and press that had, by 1789, already been established in Anglo-American law.

If the amendment does not tie us irrevocably to 1789 law, nor absolutely bar all law that regulates any speaking whatever, what is the standard for testing the freeness of speech? What speaking may be penalized, civilly or criminally, and what may not be? What guides do we have, other than today's majority decisions, to tell us where the Congress and the states must call a halt to regulation of speech?

The start on an answer to such inquiries must be in terms of social values: Has our society identified the qualities and the virtues that it values in free speech—those valued highly, against those valued lightly or not at all? To be significant, this identification must be discovered in terms of today—looking toward the future as well as the past—and not in terms of 1789, because today is when our United States Supreme Court and most of our other American appellate courts read meaning into the clauses of our constitutions.

To say that any such identification exists in precise form,

like a definition, would be preposterous; philosophers, social scientists, lawyers, and men in the street do not all agree with each other that readily. Many have not thought about the matter very seriously. Some would put the integrity of *status quo* so high in their scale of values that speech proposing change would be rated low. But their views do not help us. A useful identification must be one made by people in our society who have thought seriously and discriminatingly about the freedom of speech, and who place it in their scale of values above almost everything else that our society holds dear. If free speech as an ideal is to be something short of an absolute, that is the way it needs to be measured.

It may be that in 1789 the evaluation of free speech by philosophers and political thinkers of the time was largely made in terms of "governing" and government, or wise use of the ballot. We do not really know whether that was so or not. We do know, however, that in this last fraction of the twentieth century, the values which the freedom of speech represents to those of us who value it highly are more all-embracing than the issues which we pass upon even most indirectly at the ballot box. They include freedom to speak on every controversial matter concerning human conduct and thought, and every issue affecting mankind about which there is room for difference of opinion. They include freedom to talk about religious issues which we do not pass upon at the ballot box, matters of morals, social conduct and business behavior which our society has never regulated politically, ethical beliefs and artistic tastes that are not susceptible to regulation by law in America. By our ideal, the values inherent in the right to free speech are as broad as all the concerns of our American society.

How then do we, or should we, make our specific judgments? How do we, while effectuating our ideal, or perhaps only pretending to effectuate it, pick out situations in which free speaking will be penalized?

One mass of cases is easy. Neither frauds nor perjuries nor

most defamations have within them any of the social values for which our ideal of free speech demands protection. Libel or slander which seeks acceptance of no cultural, political, social or ethical attitude, which urges no controversial idea or opinion, which seeks nothing beyond private benefit to the speaker and possible harm to others, does not come within the ideal at all. It deserves no constitutional protection, and receives none.

But what about legal sanctions imposed against so-called subversive publications which state the strongly held societal views of their publishers, against defamations which appear in a political or social context, and obscenities for which literary or cultural quality is claimed? What about contempts and lobbyings and efforts at persuasion when competing interests assert some possibly superior claim to the law's protection? In these cases the ideal of free speech is truly involved. Any speaking which seeks overthrow of established order and system, attacks it or its spokesmen in their representative character, comes clearly within the ideal of free speech deserving the law's protection. Yet speech in these areas has often been penalized.

What the courts have decided in these difficult cases has been essentially the same as in the easy mass of cases. They have weighed the social values inherent in the particular free speech, as they saw those values, against the competing interests, and have concluded that the values inherent in the competing interests were the weightier. They have concluded, for example, that maintenance of our established form of American government is more important than the virtues inherent in free speech when the speech creates a "clear and present danger" of Communist effort to overthrow the government by force and violence. To use another example, they have held that the reputation of a state governor was more important than the free speech which was interpreted as charging the governor of Massachusetts with crime in connection with the celebrated Sacco-Vanzetti criminal-political prosecution.

There are many who believe that wrong weights were given to the competing values in these cases or in some of them. Comparable differences of opinion exist over a thousand other cases that might be cited, holding either one way or the other on the free speech issue. Some think the ideal of free expression is so important that it outweighs all others when the words spoken have any genuine societal significance; others give it less weight. Judges, like the rest of us, hold variant views. The constitution does not tell us what view is right or what weights to give the competing values. The courts decide, as they must.

Consciously or subconsciously, they decide by balancing the values as they see them at the time they do the balancing. That is the only way a court can decide between competing social values when there is no clear basic law or precedent to guide it.

That is what has happened, still is happening, and will continue to happen as the courts strive to ascertain the line that divides free speech from that which may be punished or even prohibited. The court that has the ultimate responsibility is the Supreme Court of the United States. Not until the 1960s did that court really accept its responsibility concerning freedom of speech. It did not adopt Justice Black's absolutist theory, though he restated it persistently in dissenting and concurring opinions. The court's majority shifted somewhat, as new justices and new ideas replaced older ones and as appeals multiplied. That is characteristic of judicial decisions in areas of newly developing law.

As of today (1985), however, a fair measure of stability seems to have been achieved. The constitutional guaranty does impose limits on the states' laws of libel and slander. The leading case of *New York Times Co. v. Sullivan*, 376 U.S. 254, at 279, "prohibits a public official from recovering damages for a defamatory falsehood relating to his official conduct unless he proves that the statement was made with 'actual malice'— that is, with knowledge that it was false or with reckless disregard of whether it was false or not." Other cases extended the same protection against liability to statements about public activities of other "public figures," defining the term "public figure" somewhat narrowly, while at the same time restricting recovery for all defamation to cases in which there was "fault" (negligence, or "actual malice" as just defined) in the defamer. Thus the Supreme Court has attempted to give a practical and contemporarily realistic meaning to the constitutional guaranty as it controls the law of defamation.

As to free speech, we are likely to have guaranteed to us at any given time that measure of it which the prevailing judicial philosophy thinks is good. If the state and its institutions are firmly established in the ways of civilized democracy, the law announced by the judges is likely to mirror the demand for a correspondingly large measure of free societal expression. The ideal of speech altogether free where societally significant expression is concerned may never be completely realized, but it will approach realization as rapidly and as closely as civilized democracy accepts its values. In the United States, free speech and press are more completely guaranteed today than they were a quarter-century ago (before 1964), though the words in the Constitution date back to 1789 and 1868. But the guaranty is still not an absolute one, and it is unlikely that it will ever be.

Supreme Court of the United States
Washington, D. C.

CHAMBERS OF
JUSTICE HUGO L. BLACK

February 20, 1963

Dear Professor Leflar:

Thanks for sending reprint of your article from the
Vanderbilt Law Review entitled "The Free-ness of Free Speech".
Of course you understand my very deep interest in the First
Amendment freedoms and I am happy to have your views. You
also understand, I am sure, that my views are quite different
from many of those you have expressed. One reason underlying
my own First Amendment philosophy is that I am afraid you are
right about the type of infringements on First Amendment freedoms the opposite philosophy will tolerate and, I am afraid, encourage. I refer at this moment particularly to your sentence
on page 1084 where you say:

"As to free speech, we are likely to have at any
given time that measure of it guaranteed to us that
the prevailing judicial philosophy thinks is good.
. . ."

A view somewhat like yours is expressed several times in an article
by Professor Clifton B. Kruse in the Winter 1962 Washburn Law
Journal, which discusses the historical meaning and construction
of the Establishment of Religion Clause. As I understand his
article, his final conclusion is that the Constitution means pre-
cisely what the Court says it means at a particular time to meet
what the Court considers to be current needs of the country, without giving any emphasis whatever to original meanings.

Again thanking you for the article and with my kind regards, I am

Sincerely,

Hugo L Black

Professor Robert A. Leflar
New York University
School of Law
New York 3, N. Y.

V The Law of Conflict of Laws

The Nature of Conflicts Law

Over the last half-century or so I have written some thousands of pages about various aspects of my favorite legal subject, conflict of laws, and have taught it as a law school subject almost continuously since 1927. It is a complex and unsettled subject, dealing with nearly every area of law that law study or law practice encompasses; therefore, it is normally scheduled at or near the end of a law school course of study. The thick tomes that treat it often make hard reading even for legal scholars. Yet it is not, in my view, as mysterious a subject as it has often been made out to be.

Stated simply, conflict of laws has to do with situations in which sets of facts, including lawsuits, have contacts with more than one state or nation. If only one state or nation was involved, its law would control. When two or more are in-volved, each having its own body of laws covering the infinite variety of topics that law deals with, the inevitable question is "Which law governs?" That is what the law of conflict of laws, which can be shortened to the one word "conflicts," is all about.

One constitutional principle underlies all American con-flicts law. This is that the law applied to any given issue raised by any set of facts must be that of a state (a word that here-inafter includes nations) which has a substantial connection with the facts themselves. It is said that to determine the rights and obligations of litigants by the law of a state that has no connection with the disputed facts would be as bad as to decide their case on the basis of a different and unrelated set of facts. The due process clause of the United States Constitu-tion would be violated by any such adjudication under an irrel-evant law. A case based altogether on Louisiana facts may be filed in a Texas court, and tried there, if the defendant is found and served with process in Texas. The Texas court trying the case will of necessity follow its own procedural rules, but it must determine the substantive merits of the case under the substantive law of Louisiana. That is the constitutional re-quirement, enforced by the United States Supreme Court (449 U.S. 302). A court's choice of law problem exists only between the laws of states which had real contacts with the relevant facts.

To illustrate: A man named D, a resident of Missouri, stands in Oklahoma and shoots P, also a resident of Missouri who at the time is standing in Kansas. After suffering the Kansas wound P is taken to a hospital in Missouri where he dies. Which state's law may govern D's criminal liability for the homicide? His civil liability to P's survivors for the wrongful death? All three states have substantial contacts with the facts.

Or P and D, who both live in Arkansas, there engage in

preliminary negotiations looking toward the establishment and operation of a business in nearby Tennessee. They plan to attend a convention in Nevada together and to firm up the project during their trip by airline from Memphis. While on the trip, apparently above Utah, they reach agreement and shake hands on it. Returning to Arkansas, they commence activities in Tennessee, then disagree and prepare to sue each other. Which state's laws determine their rights and obligations, if any, under the purported contract? Is Utah a possibility?

Or Mr. A, whose home is in New York, dies while on vacation in Florida. He leaves a farm in Iowa, 1,000 shares of stock in a Delaware corporation, a substantial deposit in a Connecticut bank, a wife who was suing him for divorce in Nevada, and no will. What states' laws determine who gets what?

Several hundred similarly complex sets of facts can readily be imagined, and actually do occur. It can be agreed that the law of Texas may not govern in any of the three cases just stated. Since Texas had nothing to do with any of the sets of facts, the due process clause of the Constitution bars that possibility. But among the states which do have contacts with the facts, which laws will be chosen to govern? In the absence of relevant statutes, of which there are very few, this is a conflict of laws question to be decided under the common law of the state in which the particular controversy is litigated.

My law school conflicts teacher was Professor Joseph H. Beale, who was the modern developer of the subject. He put together the first student casebook on conflict of laws, and around 1900 offered the first law school conflicts course. Books on the subject had already appeared in European countries where transactions across national lines were common. Justice Joseph Story of the United States Supreme Court and Harvard Law School wrote, in 1934, the first comprehensive treatise in English on conflict of laws. Two or three other books were published in this country during the 19th century. None of them analyzed the subject in terms of basic theory, which Beale did, and in the first half of the 20th century he came to be recognized as America's leading expert in the field. The American Law Institute's Restatement of Conflict of Laws (1934), for which he was the Reporter, set forth his views consistently. Advisers who disagreed could only resign from the Board of Advisers. His Restatement dominated judicial decision and law school teaching for decades.

Beale's basic theory, however, was severely criticized on the ground that it was too rigidly mechanical. It selected a single central fact for each standardized type of transaction or event upon which a conflicts question might arise, and specified the state in which that central fact occurred as the state whose law would govern all transactions or events within the standardized type. The standardized types, fewer than a dozen altogether, were traditional legal classifications: immovable property (land), movable property, contracts, torts, civil procedure, administration of estates, corporations, family law, all analyzed in traditional legal fashion, thus making the judicial task of choosing the governing law a fairly easy and almost automatic one, once the case was characterized as tort, contract, or under one of the other standard legal classifications. Criticism arose because the choice of law was too automatic, too easy; it too often disregarded the law's and society's proper concern with justice, with protection of justified expectations, with genuine state interests, and with other relevant considerations.

For example, tort liability in the three-state shooting case would, according to Beale, be governed by the law of Kansas since that was the state where, by the harmful impact, a tort was completed. The Arkansas-Tennessee business contract would be governed by the law of Utah if that was the state in which, or over which, the contract was made. Two or three different state laws could control the several problems left by the unfortunate New Yorker who died in Florida. For the most part, these were results produced by application of hard and fast rules unrelated to any sense of justice or practical reality. More sensible choices of governing law can readily be suggested, but conflicts law designed to assure such better choices had not yet been promulgated.

Most American courts purported to follow the Bealian rules through the 1950s, but gimmicky devices for moving cases from one standard category to another were increasingly employed to enable courts to apply the law of a different state. If there was a contract relationship in the background of a personal injury case, the case might be characterized as sounding either in contract or in tort, enabling the court to apply the law of the place where the contract was made, if that seemed to produce a more just result, or the law of the place of injury if that was thought to be the better law. If the tortious injury claim was between family members it could be characterized as either a tort case or a family law case, again enabling a court to apply the law of the place of injury or that of the family domicile, according to the court's preference as to which state's law was better. An issue such as statute of limitations, or the availability of some specific remedy, might be characterized as procedural, and therefore governed by the law of the place where the lawsuit was tried, or as substantive and governed by the law of the place, or of one of the places, where the facts occurred. A technique called *renvoi* could be employed to move the details of the chosen law from one state to another. The fact was that courts were getting around Beale's hard and fast mechanical rules at the same time that they purported to follow them, and the reasons for evading the rules were independent of and more appealing than the Bealian reasoning. The rules were not truly good law and neither, in view of persistent evasions, were they actually accepted as the law.

My disillusionment with Beale's hard and fast conflicts rules came early. He asked me to prepare Arkansas annotations (it was planned to publish annotations in each state for each of the Restatement subjects) for the Conflict of Laws Restatement. I agreed to do it, and started out by locating and abstracting all reported Arkansas conflicts cases. There were a lot of them, and on the whole they made good legal sense, as well as being realistically fair in their results. But they did not fit in with the rigorous rules laid down in the Restatement. The annotations would be negative, and useless as far as the Restatement was concerned. The upshot was that I in 1938, as my own publisher, put out the book *Arkansas Law of Conflict of Laws*. All of the 1,000 copies were soon sold, at $4.50 each, with the profits going to the University of Arkansas law school library. I am amazed that occasionally a lawyer tells me that he is still using the book. When it was published I thought it was the only one-state book on conflict of laws in America. Later I learned that *The Conflict of Laws in the Province of Quebec* by Eugene Lafleur had been published in 1898. Canadian friends eventually gave me a copy of the Lafleur book, long out of print. Oddly, the two one-state authors' names were nearly the same. And my Arkansas studies gave me some acquaintance with every aspect of conflicts law.

By the 1960s it was time for a revision of America's law of conflict of laws. New choice-of-law approaches to replace Beale's mechanistic ones had already been proposed by academic scholars in several articles in legal periodicals. Elliott Cheatham and Willis Reese of Columbia University in 1952 published an article (52 Columbia L. Rev. 959) which sought out the real reasons that justified courts in choosing one state's law over another's. David Cavers of Harvard suggested that the choice ought not to be just between the different states as jurisdictional entities. His view was that the choice of governing law should be a choice between the laws as laws, and not between states without regard to the content of their laws. Brainerd Currie of Duke University proposed that choices of governing law ought to be controlled by checking on the "governmental interests" of the states involved, with first choice going to the law of the state in which the lawsuit was filed if that state had an interest in the subject matter of the suit. A state's interests were to be measured, presumably, by the significance of its contacts with the facts. Currie's analyses, though modified by just about every court and every conflicts theorist purporting to follow them, have been more cited than any other of the various approaches to modern conflicts law. Both the scholarly writings and the judicial decisions in the field are reported and correlated in the conflicts articles I wrote each year, beginning in 1955, for the New York University Law School's *Annual Survey of American Law*.

A revision of the Conflict of Laws Restatement was commenced in 1953, with Willis Reese as Reporter, but it was not completed and published until 1971. I was one of the Advisers who assisted in drafting and editing it. The Restatement (Second) choice-of-law test, called the "most significant relationship" rule, depends less upon mechanical characterization of problems and instead upon a determination of which state had the most significant contacts with the facts as they bore upon the question to be decided in the case. The law to be applied is that of the state having this "most significant relationship" to that issue.

My own theoretical analyses were first published in 1966 (41 N.Y.U. L. Rev. 267; 54 Calif. L. Rev. 1584), and first judicially adopted later that year in a New Hampshire Supreme Court case (*Clark v. Clark*, 107 N.H. 351, 222 Atl.2d 205). They were in no real sense original, but largely based upon earlier studies such as the Cheatham and Reese article cited in a preceding paragraph. My effort was to identify and synthesize all the considerations that made good sense as reasons for choosing one state's law, as against some other state's, in any conflicts case. It finally appeared that all of these reasons, though they had previously been referred to under many different explanations, could be correlated with fairly full descriptions under five main heads. These became the "five choice-influencing considerations," listed as follows:

1. Predictability of results,
2. Maintenance of interstate and international order,
3. Simplification of the judicial task,
4. Advancement of the forum's (the court's home state's) governmental interests,
5. Application of the better rule of law.

Their conflict of laws significance is explained briefly by the following excerpts, copied for the most part from the original analyses cited above.

1. PREDICTABILITY OF RESULTS   Uniformity of results, regardless of forum, has always been a major goal in choice-of-law theory. Achievement of this goal would enable parties entering into a consensual transaction to plan it with reference to a body of law that would give them the results they desired. As a result, their transactions would normally be validated and their justified expectations thus protected. This would further the broad social policies of most forum states by sustaining legal arrangements in which parties have in good faith engaged.

Knowing in advance what state's law will govern helps to achieve validity for such planned transactions as marriages, child legitimations, trusts, property transfers, the making of wills, commercial instruments, most contracts, and other socially favored compacts. At the same time it would discourage "forum shopping," the deliberate effort by plaintiffs, or their attorneys, to file their cases in a state whose law was most favorable to their claims and least favorable to the defendant's defenses.

On the other hand, predictability as to governing law has

little or no relevance to unplanned transactions such as accidents and most torts. Advance reliance upon known law is seldom in the background of such occurrences.

2. MAINTENANCE OF INTERSTATE AND INTERNATIONAL ORDER   Both nations and states within a nation are interested in facilitating the orderly legal control of transactions that in any fashion cross their boundary lines. Smooth conduct of affairs between the peoples of different nations is essential to modern civilization; the easy movement of persons and things—free social and economic commerce—between states in a federal nation is essential to the very existence of the federation. There must be a minimum of interference with claims or aspirations to sovereignty. No forum whose concern with a set of facts is negligible should claim priority for its law over the law of a state which has a clearly superior concern with the facts. Encouragement of that measure of interstate and international intercourse which is in keeping with the interests of the forum state and its people has always been a prime function of conflicts law.

Specific clauses in the federal constitution (full faith and credit, due process, privileges and immunities, equal protection, interstate commerce, and perhaps others) as well as the inherent federal control over foreign and national affairs, all as interpreted by the United States Supreme Court, have imposed outer limits on the states beyond which they must not go in interfering with basic requisites to international and interstate orderliness. But there are factors affecting relationships between states and nations, in choice-of-law cases, that ought to be taken into account, yet which ought not (not yet, at least), to be hardened into constitutional limitations. These are properly considerations in the common law judicial process.

The free and unpenalized movement of people and goods from state to state, and freedom in commercial intercourse, are essential to the success of our federal system, and it is part of the law's task to assure them. Deference to sister state law in situations in which the sister state's substantial concern with the problem gives it a real interest in having its law applied, even though the forum state also has an identifiable interest, will sometimes usefully further this aspect of the law's total task.

It must be recognized that if nearly all of a transaction's significant contacts are with one state (X), yet the forum state (F) applies its own law to the transaction despite its lesser contacts, resentment in X may induce later retaliation in kind. Avoidance of interstate friction that can develop from this sort of retaliatory comity is a proper choice-of-law objective. The balancing process here, however, is particularly delicate, since discrimination against the interests of other governments can be a subtle thing. The most that can be safely said is that they constitute a relevant factor for consideration, and that failure to consider them may produce results that, though within the permissible limits of constitutionality as now defined, are troublesome and unfortunate. A neat and orderly system of choice of law, with states' rights clearly identified and allocated, is in our federalism an ideal that should not be discarded.

3. SIMPLIFICATION OF THE JUDICIAL TASK   An easy cliché is that law does not exist for the convenience of the court that administers it, but for society and its members; therefore, simplification of the judicial task should be a minor consideration in determining what any rule of law should be. The statement is true enough. But overcrowded dockets can become a real problem, and complicated rules of law may encourage the delay in decision that is sometimes a reason why dockets lengthen. Also, complex rules are sometimes difficult to apply, especially to complex facts, and even reasonably competent courts, both trial and appellate, may misapply them. Simplicity in law is a virtue. Judicial efficiency often depends upon it.

It has been argued that a court should apply its own local law unless there is good reason for not doing so. No one can deny the propriety of this argument so long as the "unless" clause is adequately emphasized. It will usually be easier for the forum court to apply its own law than any other. The court is presumably already familiar with it and is already accustomed to administering it.

That is without question a good reason for a court's applying its own procedural rules, since it would be utterly impracticable for a court in forum state F to import the whole procedural machinery of state X even in a case that is clearly governed by X law. But the reasons of practicality which justify that generalization stop short when the rule in question is an outcome-determinative one.

Preference for forum law is, of course, not the only approach that can simplify the judicial task in choice-of-law cases. Any simple mechanical rule, such as that the law of the place of contracting governs in contract cases and the law of the place of first harmful impact governs torts, is also easy to apply. This is a virtue, and was some justification for those purported rules. Their ultimate rejection did not deny this virtue, but was based rather on recognition that other relevant considerations were more important.

4. ADVANCEMENT OF THE FORUM'S GOVERNMENTAL INTERESTS If a forum state has a genuine concern with the facts in a given case, a concern discoverable from its strongly felt social or legal policy, it is reasonable to expect the state's courts to act in accordance with that concern. This refers to legitimate concerns, not just to the local occurrence of some facts, or to the local existence of some rule of law that could constitutionally be applied to the facts. A state's governmental interests in the choice-of-law sense need not coincide with its rules of local law, especially if the local rules, whether statutory or judge-made, are old or out of tune with the times. A state's total governmental interest in a case is to be discovered from all the considerations that properly motivate the state in its

law-making and law-administering tasks, viewed from the time when the question is presented. So viewed, circumstances may show that the forum is truly interested in applying its own law to a set of facts. If they do show this, that conclusion becomes a major choice-influencing consideration. To the extent that the elusive concept "local public policy" can be correlated with local positive law, it constitutes an affirmative pull on any court to prefer its own law over any foreign law.

Too often the search for governmental interests in a particular case, especially for the purpose of sustaining application of forum law, is artificial. Since some reasons, usually a variety of them, can be called up in support of almost any rule of law on the books anywhere, it is nearly always possible for a good lawyer to conjure up governmental interest in just about any state that has any connection with a set of facts. It is not at all unusual for one state to discover that it has such interests in a set of facts although another state's courts would say otherwise. A court is usually more discriminatingly hardboiled in analyzing another state's interests than in analyzing its own.

In the United States, increasing mobility of the citizenry serves to decrease the importance attached to the sociopolitical concept of each person having a preeminent headquarters at some one place. The fact that in this country the states are becoming more alike, less chauvinistic in their eccentricities, contributes to this change. Most of the states are becoming accustomed to the fact that a large proportion of the human beings who at any given moment are working or playing within their borders will have ties with other states as well. An effect of this is that the states are less concerned than they once were with protection of the local citizen as distinguished from the "stranger," and more inclined to promulgate and enforce laws that apply to both equally, well beyond the minimum equalities prescribed by the federal constitution. Visitors as well as residents may be protected by "good" local laws. The domicile of parties in one state or another has less significance today, and may well have far less in another generation, than it once had as a basis for locating true governmental interests.

If we classify the choice-of-law process as to some extent a search for and effectuation of the state's governmental interests, we should think of those interests in terms of the total governmental concerns of a justice-dispensing court in a modern American state. Despite the increasingly common character of the states of the United States, there are still significant differences among them on some but not on most matters. If two states really have opposing governmental interests, then advancement of the forum's interests as against those of the other state must be accepted as a legitimate part (but not all) of the process.

5. APPLICATION OF THE BETTER RULE OF LAW   The better rule of law is the most controversial of the considerations, yet a potent one. If choice of law were purely a jurisdiction-selecting process, with courts first deciding which state's law should govern and checking afterward to see what that state's law is, this consideration would not be present. Everyone knows that is not what courts do, nor what they should do. Judges know from the beginning between which rules of law, and not just which states, they are choosing.

At one time judges deciding choice-of-law cases would have self-consciously denied that they gave any weight to the quality of the rules of law between which choice was made. A vested rights approach called for a choice between states, not between laws, and there was thought to be some tinge of the unethical in the conduct of a judge who, unlike blind Justice, deliberately opened his eyes to see the consequences of his choice. Even today some jurists assert the blind ideal, though none would deny the reality, sometimes partially concealed but readily discoverable, of weight given to the content of rules and the results they produce.

Choice of law, as distinguished from choice of jurisdictions, is accepted by the courts more by deed than by word, but it is accepted, within limits. Superiority of one rule of law over another, in terms of socioeconomic jurisprudential standards, is far from being the whole basis for choice of law, yet it is without question one of the relevant considerations. When the choice is deliberately made in favor of applying the better of the competing rules of law, by the forum's standard, it is likely that justice between the litigating parties, according to this standard, will be approximated too.

Often the better law, for any given set of facts, will be the law which undertakes to uphold a fair transaction entered into by the parties in good faith. This, of course, is the "basic rule of validity," already referred to as applicable to many contracts, trusts, wills, commercial instruments, marriages, legitimations, and other socially favored arrangements. This choice-of-the-better-law process, while it normally leads to validation, could lead to invalidation if the subject matter of a contract were deemed grossly immoral or antisocial by the forum court, or if its form or method of execution, as in some sorts of adhesion contracts, savored of what the court regards as unfair advantage. In choosing between a relevant law that would sustain a transaction and another that would defeat it, the court will almost surely be influenced by its strongly held views on these matters. If it has no strongly held views the policy favoring validation will presumably win out.

It is evident that the search for the better rule of law may lead a court almost automatically to its own lawbooks. The idea that the forum's own law is the best in the world is unfortunately but understandably still current among some of our courts. There are good reasons why a court should prefer its own state's law, both for the sake of simplifying its judicial job and in order to advance the forum's governmental interests, if it has any, in the litigation. Those two relevant considerations have already been discussed. Furthermore, it is altogether possible that a court may conscientiously conclude, after intelligent comparison, that its local rules of law are wiser, sounder, and better calculated to serve the total ends of justice under law in the controversy before it than are the competing rules of the other state or states involved in the case. Such a conscientious conclusion is to be respected. But it does not amount to an automatic preference for local law, nor is an automatic preference justifiable. Most courts today do not employ any such automatic preference.

Judges can appreciate as well as anyone else the fact that in some areas their forum law is anachronistic, behind the times, a "drag on the coattails of civilization," or that the law of some other state has these benighted characteristics. When a court finds itself faced with a choice between such anachronistic laws still hanging on in one state, and realistic, practical, modern rules in another state, with both states having substantial connection with the relevant facts, it would be surprising if the court's choice did not incline toward the superior law. A court sufficiently aware of the relation between law and societal needs can recognize superiority of one rule over another and will seldom be restrained in its choice by the fact that the outmoded rule happens still to prevail in its own state. One way or another it will normally choose the law that makes good sense when applied to the facts.

A lawyer representing one side or the other in a case starts, at least approximately, with the result he wants to reach, whether the case involves choice of law or something else. In non-conflicts cases he first endeavors to characterize his problem, to determine what field it falls in; then, when he finds that the governing rule is unsettled he builds an argument for the rule that for his purposes seems the better one. At the same time he seeks a legal characterization of the problem under which he can with reasonable hope of success argue for the preferred rule.

In choice-of-law cases the customary process is much the

same, up to a point. The typical lawyer, knowing the result he wants to achieve and having characterized his problem sufficiently to know what rules of law he is concerned with, checks the laws of the connected states and ascertains those favorable to him. Then he looks at the mechanical conflicts rules which choose a state rather than a law, and selects anew a characterization or a conflicts theory that will, under the mechanical rules, lead him to the previously chosen law with its desired result. When he comes before the court, he reverses the reasoning process and argues first for his ultimate characterization and conflicts theory, then leads on to the concluding result which was in fact his starting point. Since both sides normally present their choice-of-law reasoning in this form, it is understandable that courts accept the form, and in their decisions adopt it as presented by one side or the other. But it is also expected that a court will see through what the lawyers have done, follow the order of their unstated as well as their stated argument, and weigh it also in the judicial balance. The court's desire to achieve justice is just as real as that of the opposing lawyers, the difference being that the court's definition of justice is not controlled by the identity of the lawyers' clients. The court can concern itself with the quality of opposing laws between which it has to choose, and there is plenty of evidence that courts do concern themselves with this question of quality even though they do not often phrase their opinions in terms of it. The lawyer who omits argument on the inherent superiority of opposing laws, apart from their territorial origins, is crediting the average court with less understanding and wisdom than it really possesses.

No one can sensibly contend that this fifth consideration, favoring application of the better rule of law, outweighs the other four considerations. I gave it special emphasis because in years gone by the other considerations, or at least their content, were more often discussed while this fifth one was not clearly identified. The fact remains that it is only one of the five, more important in some types of cases than in others, almost controlling in some, but far in the background in others.

What have our courts said or done about the five choice-influencing considerations in conflicts cases adjudicated after the considerations were synthesized?

The first judicial opinion to make use of them was *Clark v. Clark*, 107 N.H. 351, 222 Atl.2d 205 (1966), written by Chief Justice Frank Kenison of New Hampshire. On its facts, the case was simple. A husband and wife left their New Hampshire home in the husband's car, he driving, to spend an evening at a bowling alley in another New Hampshire town, intending to return home the same evening. Their route took them briefly onto a Vermont road, across the state line. While on the Vermont road the husband's negligence caused a car wreck, injuring the wife. She sued him and his insurance carrier in New Hampshire for that injury. New Hampshire law would allow such an action, but Vermont's host-guest statute barred ordinary negligence actions by an automobile guest against a host. The question was which state's law should govern.

A standard tort characterization of the problem would have led to application of Vermont law, since injury occurred in that state. Recovery would be denied. The New Hampshire court, overruling earlier precedents, rejected that approach and, after reviewing the five choice-influencing considerations, applied them to the specific facts:

. . . a lawyer advising these parties—either the plaintiff or the defendant, or insurance company—after the accident could anticipate with reasonable certainty that the lawsuit would be brought in a New Hampshire court under New Hampshire law. Predictability of legal results in advance of the event is largely irrelevant, since automobile accidents are not planned. The expectations of the present parties, if they had any, as to legal liabilities and insurance coverage for accidents, would be with reference to their own state, and they would think in terms of lawsuits brought in New Hampshire courts under New Hampshire law, if they thought about the matter at all.

Maintenance of interstate orderliness presents no problems, one way or the other. Interstate travel by residents of the two states will not be affected, nor will the sensibilities of either state, whichever law is applied.

Simplification of the court's task is almost irrelevant here too. We are accustomed to applying our own ordinary negligence rule, and our judges could administer a trial under it a bit more confidently than under Vermont's gross negligence rule, but they could with relative ease use either rule.

As to New Hampshire's governmental interests, it is our duty to further them. We in this instance believe in our own law. Our negligence rule is common law, made by this court, and our Legislature more than once has refused to change it. We have an interest in applying it to New Hampshire residents, especially when such advance expectations as they may have had, based upon their domicile in New Hampshire, their maintenance of a car under our laws, and going on a short trip that was both to begin and end here, would have led them to anticipate application of our law to them. Unlike "rules of the road," as to which every consideration requires obedience to the rules that prevail at the place where the car is being driven, the factors that bear on this host-guest relationship all center in New Hampshire. . . . Our primary interest arising out of our ordinary negligence law . . . applies to suits in our courts affecting people and relationships with which we have a legitimate concern. That interest in this case is a real one.

Finally, we conclude that our rule is preferable to that of Vermont. The automobile guest statutes were enacted in about half the states, in the 1920s and early 1930s . . . Legislative persuasion was largely in terms of guest relationships (hitchhikers) and uninsured personal liabilities that are no longer characteristic of our automotive society. The problems of automobile accident law then are not what they are today. New Hampshire never succumbed to this persuasion. No American state has newly adopted a guest statute for many years. . . . Though still on the books they contradict the spirit of the times . . . we should not go out of our way to enforce such a law of another state as against the better law of our own state.

The California Supreme Court, without specifically citing the choice-influencing considerations, reached a comparable result in *Offshore Rental Co. v. Continental Oil Co.*, 22 Cal. 2d 157, 148 Cal. Rptr. 867, 583 Pac.2d 721 (1978). The California lawsuit was brought by a California corporate plaintiff against a Louisiana corporation to recover for loss of services of the plaintiff's key employee who was injured by the negligence of the defendant Louisiana corporation while engaged in business on the defendant's premises in Louisiana. An early California statute which gave a cause of action for "any injury to a servant which affects his ability to serve his master" (Civil Code Sec. 49) would have allowed the plaintiff to recover. Louisiana law allowed no such recovery by a "master." The California court denied recovery, holding that Louisiana's law governed.

On "predictability," the opinion said only that "defendant would most reasonably have anticipated a need for the protection of premises' liability insurance based on Louisiana law," since the premises on which injuries might occur were in Louisiana, although insurance against employee injury could just as readily have been taken out by the California employer. 'Maintenance of interstate order" or good state relationships and "simplification of the judicial task" were scarcely touched on. They seldom have much bearing on choice between substantive laws in tort cases. California's "governmental interest" was identified, but minimized:

California is interested in applying its law in the present case to plaintiff Offshore, a California corporate employer [but] . . . we have determined that the California statute has historically been of minimum importance in the fabric of California law . . .

Louisiana's interest may have outweighed California's. California's interests, at best, were slight.

What the court dwelt on was the "better law" aspect of the two states' laws. Professor Paul Freund's work (59 Harvard Law Rev. 1210, 1216) was quoted at length:

If one of the competing laws is archaic and isolated in the context of the laws of the federal union, it may not unreasonably have to yield to the more prevalent and progressive law, other factors of choice being roughly equal. . . . Perhaps one of the functions of conflict-of-laws decisions is to serve as growing pains for the law of a state, at all events in a federation such as our own. . . . a particular statute may be an antique not only in comparison to the laws of the federal union, but also as compared with other laws of the state of its enactment. Such a statute may be infrequently enforced or interpreted even within its own jurisdiction, and, as an anachronism in that sense, should have a limited application in a conflicts case. . . . [a] statute which was once intended to remedy a matter of grave public concern may since have fallen in significance to the periphery of the state's laws.

Then the California court itself, no longer quoting Professor Freund, pointed out that:

The majority of common law states that have considered the matter do not sanction actions for harm to business employees, recognizing that even if injury to the master-servant relationship were at one time the basis for an action at common law, the radical change in the nature of that relationship since medieval times nullifies any right by a modern corporate employer to recover for negligent injury to its employees.

The court then concluded that the law to be applied should be Louisiana's modernized view rather than the "archaic and isolated" rule set out in California's Section 49. Though the court did not cite the choice-influencing considerations as such, both its analysis and its conclusion were clearly based upon them. In that respect the opinion set out the court's true reasons more honestly than do other courts which cover up their true reasons by employing gimmicks such as characterization, *renvoi*, and the like to direct their conflict-of-laws choice to the preferred rule of law.

At least a half-dozen different approaches to choice-of-law decision, all designed to replace the mechanistic rules promulgated by Professor Beale during the first half of the twentieth century, have some academic and judicial acceptance in America today. The five choice-influencing considerations, as a technique for making the choice between competing laws of two or more states, is only one of the several current approaches. Most courts deciding choice-of-law cases in the 1980s have not actually committed themselves to any single one of these approaches. Their opinions tend to speak simply of the "new" choice of law as distinguished from the "old," and to conclude that results arrived at can be supported by citation to the work of just about any of the conflict-of-laws writers who have proposed new ways to solve the old problems.

A 1977 Arkansas case, *Wallis v. Mrs. Smith's Pie Co.*, 266 Ark. 622, 550 S.W.2d 453, illustrates this eclectic method of decision. The plaintiff was an Arkansas resident returning to Arkansas from a motor trip to Ohio. While crossing Missouri on an interstate highway deeply covered with ice and snow, he drove on the left, or inside, lane. A Missouri statute required driving on the right, or outside, lane at all times except when passing other vehicles. The defendant was a Pennsylvania corporation whose truck was being driven from Pennsylvania to Oklahoma. As the truck approached the plaintiff's car from behind, the truck driver moved from the outside to the passing lane, but due to the ice and snow the truck was not brought under control at once and rammed the back end of the plaintiff's slower moving car, causing the injuries complained of. The defendant's driver was clearly negligent, but by Missouri law the plaintiff was negligent also, because he was violating the Missouri statute by driving in the wrong lane. By Missouri law the plaintiff's contributory negligence barred all recovery. The Arkansas comparative negligence statute would permit a proportional recovery if the plaintiff's negligence was less than the defendant's.

The Arkansas Supreme Court, speaking through Justice Elsijane T. Roy, first indicated that its earlier *lex loci delicti* decisions were no longer controlling. It then analyzed the facts in light of the five choice-influencing considerations, and concluded:

We therefore find that this state has a predominant interest in applying its comparative fault statutes to its own citizens and those who seek relief in its courts. . . . For equally compelling reasons we find Missouri rules of the road are applicable to questions of alleged negligence in the actual driving of the vehicle. At the time of the accident, the parties were traveling the highways of Missouri and were under a duty to obey the traffic laws in force there.

Though the choice-influencing considerations were relied upon, they were by no means the sole support for the decision. The result was also specifically supported by a showing that the "dominant contacts" of the facts were, concerning each of the two issues, with the state whose law was chosen to govern the issue, and that the 1971 Restatement's "most significant relationship" test would lead to the same conclusions, as would a "governmental interest" analysis based upon Professor Brainerd Currie's writings.

No court can in a single case follow all the theories that are currently proposed, but it can agree with their general effect, which is that there are better ways of deciding choice-of-law issues than under the old mechanical rules prescribed by Professor Beale and the first conflicts Restatement. Every one of the new proposals calls for decision based upon real reasons relevant to the functions of law in our society, as distinguished from decision based upon formulas merely. Some of the proposals call for less judicial honesty in stating the real reasons for decision than do others, and a theory which leaves room for discreet cover-up of some real reasons has lingering appeal for judges still tied to the notion that all law must consist of rules and formulas. But real reasons generally underlie all of the modern approaches.

It is easy to understand why the courts are running the approaches together. They relate to each other, and each has sustainable merits, yet there are too many of them, and some of them are subtle and call for fine distinctions. Busy judges have no time to study and master all of them, then choose among them. Some afford more flexibility than others. The personalities of proponents influence some courts. Courts are also avoiding conflicts issues when they can reasonably do so. Explanations are easy, but the fact is what is important. The fact is that most American courts today are moving to what they call "the new law" of conflict of laws. It is a conglomerate, and not a bad one.

A Marital Property Problem

There is nothing unusual about one's legal writings being cited, or even followed, in judicial opinions. That is one of the purposes for which a law school professor writes them. At least he hopes they will be read by a few lawyers and judges, in addition to his own law students who think that such reading will help them pass his courses. I once experienced an odd variation of this sort of thing. It involved a conflict of laws article dealing with marital property problems that I wrote for the California Law Review (21 Calif. L. Rev. 221). The incident illustrates the complexities—some would call them frustrating technicalities—that inhere in a national legal system comprising more than fifty different and independent bodies of law operative in geographical areas between which citizens are free to move at will.

One part of the article dealt with a difficulty faced by an elderly married couple moving to California, a community property state, from any of the 42 common law states (such as Arkansas) in the United States. Typically, the property acquired in the common law state would be owned by the husband; the wife's dower interest is inchoate and would vest in her only if she survived him. California's community property law does not recognize dower; it takes care of wives' interests by giving each spouse a half-ownership in the earnings of the other from the moment of acquisition. On a California husband's death, which would often occur before the wife's, the widow would already own her separate half of what they had acquired, and all of his separate property would go to his own heirs, not to the widow, unless he left a will giving it to her.

The effect of all this upon our elderly couple newly moved to California was harsh. When he died, all the acquisitions during marriage were still his property; by the law of his California domicile at death, since he left no will, all his property (and all of it was still his) would go to his heirs (who might be nephews and nieces), and his widow would be left penniless.

The California legislature in 1917 attempted, in an uninformed manner, to rectify this injustice. Unfortunately, it did so by providing that if separate property acquired elsewhere would have been community property had it been acquired by spouses domiciled in California, the separate property automatically became community property upon being thereafter brought to California by a spouse later becoming domiciled in California. In my article published in early March, 1933, I pointed out that this taking of one-half of a person's property and transferring title in it to another person, spouse or whomever, based upon nothing more than the owner's moving with the property to the new state, was a taking of his property, one-half of it, without any legal process whatever, and was prohibited by the due process and privileges and immunities clauses of the Fourteenth Amendment to the Constitution of the United States.

A few days after the article appeared, I received a letter dated March 7, 1933, from one M.D.L. Fuller, a lawyer with the firm of Pillsbury, Madison & Sutro in San Francisco. In it he wrote:

In view of your recent article in 21 California Law Review, I am sending you herewith a proof copy of the decision of the California

Supreme Court in the *Estate of Thornton*, and would be pleased to have your comments.

The Supreme Court opinion, dated March 1, 1933, upheld and applied the 1917 statute, on a set of facts involving an elderly husband's move from Montana to California. The unanimous decision (19 P.2d 778) was that California could constitutionally change the husband's 100 percent ownership to a 50 percent ownership upon his acquiring a California domicile and bringing his property to California. Mr. Fuller's firm was listed as having lost the case.

I replied at some length, reaffirming what was set out in the article. My letter sympathized with the purpose sought by the well-intentioned 1917 enactment, but added:

The main weakness of the decision [is] that it deprives a non-citizen of vested property rights as a condition to his doing something which the state has no constitutional right to prevent him from doing, viz., coming into the state and making his home there. Had California's statute been applied a step further down the line (to subsequent events or transactions affecting the property) the result reached would be supportable, since then California would be merely determining the legal effect on California titles of a California transaction. But [that] was not . . . in the facts of the case.

I made the obvious recommendation, that a motion for rehearing be filed, and learned later that this was done.

The next that I heard about the case was that the earlier decision was, in mid-1934, superseded on rehearing. The new opinion held the 1917 statute unconstitutional since it provided for a taking of property prohibited by the privileges and immunities and due process of law clauses in the state and federal constitutions (1 Cal. 2d 1, 33 P.2d 1). My article was not cited except in a dissenting opinion. I wrote twice to Fuller asking him to tell me more about the case, but received no reply.

Needless to say, I felt bad about having helped produce an

unjust though legally correct result. A widow had been left with nothing. The remedy for the future, however, was for California not to take an owner's property away from him the moment he moves to the state, but rather to regulate subsequent California events and transactions which relate to a spouse's property interests. Ultimately the California legislature did just that.

Today, two basic enactments take care of the problem. One, enacted a year after the final *Thornton* decision, governs distribution of property on the death of an owner domiciled in California, the other adopted later governs the division of property between California spouses securing California divorces. Both prescribe, subject to designated exceptions, that there be a 50–50 division of property that would have been community had it been acquired under California law. Thus ownerships remain in original owners until the occurrence of new California events or transactions that may traditionally be controlled by the law of the state where the new occurrence is centered. A few other community property states have enacted similar statutes. All of them (in addition to California, they are Louisiana, Texas, New Mexico, Arizona, Washington, Idaho and Nevada) should.

When spouses move and take property from a community property state to a common law state, comparable problems, fortunately not as serious, can arise. A uniform act promulgated by the National Conference of Commissioners on Uniform State Laws deals with that situation. It has been enacted in Arkansas and a few other states.

These conflict of laws distinctions may seem, to non-lawyers, to be overly technical. Perhaps they are. Within a nation governed by a single principal body of law, as is true for most European and many other countries, conflicts of law would not arise, but they do in the United States because ours is a nation of federated states. And there are means available in our law whereby these complexities can, at least ultimately, be fairly resolved, either by the adoption of uniform state laws, by wise rules of conflict of laws, or through the enactment by Congress of a single national law for areas in which that is constitutionally permissible.

Sister State Judgments

According to political theory, and to a large extent in actual fact, the United States and its several states constitute governments "by law and not by men." Even our governors and our millionaires are subject to the law. The courts enforce the law, and on the whole do a fairly good job of it. The judicial process produces judgments rendered by the courts, which may be appealed to higher courts, until eventually they become final. It is the enforcement of these judgments that gives ultimate meaning to the assertion that ours is a government by law. But judgments do not enforce themelves; levy of execution or other procedures for enforcement must be available.

Most American judgments are rendered by courts of one or another of the fifty states. Even the federal courts are for some purposes courts of the states in which they sit. At common law a state provides enforcement procedures only for judgments rendered by its own courts. If P secures a judgment for $10,000 against D in State F, and all of D's assets are in State X (perhaps purposely removed from State F) no effective levy of execution can be had in F. If "government by law" is to be achieved, P must be allowed to levy execution on D's assets in State X where they are located. For this to be permitted it would have to be authorized by X's own law, or by a federal law which could be law throughout the nation, in all the states.

The framers of our nation's Constitution dealt with the problem by providing (Art. 4, § 1) that "full faith and credit shall be given in each state to the . . . [judgments] . . . of every other state," but they left it to Congress to implement the clause. Congress, in turn, did no more than require, for the mass of state judgments, that they receive in other states the same faith and credit that they have in the courts of the first state (28 U.S. Code § 1738). No procedure for sister state enforcement was prescribed.

What the sister states did nearly two hundred years ago was to require a new lawsuit to be brought on the first state's judgment as a new cause of action, with new service of summons on the judgment debtor, a new trial, and a new judgment rendered in the second state so that levy of execution could then be had in the second state (X) on its own judgment. This was a slow, circuitous, and expensive way of enforcing a right that was already adjudicated and against which no new substantive defense could be raised. Congress could have enacted a law prescribing a system for registering other-state judgments so that they would be enforced without the cumbersome and costly formality of new suit and new judgment. Such a law was eventually enacted for judgments of federal courts, allowing them to be registered and enforced in any federal district anywhere in the United States, but no such statute was adopted for state court judgments, and the states themselves for a century and more made no change, either legislatively or by judicial decision, in the settled procedure.

Finally, in 1946, the National Conference of Commissioners on Uniform State Laws decided that, if anything was to be done about the problem, the states would have to do it. A committee was set up to draft a uniform act for state adoption. Though I was a new Commissioner I was made chairman of the committee, presumably because the problem could be classified as falling in the area of conflict of laws.

We first assumed that a procedure for registration of sister state judgments, with enforcement permissible at once after registration, was needed. All of us agreed on that. Yet doubts were expressed. Lawyers are cautious, sometimes overly cautious. If a State F judgment registered in State X were to be enforced in X the same as an X judgment it would for all practical purposes be an X judgment, and the due process clause of the Constitution clearly prohibits the rendition of any judgment in any state without first going through the standard legal procedures of service of summons and formal trial, or at least affording a fair opportunity to have a trial. We feared that levy of execution on D's property in the second state without any trial, or opportunity for trial there, might be deemed a taking of his property without due process of law, and therefore unconstitutional. Accordingly, what we came up with in our cautious mood was a summary judgment procedure. It required the judgment creditor to bring a new lawsuit in the second state but specified minimal procedures that would be enough, though just enough, to satisfy due process requisites. The Conference in 1948 approved and promulgated the act in that form, and it was subsequently enacted in several states, including Arkansas. Enforcement in State X of rights conferred by a State F judgment was thus simplified, but not made easy. The State F judgment, though it had completely settled the rights of the parties, still had to be sued on anew.

The more we thought about this the less sense it made. It seemed that due process of law demands notice and opportunity for a fair hearing only one time, not a succession of times. The judgment debtor has had his notice and opportunity for hearing in the first state (F), and is not entitled to re-litigate substantive defenses that were available to him there. Those are foreclosed in any event. The only defenses later available to him anywhere are that he has already satisfied the judgment or that he was not legally before the State F

court which rendered the judgment against him. If these defenses do exist, all that the debtor needs is an opportunity to
present them, and them only, in the second state. This presentation could be made in the same manner in which the
same defenses might be raised against the second state's own
judgments.

Finally, in 1964, the Commissioners concluded that such a
registration procedure would not be successfully attacked under
the due process clause. We became convinced that a new judgment in the second state was not necessary if the first state's
judgment satisfied due process requisites, and if the second
state would refuse enforcement on a showing that the purported first state judgment had in fact not been validly rendered or had been satisfied. That could be shown on motion to
set aside the registration. The judgment debtor's due process
rights would in this way be fully protected. They need not be
protected twice. A new uniform enforcement of judgments
act, promulgated in 1964, prescribing a registration procedure,
has now replaced the 1948 act in most, but not in all, of the
states.

The long delay in establishing this equally fair and far more
efficient method for enforcing fully adjudicated rights constitutes a sort of monument to two common characteristics of
lawyers (myself included) and legislators: (1) excessive caution
about overturning traditional though uselessly cumbersome
legal procedure, and (2) a tendency to overlook injustices that
do not spectacularly attract public attention. If it were not for
groups such as the Commissioners on Uniform State Laws, this
particular inefficiency might not have been actively noticed
and remedied for another hundred years. Today, for the states
that have enacted the newer uniform act, "government by
law," achieved by means of the efficient enforcement of sister
state judgments, is more complete than it was only a few years
ago.

Light v. Light

Legal issues which appear to be abstract and wholly imper-
sonal can turn out to affect intimately personal matters. An
odd example of this happened in connection with the uniform
act which I helped to draft in 1948 and an Illinois lawyer who
later corresponded with me at some length about it.

This was the first Uniform Enforcement of Foreign Judgments Act, described in the preceding section. It was designed
to simplify the enforcement of valid state judgments in sister
states. The basic principle is that due process of law entitled a
judgment debtor to one fair opportunity to defend the claim
against him, but not to two or more. A valid judgment once
fairly rendered should be enforceable. The new act satisfied a
felt need in the law and was soon enacted in a number of
states, including Illinois.

Not long afterward I began to receive letters from Ivan H.
Light, Illinois lawyer, who contemplated writing an article
about one aspect of the act, especially having to do with its
bearing upon sister state alimony awards. Such awards, accom-
panying divorce decrees, are typically kept on the divorce
court's docket, not final but modifiable so that the award may
be changed up or down as the situations of the parties change
in the future. His special concern was whether the new judgments act applied to such modifiable decrees.

The question was one that we had considered when drafting
the act. There are United States Supreme Court decisions
holding that modifiable, therefore non-final, judgments are
not absolutely entitled to full faith and credit in sister state
courts. These decisions did not mean that non-final judgments
must be denied faith and credit (enforcement) in the second
state, but only that the second state was free to deny their enforcement. The second state could frame its law either way it
pleased. With that in mind, we worded the uniform act to ap-

ply not just to judgments entitled to full faith and credit under the United States Constitution, but to all judgments "entitled to full faith and credit in this state."

In response to Light's inquiries I sent him a copy of a law review article I had written explaining the act, and wrote him that "if a state wanted to give faith and credit to foreign judgments beyond what is required by the (federal constitution), that should be its own business and a state should be free to do so, but our statute was not designed to require any state to do so." He then wrote an article which was published in the Chicago Bar Record presenting his interpretation of the uniform act, suggesting that parts of it were unsound and should be revised, and particularly urging that a second state's enforcement of a sister state's judgments be limited to final non-modifiable ones, as under the Supreme Court decision. When I read his article, I assumed that it was an impartial though critical analysis of the uniform act, and I even considered a restudy of the act by the Conference of Commissioners.

In about a year I learned what was wrong. Justice Walter V. Schaefer of the Illinois Supreme Court sent me a copy of his court's opinion, which he wrote, in the case of *Light v. Light*, 12 Ill. 2d 502, 147 N.E.2d 34 (1957). From that opinion I learned that Light himself had been divorced in Missouri and ordered by the Missouri court to make periodic alimony and child support payments to his former wife. Typically, these were modifiable *in futuro*. Light had then moved from Missouri to Illinois, apparently taking his assets with him, and had failed to make the periodic payments. His wife brought action in Illinois, under the uniform act, to collect what was due her. His "scholarly research" was motivated by an effort to defeat his wife's lawsuit, in which he appeared as his own attorney, and thus to evade his adjudicated liability to her. The Chicago Bar Record article was presumably designed to establish a favorable atmosphere for his impending appellate argument. The effort was unsuccessful. The Illinois court's unanimous decision was that, under the act, the Missouri award was entitled to full faith and credit "in this state" even though the United States Supreme Court's interpretation of the federal constitution did not require that result. He had to pay up.

Incidentally, it is probably not a good idea for a litigant to try his case either in the newspapers or in the legal periodicals. Or if he does so, it will leave a better feeling in the minds of his correspondents and readers generally if he admits what he is doing when he does it.

A Conflicts Casebook

The 1983 casebook on conflict of laws, designed for use in advanced law school classes, constituted a somewhat incidental piece of work, as far as I was concerned. My treatise *American Conflicts Law* went into its third edition in 1977, and was mildly successful. The Bobbs-Merrill Co., which had published all my conflicts books, shortly afterward sold its lawbook business to the Michie Company of Charlottesville, Virginia, a more aggressive organization. Michie wanted a casebook to go along with my treatise, and asked me if I would prepare one. The task did not particularly appeal to me, since it would involve going over the same materials that were in the treatise, but at lesser depth. I did not agree to undertake it.

Michie then approached Professor Robert L. Felix of the University of South Carolina and Professor Luther L. McDougal III of Tulane University, successively, and asked them to offer to join me in working up a casebook. After further delay, I saw a light, dimly. Each of these excellent conflicts scholars was willing to do the bulk of the work. If both of them joined me, the labor would be less for each of us, certainly less for me, and the combined efforts of three experienced conflicts teachers could well produce a better book. So, after exchanging ideas, we met in New Orleans in August of 1981, laid out a table of contents, divided up the topics, agreed on a three-way review system, and went to work.

One thing we agreed on was that our book should be shorter than others in current use. In years gone by, conflict of laws had been taught in all law schools as a four semester-hour course. In the last sixteen or twenty years the mushrooming mass of American law has so expanded law school curricula that the conflicts course had to be reduced everywhere to three semester hours. Yet every new edition of a conflicts casebook was lengthened, so that the materials available for three-hour courses were sometimes twice as long as those formerly studied in four-hour courses. The inevitable consequence was that not all could be covered, and the parts omitted were often by happenstance, not based on good legal pedagogy. This we tried to remedy by shortening the number of pages, and printing basic source materials combined with questions for students to answer for themselves on hundreds of additional issues on which lengthy explanations might have been printed.

Also, we attempted to organize the course so that it could serve as a sort of introduction to legal philosophy, and to the broad principles of Anglo-American jurisprudence. Conflicts students must accept the fact that the subject is still in a stage of growth; it is not a maturely developed body of law. Today's law students must plan to participate in its further development.

As a kind of postscript added in the late fall of 1984, I report that the Michie Company is now asking for a fourth edition of my treatise American Conflicts Law. Professors McDougal and Felix have agreed to work with me on this new edition, as they did on the casebook. That should keep all three of us busy in our spare time for the next year or so.

VI Law Teacher

A Good Law School or a Poor One

It is much easier to talk about a good law school than it is to establish or maintain one. The difficulty is enhanced by the fact that there is no single clear pattern of law school quality. There will be differences between the best for a school with 500 students and for one with 1500. The best for a school that has only $500,000 a year to spend would not be the best for a school that has $5,000,000. There are some standards that apply everywhere and always, and some that don't. Every dollar ought to be spent wisely wherever it is spent, but what constitutes wisdom in spending a $50,000 foundation grant is different from wisdom in spending one's last dollar, or one's last $50,000.

I am not talking about schools like Harvard or New York

University, except incidentally, but rather about smaller state law schools. I will assume a school which is part of a university, because no school that is not part of a university, partaking of its university's cultural and academic atmosphere, has ever amounted to much. There is not a single top-quality non-university law school in the United States, and the quality of a law school directly correlates with that of its university. The law school I am talking about would have 250–500 students, because a smaller school would not be as efficient in its operation and probably would not have enough money to operate on.

It is obvious that, in the United States, a good law school would be approved by the American Bar Association's Section of Legal Education and would be a member of the Association of American Law Schools. The standards prescribed by these organizations have been formulated by thousands of lawyers and law teachers counseling together on the problems of legal education, and they constitute the consensus of the legal profession's thinking, in terms of minimum requirements. Any school that does not comply with them is trying to get by with less than it should. We must remember, too, that the association standards are minimal, and a law school that barely complies with them is not a very good school.

Sometimes it is argued that economically disadvantaged students need to go to inexpensive schools, which may mean unaccredited ones. That is as wrong as can be. A poor boy or girl should have the same opportunity to attend a good school as does the child of wealthy parents. There is no justification for any law school subjecting anyone, wealthy or poor, to a legal education that does not at least come up to decent standards.

The first test of a law school's quality is its teaching, and nothing is harder to measure. The casebook system of teaching is basic to American legal education, yet there are almost as many different case systems today as there are law teachers. The system devised by Langdell of Harvard more than 100 years ago called for a student to state each case, after which there was a Socratic dialogue between teacher and student, in the course of which the full inner meaning of the case and all that it stood for was revealed, preferably with subtlety and wit, while eager classmates listened avidly and recorded what they heard in bound notebooks. This was an improvement over the old textbook and lecture method of teaching, because it centered upon actual materials of the law, the cases, rather than upon second-hand digests of them, and because it engaged the reciting student's whole mind, not just his memory, in the learning process. Yet the virtues of the method decline significantly as the student's law study moves on. By the end of the first year a law student knows how to state a case and to analyze it on his own if he is ever going to learn how. The case-stating experience remains valuable for the individual who states the case, but it becomes deadly dull for the other 49 or 99 class members.

So law teachers often skip the statement of the case and move into its analysis, on the not-always-correct assumption that the students already know what the case says. Or we devise problems that call upon the students to apply what they got out of reading the cases. Or we ask the students themselves to come up with the rules and principles, and the policies behind them. Or we lecture and the students take notes.

Whatever we do, we worry about our inability to cover all the material in the casebook and the student's inability to study in three years all the law that a well-rounded lawyer ought to know about. We worry about the fact that our students, even the best of them, are graduated without knowing all the law and possessing all the skills they will need when they start practicing.

The only complete answer to that, I suppose, is Dean Prosser's "ten-year curriculum." We are not going to teach our students all the law and all the practice skills they will need unless we keep them in law school a lot longer than three years. Yet three years of law school, after four years of college, is all the time we are entitled to ask for. A competent adult law student ought not to expect support from parents or spouse forever. I have concluded that law school, recognizing that mastering the law is a lifetime and not a three-year job, ought to use its limited time to inculcate in the student four things:

1. Understanding of the fundamental rules, principles, policies and organization that make up our legal system as a whole, and all its branches;

2. Mastery of techniques for study and analysis of narrow problems in minute detail;

3. Appreciation of the law's relation to our society—past, present and future, and

4. An interest in the law sufficient to induce him to spend the rest of his life trying to learn something about it.

All of these contemplate scholarly but critical study of a mass of materials that either constitute or bear upon what we call "the law." We could not include in the regular law school course much room for the skills training, the "how-to-do-it" courtroom and law office vocational courses that some practicing lawyers have urged upon the law schools. I think the answer is that the 27 months in law school had better be spent on more basic matters, and that the arts and skills of practice can best be learned on the outside, from men who know them better than most of our law teachers do. Part-time internships with law firms, preceptorships for summer work, legal aid assignments, clerkships with judges and with government agencies or law firms immediately after graduation, beginning practice under the guidance of older lawyers—these opportunities are more efficient.

This does not leave out the law review. For students good enough to make the staff, the law review gives the best education that law schools afford. That is as true of the small school's local law review as it is of a large school's national review. What a person works out for himself stays with him better than what any teacher tells him. Law review editing and writing is self-education at its best because it is done within a containing pattern that eliminates much of the wasted effort and unguided going-off-in-all-directions that too often defeat honest effort at self-education.

The relation between curriculum and bar examinations needs more study. Bar examination subjects ought never to control curriculum, though curriculum may very well influence the choice of bar examination subjects. No student should ever take any course, nor should any course ever be required, merely because it is on the bar examination. The "diploma privilege" is bad, but the fact remains that any student who is graduated by a good law school ought to be ready for admission to the bar. He ought to be able to pass a fair bar examination if he studies seriously for it. If that is true, then the main value of a bar examination is that it compels the student to engage in a comprehensive review of all that he has studied so far, at the close of his period of formal education. I think that value alone justifies bar examinations.

Apart from the faculty, the law library is the most important part of any law school setup. This means books, the right books and plenty of them, which can be expensive. It means modern computerized facilities for legal research. It also means that the books and other facilities should actually be used by both students and faculty. A vacant reading room marks a poor law school and a poor law library. If the faculty does not, by example or otherwise, induce the students to use the books, the faculty is falling down on its job. The librarian's job is to have the books and other facilities there and always easily available for use. Otherwise the law review cannot operate as it should, faculty research and writing cannot proceed, and student learning outside the classroom and casebook, which is the best part of student learning, is stymied. The importance of a comprehensive and efficient library cannot be emphasized enough.

Probably the building that houses the law school is less important, comparatively, than we sometimes think it is. For the library to be any good it has to be well housed, with adequate reading and research space. There have to be usable classrooms and seminar rooms, and plenty of them. The faculty cannot work very well unless they have offices to work in. The law review must have editorial quarters and storage space. Students need book lockers, a place to hang their raincoats and, nowadays, typing rooms. The dean and his assistants need a corner somewhere. Space should be allocated for visiting members of the bar. Efficiency can be considerably increased if there is air conditioning in the summer and adequate heating in winter. It is well for the building to have a dignified and attractive appearance. My only reservation may be summed up: If a law school has an adequate building, or plans for one, and has another $500,000 to spend, it would be better to spend it on the library or towards improving the faculty than on extras for the building.

Many matters connected with university and law school administration, and their interrelationship, are important. The law school dean's job is to make his law school as good as possible. The university administration's job, with reference to the law school, is to help the dean in every way it can, in view of the university's total situation, to do his job well. We hear much of law school autonomy as an ideal, but what is meant is reasonable autonomy within the university structure, not outside it. The ideal autonomy is one which permits freedom within the law school, to do things that it can do better than the central administration. What these things are will differ somewhat from school to school, but nearly always the law school must maintain its professional ties with the bar of which it is a part, must control its own library, and must conduct its own continuing education programs for members of the bar.

Law schools are different from English departments and colleges of education, and should not be lumped together with general undergraduate or even graduate divisions in determinations concerning faculty appointments, salaries, teaching schedules, libraries, teaching methods, public relations and a score of other matters upon which the university administrator's first impulse is to fix single unified policies for a whole campus. Law is one of the few fields in which the effort to secure good faculty members has to compete with high financial returns in private professional practice. It is one in which alumni loyalties tend to center in the particular school rather than on the university as a whole. The law school has more fund-raising potentialities as a separate donee than as an unseparated unit in a larger institution. Its goals can be independently identified to an extent that is not possible with most university divisions. All this deserves autonomy, but there can be such a thing as too much autonomy. The American law schools which have the most complete autonomy are those which are not on university campuses at all, a few without any university connection. Their lack of university contacts creates for these schools disadvantages far greater than what they gain from their independence. The vital importance to modern law study and legal research of collaboration between disciplines must constantly be emphasized.

The task of the university's central administrators is to facilitate, not slow up, law school administration. Maximum control over details must be left to the law school dean. A good central administrator makes it his business to show the dean how a proposed program can be carried out within the requirements of university rules and policy, not why it cannot be. He must endeavor to understand the law school's problems, along with a hundred other problems, and be ready to discuss them intelligently and sympathetically, but he must not supersede the dean in determining what is to be done about them.

The greatest waste, especially of human resources, in today's academic world is caused by overorganization, bureaucratization by and for administrators. It has not been as bad in law schools as in other divisions. Law school deans have usually resisted the administrator's "too busy to teach" reaction to their high offices, and have continued to meet regular classes. Few deans in other fields have been willing to do this. Thus they have deprived their students of what was often the finest scholarship and pedagogic talent in their academic disciplines, and at the same time have removed themselves further from their main goals—providing good teaching to students. Even in law schools we see too often the time of our ablest teachers used up in the guise of administration on what are no more than high-class secretarial or janitorial jobs. The difference between low-class administrative work and high-class clerical work is hard to identify, but when highly paid academic staff members immerse themselves in tasks that are near the borderline, the loss to scholarship and teaching is evident. Delegation of some dean's duties to young assistants who also teach, and to competent secretaries, is a clear mark of good administration, not because it eases the dean's work but because it enables him to enhance his administration by doing more teaching and research of the higher quality which, if he is a good man, he can perform better than can those who do the lesser jobs for him.

The waste of faculty members' time in committee meetings can be as bad as the waste of a dean's time in doing janitor work. Fairly selected, committees constitute an excellent device for considering general policies, because all attitudes can be represented and presented. But for handling administrative matters, even those of major importance, or for carrying out an already established policy, a faculty committee is probably the least efficient and one of the least effective agencies ever devised. It requires three, five, or seven teachers to spend their presumably valuable time doing what one of them could do as well or better in one-third or one-fifth or one-seventh of the same clock time. It is quite true that if a professor is not going to be doing anything else that is more useful during his afternoons—and some will not be—he might as well be assigned to administrative or clerical tasks, but that does not justify disregard of efficiency and effectiveness in performing the tasks any more than it justifies a device tht achieves a mere pretence of busyness. Above all, there is no justification for taking good lawyers away from serious work—research, writing and preparation for teaching—that they would actually be doing if it were not for unnecessary time-consuming committee assignments.

Everyone agrees that a good faculty, with as low a student-faculty ratio as is reasonably possible, is the most important feature of any law school. Classes with 100 or more students are seldom effective, and should be allowed only under teachers who are exceptionally qualified to handle them. A good faculty is hard to get, and harder to keep. Most law school graduates we would like to have on our faculties prefer to go into practice, or want to stay in practice long enough to make a nest egg before they start teaching, which usually takes so long that they are spoiled for teaching before they ever start. A long period of successful practice is seldom good training for a law teacher, though a short period can be. No one will be a good law teacher unless he really wants to teach, and then only if he is willing to work at it.

A law professor in his first year or two of teaching has all he can do to keep up with his classes, and normally ought not to try to do much else. But after that, if he teaches most of the same courses, he is not really a full-time law teacher unless he does do something else. He is hired to do more than meet his classes. Research and writing are the most common tasks; every mature law teacher owes at least one full-length article each year to his own school's or some other law review. In extra-curricular areas, efforts to improve state or national law, interest in continuing legal educational programs, administrative duty in the law school or the university, all suffice to fill out the full-time teacher's schedule reasonably. A bit of remunerative outside practice in his special field is appropriate. It gives a sense of reality and practicality to his teaching, and ought to be encouraged, but this can neither supplant nor suffice as scholarly research or writing. The teacher is expected to be a scholar, at least some of the time.

The law teacher's main job is teaching. If he is not a good teacher, or does not take his teaching seriously, he ought not to be teaching. There are many kinds of good instruction, running all the way from the technique of persistently raising unanswered questions in students' minds so they will be impelled to seek out answers for themselves, to the technique of making everything so clear that every student thinks he knows all the answers when he leaves the classroom. A well-chosen faculty ought to run the gamut between these methods. Above all, a law teacher should realize that his job is not to train lawyers for yesterday's types of practice, but for tomorrow's, for work that they will be doing ten or twenty years hence. He can ask himself, "How have the law and practice changed in the last twenty or thirty years?", and he can be sure that change will be swifter in the years that lie ahead. The task of prophecy is not an exact one, but there are tangible materials from which we can pursue it, and a good curriculum committee knows what these materials are.

The selection and admission of students, and even their recruitment, have become major problems. A few of the great American law schools now have eight or ten times as many applicants as they have places for first year students. These schools employ college grade records plus law school aptitude test scores in making their choices. Other schools accept all applicants with the standard minimum qualifications, then weed them out on the basis of later performance. This is unfair to some of those who are admitted. We ought not to take a year out of their lives, and waste our own and their fellow students' time with them, when they are sure to fail out at the end of a year. The trouble is that we are not yet sure of our ability to predict success in law school. Motivation and personal drive are hard to measure. They ought to show up in prelaw grades, but sometimes they don't. Law school aptitude testing is still being improved. One of these days we should be able to do a better job of picking our students. Certainly we should not try to build enrollment records nor statistics on hard-boiled flunking at the expense of students who should have been excluded in the first place.

We cannot settle the matter of prescribing what prelaw courses our students should take. We know that courses in English, history, government, economics and sociology, and some accounting, are desirable, but the best student in the class may turn out to have an engineering degree or a major in mathematics.

As the costs of law school operation rise, the cost of going to law school steadily increases. This presents a danger that law study might become an occupation limited to children of wealthy parents. That would be a national disaster. The nature of our government and society demands that the profession of law, perhaps above all other callings, be open to all classes, races and conditions. No limitations on admission to the bar save intellectual and moral ones, plus compliance with reasonable procedures, should be imposed. Law schools are not the only educational institutions facing this problem today; protracted and expensive graduate work looms as a barrier to every learned and scholarly calling. Scholarships are the answer. They are available in other fields. We in the law schools must offer more of them than we do, along with low-interest loans, else we will lose our talented but unfinanced prospects to other disciplines, or to uneducated mediocrity. That is a loss we cannot afford.

A placement service which brings law firms and employers of law personnel together with current and recent graduates is a necessity today. Student organizations such as the honor council, the student bar association and law fraternities need guidance and encouragement in performing their useful functions. A law school alumni organization ought to be created and fostered. The importance of the law review has already been emphasized. A moot court program, assisted by practicing lawyers as judges, is always worth more than the trouble it causes. Close relationships with bar organizations and with the courts are essential if a truly successful program of continuing legal education is to be carried on, and are useful in almost every other law school context. Faculty participation in efforts to improve the law, in addition to its intrinsic value, serves to aid the law school's public image, as do published research articles generally. The law school faculty is obligated by a clear duty to perform its fair share of university tasks, whether they relate to athletics, the discipline committee, or general university planning. And national professional organizations, whether related to law teaching, as is the Association of American Law Schools, or to the teaching profession generally, as is the American Association of University Professors, deserve the law teacher's active participation and support.

An obvious limitation is that one man cannot do everything, nor can one small law school. A school that tries to do too many things may wind up doing nothing well, and doing some things poorly. The danger in a small law school is that a limited budget may be spread too thinly by adding extracurricular programs that take away funds and manpower from the law school's main purpose. The point is that any law school considering a new program should first ask what the school's real function is, in the territory it serves, and then consider if the costs and benefits of the new program, taken all together, will further its performance. Often they will improve it, but not always.

No law school ever became great by merely continuing to do what it did in the past. That is the way to lose greatness.

A Message to English Law Teachers

The contrast between legal education in England and in the United States is striking. England has no professional law schools such as we have in this country. Law study in English universities is essentially an undergraduate program, like history or geology, with professional law study for the most part undertaken privately after the would-be barrister or solicitor has finished his college courses. One consequence of this academic arrangement is that in England law teachers generally do not have the status accorded by the legal profession that American law teachers enjoy. There are, of course, exceptions.

English law teachers have naturally been curious about the professional activities of their American brethren. I was asked to write a short article for one of the English journals on "the law teacher's place in the American legal profession." This was some years after we had established the Appellate Judges Seminars at the New York University Law School. English lawyers and law teachers could hardly believe that appellate judges would voluntarily come back to law school for refresher courses. They knew about the program because we had invited Lord (Judge Kenneth) Diplock and a few other English judicial scholars to serve as members of the Seminar faculty. They wanted to know more about law teachers over here. What I wrote (in 1963) was in part as follows:

It is only in recent years that American lawyers have taken to speaking of "the three branches of the legal profession", meaning the judiciary, the practicing bar, and the law teachers, with an implication that the three are about equally important in their professional functions.

During the presidency of Franklin D. Roosevelt, American law teachers were first called in considerable numbers into government service. President Roosevelt consulted frequently with Professor Felix Frankfurter of Harvard about bright young (and middle-aged) lawyers who might work for the government, and dozens of Frankfurter's "little hot dogs", as his protégées were facetiously called, began careers in Washington during Roosevelt's New Deal days. Frankfurter was himself appointed to the United States Supreme Court by Roosevelt a little later. In the same period several other law professors became distinguished federal judges. One of these was William O. Douglas of the Yale Law School, who was named chairman of the federal Securities and Exchange Commission, then went on the United States Supreme Court. Others included Dean Charles E. Clark of Yale, Dean Herbert F. Goodrich of the University of Pennsylvania, Dean Herschel Arant of Ohio State University, Professor Calvert Magruder of Harvard Law School, Dean Armistead M. Dobie of the University of Virginia, and Professor Thurman W. Arnold of Yale, all of whom were named to the United States Court of Appeals.

Judicial service by law teachers in the United States was by no means limited to the New Deal period. Judge Joseph Story, who went on the Supreme Court in 1811, served simultaneously as a professor in the Harvard Law School. William Howard Taft, after he had been President of the United States for four years, was for nine years Professor of Law at Yale, then in

1921 became Chief Justice. Harlan Fiske Stone was for many years a professor, then Dean, of the Law School at Columbia University, before he became Attorney General of the United States, then in 1925 Associate Justice and finally Chief Justice of the Supreme Court in 1941. Oliver W. Holmes, Jr., was just starting on the Harvard Law School faculty when appointment to the Supreme Judicial Court of Massachusetts turned him to a judicial career instead. Charles Evans Hughes, who served as Chief Justice of the United States from 1930 to 1941, had taught at the Cornell Law School for two years while a young man. Arthur T. Vanderbilt, sometime President of the American Bar Association and Chief Justice of New Jersey, taught part-time during most of his adult life at the New York University Law School and as Dean furnished the inspiration which made that institution the great law school that it is today. Two of the nation's greatest modern judges who were law teachers are Roger J. Traynor, who taught at the University of California for a dozen years before going on the Supreme Court of California in 1940, and Walter V. Schaefer, who taught law at Northwestern University in Chicago before becoming a Justice of the Supreme Court of Illinois. Two score or more other instances could be named in which American law teachers have become state appellate judges.

At an earlier period, most of the teaching in our law schools was by practitioners who taught part-time, often in night classes. This arrangement has today been largely superseded by the employment of full-time teachers in full-time law schools, but some part-time teachers remain in nearly every school. These are often former full-time teachers who have gone into private practice but do not wish to give up their academic connections altogether, or lawyers who have specialized in some particular area of practice and who are asked to teach courses, often at the graduate level, in their fields of specialization.

The occasional desire of middle-aged or elderly lawyers to

"retire" from the rigors of active practice to the presumably quiet and peaceful life of the law teacher sometimes presents a problem for the law schools. Many members of the bar are inclined to think that any experienced lawyer with a reflective bent would automatically make a good law teacher, and that the presence of such men on law faculties would assure the students of "practical" and "realistic" training which they might not receive from "theoretical" teachers whose background was primarily academic. Hundreds of men came to American law school faculties on this basis in years gone by. Some of them became excellent teachers. Too often, though, they were the poorest teachers, but the highest paid, on their faculties. They had trained themselves to types of thinking, analysis, and presentation which were different from those required for effective teaching; they were often too set in their ways to retrain themselves in new techniques; and they knew much less of the whole body of the law than when they had finished law school two or three decades previously. Law students, of course, noticed these deficiencies and as recent generations of law students came to make up the practicing bar, the demand that such "practical" old-timers be added to the law faculties has decreased.

Full-time law teachers in the United States often engage in some outside practice. Frequently this is in their teaching fields, in which they become known as specialists so that they are asked to assist other lawyers who have cases in their fields. Other work related to their teaching subjects, such as the arbitration of labor disputes, is sometimes offered to them, as are temporary assignments in local, state and national government. Law school faculty rules normally permit a fair amount of such outside work, the discretionary test being whether it in general aids the teacher in his main job as a legal educator and is not so extensive as to interefere with his day-to-day performance of that job. Leave of absence may be given for more demanding outside assignments.

Law teachers have always been welcomed as members of the American Bar Association and its state and local counterparts. The formal programs and annual meetings of state bar associations, as well as programs of "legal institutes" and other special sessions held in between annual meetings, nearly always include names of law professors. Perhaps this is because teachers not only have the background but the time, or are willing to take the time, to prepare addresses for such occasions. This may be another facet of their law teaching. One famous example of such an address was delivered in 1906 by Roscoe Pound, then a University of Nebraska law teacher who had already served on the Nebraska Supreme Court, before the American Bar Association in St. Paul, Minnesota. It was entitled "The Causes of Popular Dissatisfaction with the Administration of Justice", and has had a lasting influence upon efforts to improve judicial administration and the law generally.

Law teachers also participate regularly in other professional work of the bar, of a public character, such as that of the National Conference of Commissioners on Uniform State Laws and the American Law Institute. The monumental new statute called the Uniform Commercial Code is the joint product of the two bodies, with law teachers taking the lead in the drafting job while practitioners largely assumed the responsibility for convincing legislators that the Code should be enacted as law. The American Law Institute's Restatements of the law have an even stronger law school connection, since most of the original drafting is by reporters who are law school teachers, but the hammering out of final drafts is always done by the reporters and their non-teaching brothers working together.

At an entirely different level, the "continuing legal education" programs that are now popular in the United States bring law teachers, practicing lawyers, and judges together constantly. These programs include short courses for insurance counsel, personal injury claimants' attorneys, defense attorneys, prosecuting attorneys, tax lawyers, bank and building and loan association lawyers, family law practitioners, and for specialists in every line of practice.

Many interrelated activities of American law schools, the bench and practicing bar, and the cooperative attitudes which grow out of these activities, are attributable to the professional character of American law schools. Our early law schools were nearly all conducted by lawyers or judges with a view toward training men to engage immediately in the practice of law. That was true of the Litchfield Law School, the first in America, and of all the proprietary schools which succeeded it. When the superiority of modern full-time law schools with university connections came to be generally recognized, so that in the competition of the educational marketplace they forced out the old private moneymaking schools, the basic premise remained. The function of the law school was not general education; it was (and is) the professional education of young men and women who intend to practice law, or engage in law-related work.

The difference between undergraduate college work, required as a prerequisite to law school admission, and professional work in the law school itself, is constantly emphasized. Prelaw liberal arts college curricula include courses in government, constitutional law and international law, and the curricula of business administration colleges which enroll many prelaw students include courses in commercial law. However valuable these classes be, they are not taught with the intensity that characterizes law school teaching. Modern law school courses are incorporating much material from other academic disciplines—such as economics, sociology, political science, psychology and philosophy—but it is dealt with as part of the stuff that affects legal problems as they are solved either in the courtroom or in the solicitor's office. It is studied on the assumption that it is part of the professional lawyer's equipment for legal work.

The Association of American Law Schools, born in 1900 as the official organization of the better law schools in the country, is a child of the American Bar Association. It grew out of the Bar Association's concern with standards of legal education and its desire to establish an agency which could deal with them directly. The Bar Association has its Section of Legal Education and Admissions to the Bar. The two bodies work together. The policing of law school performance in terms of minimum requirements for accreditation is attended to by the Section, while the law school association devotes itself largely to improvements in legal education above and beyond the minima. Both groups sponsor formal visits to law schools by experienced teachers from other schools, either to determine whether there shall be accreditation by the Section or to assist in improving the general performance of an already accredited school.

Standards for admission to the bar, set separately by each of the fifty states, fall within the province of the courts and the organized bar rather than that of the law schools. Each state has its board of bar examiners made up of lawyers who usually are not law teachers. Cooperation with the law schools is called for, however, since it is unfair to examinees to give them a type of examination for which the law schools have not prepared them, or which is not up to the standards for which the good law schools have prepared them. Examinations which were unfair in these senses were at one time not uncommon, but today the National Conference of Bar Examiners makes law school type examinations available to examining boards throughout the nation. Some states, including California and

Minnesota, pay law teachers from outside those states to prepare questions for them, with model answers. Bar examiners
generally try to cooperate with law schools by giving the sort
of examinations for which the better schools undertake to prepare their students.

The law school origin of most of the great legal treatises has,
in the United States as in England, served as a tie between the
schools and the more scholarly members of the bench and
practicing bar. Judge Joseph Story produced his series of treatises as part of his duties while professor of law at Harvard, and
such pioneer works as Greenleaf on Evidence and Washburn
on Real Property, written by professors at the same law school,
did much to shape the law of all the American states in their
respective fields. So did the monumental sets by Williston of
Harvard, on Contracts, and Wigmore of Northwestern, on
Evidence, in the early 1900s. A few years afterward came the
great treatises by Scott (Harvard) on Trusts, Corbin (Yale) on
Contracts, Bogert (Chicago) on Trusts, Prosser (California)
on Torts, and Harper and James (Yale) on Torts. There are
scores of others as well.

The American system of student-edited legal periodicals,
unique in the educational world and constantly amazing even
to those of us who live with it daily, furnishes another basis for
close ties between bench, bar, and law school. Nearly all
American lawyers subscribe to one or more of these journals,
and often bind them as permanent sets for their office libraries.
Bound sets are maintained in all appellate court libraries.
Though courts in an earlier time, and some judges today, have
not cited law reviews in their opinions, most American judges
cite them freely, and the citations may refer not only to the
leading articles, usually written by law teachers or scholarly
practitioners, but to the better student pieces as well. The latter, representing group work by intelligent and inquisitive
scholars, often surpasses in quality the individual work of com-

petent legal writers. After these student editors are graduated, they tend to become leaders of the bar, and judges too, and they do not forget their editorial experience nor overlook the product of their successors.

The case method of teaching also enhances law school-lawyer relationships, primarily by helping to establish the professional character of law school study. The case method is the central professional aspect of law school work, and that feature in turn binds the law schools more closely to practicing members of the profession. Lawyers work on cases in their offices and in the courts just as they started to do in their first weeks of law school study.

It should not be thought that every practicing lawyer approves of all that is done in the law schools, nor that they are quiet about their disapprovals. A natural consequence of the lawyers' sense of responsibility for legal education is that they may feel an obligation to tell law school deans and faculties how their schools ought to be run. It is an exceptional visiting committee that will attempt to interfere with the pedagogical performance of a good law school by trying to change its curriculum, or by telling its teachers how to conduct their courses. That sort of thing does sometimes happen, however, and proposals for change may not always be pointed in the right direction. This is an inevitable penalty that is inherent in the interrelationship which American law schools generally maintain with the practicing bar. The interrelationship is nearly always useful to the law school, but it can be a nuisance.

There was, for instance, a vigorous demand by some practicing lawyers that law schools offer more "practical" training to their students. It was pointed out that law school graduates were not really prepared to do all the jobs that a practicing lawyer is supposed to do, on the day they finish law school, and it was asserted that more "how-to-do-it" courses or subject matter ought to be included in law school curricula. A veritable campaign toward this end was undertaken. This effort to influence law school teaching would not have occurred if the lawyers involved had not felt a deep sense of professional relationship to the schools, and responsibility for them. Law faculties aided by knowledgeable practitioners had to present publicly a vigorous defense of their position favoring broader academic educational policies, along with clear explanations of what the law schools were really trying to do. The controversy was disturbing for a time, and if no defense had been made the result might well have been to force some more susceptible schools into unwise and backward-looking curriculum changes. The final effect, however, was a fortunate one. The whole function of law schools in a modern society was openly re-examined, some skeletons were cleaned out of half forgotten closets, true curriculum reforms were undertaken in a number of law schools, and the atmosphere surrounding legal education and the proper concern of practicing lawyers with it, were usefully clarified.

One major consequence of the professional status of American law schools, and of the loyalty which their alumni feel toward them, is a prestige that often sets them apart in their university communities. Most law schools are to a large extent autonomous in their internal operations, and are frequently so with regard to such external activities as fund-raising campaigns. Gifts for endowment, scholarships and student loans, buildings and furnishings, prizes and awards, research projects, support of designated professorships, library development, and for dozens of other law school purposes, are fairly common.

A close interrelationship between law teachers, representing their schools, and the rest of the bench and bar clearly has disadvantages as well as advantages. It subjects the schools to pressures such as that for an unsound revision of the curriculum which was successfully withstood a decade ago. It produces outside interferences with academic freedom. It carries responsibilities, both affirmative and negative, which may be different from the typical academic ones but nonetheless are likely to center on the preservation of academic standards in a professional atmosphere. It creates new obligations and new duties.

But the advantages pretty clearly outweigh the disadvantages, at least from the point of view of those of us who are used to both of them. The law teacher's life and function are by reason of the relationship broader and more significant, and more fully related to the society in which he lives. There is a readier willingness to re-examine preconceptions about both law and pedagogy, leading to better teaching and more assurance as to what ought to be taught. There is greater student interest and participation in the educational process. Putting it shortly in an aspect that sums up nearly all the rest—the interrelationshp leads the law teacher into a fuller and more vigorous intellectual life. That, above all else, makes for good teaching.

Taught Law Is Tough Law *

"Taught law is tough law." All of us have heard this expression. What does it mean?

I can give one example easily. It's been 35 years since I finished law school, yet I still remember some of what I learned there, and part of it I have had no occasion to re-examine since then. (In 1984, 57 years afterward, this is still true.) When I hear or read something that contradicts what I learned in law school, which I have assumed without thinking anew

* These remarks concerning the relation of legal education to modern law are taken from the Hepburn Memorial Lecture presented at Wayne University Law School in Michigan on May 4, 1962, which was subsequently published in 8 Wayne Law Review 465. What was said then seems still relevant in 1984.

for 35 years to be sound and accurate, I bristle up and say "They can't do that to me; that's something I already know, and they can't change it on me." I have a vested interest in what I already know, or think I know. Besides, I don't like to put out the brain-straining effort that it takes for an old dog to learn new tricks. I like for the law, once I've learned it, to stay put. With me, and with other lawyers too, the law we learned in law school is "tough law." We don't give it up easily.

Back in 1927 when I first heard Dean Roscoe Pound use the expression "taught law is tough law," the words caught my imagination and, as apt aphorisms do, conjured up vistas of thought and some insight into ultimate truth. I was then about to embark upon a career of teaching law, and the words in that context gave me a sense of prospective participation in the great glacial process by which law and legal system are handed down from generation to succeeding generations in our common law society. I was about to take part in the transmission of our legal heritage. The law I was about to teach would be "tough law"; it would be hard, persistent, enduring law. If I had any doubts about the "toughness" of the law which I would teach, they were resolved by reflection on what I could teach, which was certainly not much more than my own teachers had just attempted to impart to me. There was one generation of persistence established already.

As I thought more about it, however, I realized that Dean Pound was speaking of something larger than the effects of law school classroom teaching on successive generations of law students, and of something even larger than the congenital laziness and conservatism of lawyers which makes many of them oppose almost any kind of change in the law. He was speaking of the self-perpetuating nature of our law, the doctrine of precedents and *stare decisis*, the fact that law, particularly the common law, repeats its own patterns almost perpetually, even to the extent of disregarding changes in the society and in the civilization within which the law operates. He was speaking, for one thing, of the attitude which induces many citizens, both lawyers and laymen, to criticize appellate courts—the Supreme Court of the United States, the Supreme Court of Michigan, the Supreme Court of Arkansas—when these courts break away from old lines of decision, overrule old precedents, look beyond *stare decisis* to liberalize the law. "Tenacity of a taught legal tradition is much more significant in our legal history," says Pound, "than the economic conditions of time and place."

Rules of law sometimes persist simply because they have once been announced as such, regardless of changes in society that have made them practically unexplainable except as bits of history. Referring to the continuity of common law, Pound points out that "it has a real unity at least from the age of Coke (1552–1634) to the present. As a mode of thinking, as a mode of reasoning upon legal subjects, it is the same in England, the United States, Canada, and Australia. It is the same in its technique of decision, in its judicial and juristic craftsmanship, and in its characteristic institutions. It is the same in its reasoning by analogy from decisions rather than from statutes. It is the same in its distinction of law and equity . . . [it] is the same in substance in one century and in the next. And yet between Coke and the present, equity has developed; the law merchant, which Coke had not much more than heard of, has been absorbed into the common law. . . ." 1 Pound, Jurisprudence 323-4 (1959). Uncounted other rules have been brought into and taken out of the body of the common law. Yet a common law decision from Arkansas or Saskatchewan can be understood and respected in Michigan or in New Zealand, because the system is the same. A contracts case written in Queensland might read almost the same as one written in Michigan. And a criminal law case decided in England or in Massachusetts 150 years ago might be cited as authority by a court sitting in Illinois today.

We all know about the common law's background in history and tradition, and how a decision in one case is drawn from the decision in another, or others. This is the common law method, which preserves and continues established custom and tradition. It is the historical method. What I want to dwell on now, however, is growth and development in the law, change as distinguished from constancy, and the way in which the tough old trunk of taught law puts out new shoots and branches and leaves and even new stalks that grow up from its roots, and the way in which these new growths themselves become tough taught law, and something about the relationship of legal education to tough law and tender law.

In the early days of our Republic, young men studied law by reading Blackstone and Kent and Story. When there were no law schools, or few law students in few law schools, law was studied by the mastery of textbooks, which was for the most part an acceptance of what was in them. Originality and imagination in the student were not virtues in that kind of study; they could only get a young man into trouble when he was examined on the texts. In the later 1800s and well into the present century, for most young men who attended a law school, the lecture method of law teaching was used, and it, too, put a premium on memory rather than on original thought. Those days were great days for the toughness of taught law; those were the days when the textbook and the lecture were *the law*, the gospel according to Saint Blackstone and Saint Greenleaf, or sub-saint local lecturer.

Then in the 1800s came Dean Langdell of Harvard and his case system for law teaching. At first it made small difference, for more than one reason. The most obvious was that for thirty or forty years there were few students in case system law classes. More importantly, the case system itself, in the hands of Langdell and his immediate successors, did not encourage students in the classroom to question the social policy of a case, but only to question its logic, its historical verity, and its correlation with other cases. The early case system under a good Socratic teacher compelled the law student to think for himself, which mastering textbooks and listening to lectures never did compel him to do, but to think for himself *about what?* Mostly about the analytical structure of the law and how a case fitted into that analytical structure, the legitimacy of its historical antecedents, the factual and probative accuracy of its syllogisms. There was little in that mode of teaching to encourage young lawyers to seek improvement in the law, or strive for changes that would make law fit better the needs of society. That casebook teaching left the law that was taught as tough as ever, but only taught it better. Emphasis was on cases which were supposed to follow the precedent of prior cases, leaving improvement in the law to legislatures whose ephemeral product was no proper subject for serious law study until it had lain in the books for 100 years.

On the face of it, this does not describe what takes place, or is supposed to take place, in the classrooms of today's law schools, though we still say that we use the case system for law study. What has happened?

We have all heard it said that there are as many case methods for teaching law as there are law teachers using casebooks, and that each teacher devises his own system. That, of course, is not quite true; there can't be 2000 genuinely different systems. But with 2000 or more law teachers in the United States, each on his own and with no obligation to do homage to Langdell, we do get teaching methods that are pretty far away from what the men of Harvard envisioned three-quarters of a century ago. It is a rare law teacher today who would ask a second or third year class to state a case, discuss it, state another and discuss it, and so on until the end of the class period. Such a routine procedure has real value only for beginning students, but we know its value quickly wears out, and even the second semester student begins to demand something that goes deeper beneath the surface. The law teacher today can assume, or should be able to assume, that a student has read the assigned cases, and has them in his mind as background and foundation, so that we can take off *from* there. But take off *for where?*

I suspect that a big break in American law teaching came with the development of what Roscoe Pound called sociological jurisprudence. This new school of thinking about law placed emphasis on the idea that it is law's function to serve the best interests of the society which it governs—to serve that society's interests in terms of its culture, its economics, its social institutions, its life, and its aspirations. This was in contrast to analytical jurisprudence which treated law almost as an end within itself and was content to study the systemic character of law and the interrelationships of its parts with each other. It was in contrast too with historical jurisprudence which studied law primarily in terms of its past, its origins and lines of prior growth, more than its future.

There have been many philosophers, and few of them have avoided the temptation to philosophize about law. Most have centered upon some ultimate ideal, some end or ends that human life should serve, such as individual freedom, or the greatest happiness of the greatest number, or virtue in mankind, or the survival of the fittest, or a finer civilization, or equality in the distribution of economic goods, or the like. Many, though not all, of these were abstractions, as broad or as narrow as the beautiful large words in which they were phrased, or as the content which the particular philosopher read into the beautiful large words. Sociological jurisprudence, though it could be called a philosophy, or part of a philosophy, was both similar to and different from most of these. It was concrete. It dealt not just with ideas and ideals, but with the facts of life, the facts of our society, and how law could implement accepted philosophies.

Sociology is the study of our society and all its institutions—economic, cultural, familial, religious, political,—its ways of life and living. Sociological jurisprudence sees law as the servant of the society of the time and place, the body of norms which that society creates for itself to further and effectuate the perceived interests accruing from its activities and its aspirations. This is a conception of law that unites the study of law with the study of society. It forces the student to look outside the law itself for his justifications. It directs him to look not merely at Coke's "the reason of the law," which was a rather specialized kind of logic; nor merely at the history of law, which in some areas has more to do with folkways of the past than with the living present; but also to look at the job that the law has to accomplish today. The law student now is allowed to ask whether the law, or any particular rule of law, is doing its work in *this* society well or poorly. He is entitled to ask first what the law's job really is, then to check on how it is being performed, and then to compare, and see whether it is the best and most effective way in which this task can be performed.

I realize that far fewer than all the lawyers, judges, and law professors in America would go along with what Roscoe Pound and his disciples have written under the head of sociological jurisprudence. The natural law philosophers would not accept the materialistic implications of a functionally-tested jurisprudence, yet the fact remains that most of them have come in practice to advocate essentially the same approach to actual legal problems though they still idealize other ultimate values and condemn sociological jurists for not idealizing those values. At another extreme the so-called realists also proclaim their differences and disagreements, yet their point in fact is that they accept the function-tested approach to law, but would temper it with something of the opportunist's crassness and the cynic's defeatism. Nor does the sociological jurist deny the reality of this realism; he merely refuses to make it the central feature of his legal philosophy. What we have in America today, despite debate about ultimate ideals at one end and courthouse practicalities at the other, is a general agreement among legislators, judges, and ordinary citizens, plus law professors chiming in with their own minor discords, that the function of law is to serve the functions of society, and that every society is free, or at least should be free, to remake its law in its own functional image.

A corollary to this societal emphasis in legal theory is well expressed in another of Dean Pound's favorite phrases, "the efficacy of effort." If a body of law ought to serve the needs of a society, then the effort to make it serve those needs well is a worthwhile effort. If that is the nature of law and its function, then we as members of the legal profession are under an obligation to do what we can to make sure that not only in the law's administration but in its substance these ends are served. This is an effort in which every one of us may properly engage. More than that, it is an effort in which success, at least some measure of success, is possible. That is what is meant by "the efficacy of effort"; a belief that the law's administration and its substance can be improved, and will be improved if we work at it with enough intelligence and energy.

We in America were once less hospitable to changes in our substantive law, especially judicial changes, than we are today, and we are more hospitable to changes now than our fathers were a few decades ago. Our methods of legal education, influenced in turn by new jurisprudential theory, have had a great deal to do with our changing attitudes toward law itself. It will

be instructive, I think, to look at the attitude-producing effects of some specific features of modern legal education.

One never-ending feature of modern legal education is casebooks. That is what law teachers still call the books we use as
teaching tools in our courses, though Langdell wouldn't recognize many of them as casebooks in the classic sense. Today
they are mostly labeled "Cases and Materials on" whatever the
subject may be. The "Materials" parts of these books normally
deal with the business situations, the social, political, economic, psychological, and cultural problems that the law works
with in a particular field, the factual difficulties inherent in
these problems, differing points of view as to how the best interests of society can most effectively be served in connection
with these problems, and the like. The choice of cases to be
printed in most casebooks today is based on the adequacy of
discussion in the reported case of such "facts of life" as are
relevant to it. If an opinion relies merely on authority, without
analysis of the social or economic problems inherent in it, it is
not likely to be regarded as a good casebook case, whereas current cases selected for inclusion in the new casebooks are
likely to deal with both the legal authorities and societal considerations bearing upon the legal question in the case.

Furthermore, the parts of the good new casebooks that deal
with cases today do not just print the cases plus related citations, nor do they just ask questions about the logic of the
case, and what answers that logic would call for in the slightly
different sets of facts that students are expected to discuss and
pass judgment upon. They raise questions of policy. Their text
notes and footnotes call upon the law student not only to dif-
ferentiate deductive from inductive reasoning, to formulate or
complete the formulation of syllogisms, to reason from analogy after a fashion, or after various fashions, and to enjoy a
good *reductio ad absurdum*. These materials actually require

students to make value judgments, to make choices concerning what the law ought to be, and to make up their own minds about whether particular cases were rightly or wrongly decided, not just in the light of earlier decisions but in the light of all considerations that a free-wheeling jurist might bring to bear on the case. These considerations are at least partly the same ones that a statesmanlike legislator would take into account in dealing with the same broad substantive problem. It is pretty obvious that this student experience does not make for an attitude of unlimited reverence toward old law, but rather will influence the kinds of reasoning that he will later, as a practicing lawyer, present in cases that he hopes to win in the courts, or that he will employ as a judge in deciding other lawyers' cases.

What is the significance of the fact that today every good law school publishes a law review, that the pressure is tremendous on faculty members and better students to write constantly for these legal periodicals, and that there is at least some pressure on practicing lawyers and ordinary law students to read what is printed in the law reviews? What does this new facet of legal education, peculiarly American, do to the old "taught law is tough law" tradition?

We had better admit, without arguing the point, that much of the mass of writing in law reviews is writing for its own sake merely. It is useful, but not basic. This is true both for lead articles by law teachers and for casenotes and comments written by student editors. These writers have to "produce" in order to get ahead, to get promotions or better jobs, to get their names on editorial mastheads so they can move into the better openings in good law offices.

It is not often that law review material is written in the light of an inner fire, to say things that must be said to ease the writer's soul and make his conscience free. Such writing does turn up, sometimes, it's true, and fortunate indeed is the law review that receives it—unless it has to be rejected because the scholarship is deficient, the grammar bad, and the conclusion unsupported by the reasoning, all conditions sometimes coexistent with surging fire in a zealot's inner being. But some of the world's finest writing, including some in the law, has come from hands and minds that simply had to express ideas that could not be stayed. Every one of us could cite such writing, and such teaching, that has moved us deeply. It is too bad that we do not find more of it in the average issue of an average law review.

Nevertheless, what we do find is for the most part writing done conscientiously after careful research and under standards of control which assure thoroughness and competency. There are, of course, considerable variations in quality. Some of it is pretty mediocre. The feature that is most significant in respect to nearly all of it, however, is that it *not* merely descriptive, not setting out in Corpus Juris-Ruling Case Law fashion the holdings of collected cases side-by-side or pile-on-pile; rather, it is question-directed.

Almost every law review writer starts with a doubt in his mind as to whether he can or should agree with the case or the line of cases he is writing about. Was this case for some reason, any reason, wrongly decided? Have the courts appreciated properly the true problem underlying sets of facts like these? Have the right social or economic considerations been taken adequately into account? Are there opposing theories, doctrines, policies that need to be reconciled? Does the case set out good guidance for the future and reflect good history from the past? Possibly the writer's question reduces itself to: Are the results and reason what *I* would have arrived at had *I* been deciding the case?

Whatever the form, the process of questioning has become part of standard operating procedure in law review writing. By the same token, it has become *a* standard method of law study among those who write for the law reviews (which includes a good percentage of our better law students) and to a lesser extent by those who merely read them. They question as they go, seeking not black letter rules to be memorized, but rather to discover for themselves what the rule ought to be. It would be foolish, of course, to say that this is true of all law students, but it is true of enough of them to make a difference. And the fact that our appellate courts today cite law review writing, including student notes and comments, freely, has given added respectability to the law reviews and to the questioning attitude that they generate.

This doubting, questioning approach to law study is bound to have an undermining effect upon the authoritarian character of old legal rules and old bodies of law. Law whose only claim to authority lies in its age is certain to be criticized when so approached, and criticism may lead to ultimate rejection. "Taught law" loses some of its tough persistence when it is subjected to this sort of process.

A heightened awareness on the part of law faculties that other academic disciplines have much to contribute to law study is another major development. Increasingly we are recognizing that law is not an academic occupation complete within itself, to be studied altogether in isolation from other academic fields. Interdisciplinary study and research is becoming the rule rather than the exception in our good law schools. We have much of it in upper class and graduate seminars on medico-legal problems, family law, law and psychology (including insanity), criminology generally, the treatment of juvenile offenders, urban housing and land use problems, the economics of taxation, labor relations and labor law, civil rights, trade regulation and antitrust laws, corporate promotions, and a dozen other fields. Information concerning installment buying and financing practices relates the law of sales to the facts of daily life. A fairly thorough understanding of liability insurance policies and statistics is essential to any realistic appreciation of the law of torts. A course in crimes and criminal procedure has infinitely greater meaning when it includes something more than the thirdhand materials of appellate cases. Law teachers and casebook editors today realize this, and are acting accordingly. Seminars conducted by law teachers jointly with economists, criminologists, psychologists, physical scientists, or with experts in some special area of government or private industry, are increasingly common. Whenever this interdisciplinary study occurs, either in separate seminars or as a part of regular law school courses, it tends to break down the law's stolid insularity. It makes law students understand that law justifies itself only by its sensible relation to the problems that arise in our daily lives, and that the function of our law is to serve the needs of our society.

Furthermore, legal education today is by no means limited to work with law students. Post-admission study, so-called continuing legal education, has come to be a major activity in many law schools, and a fair fraction of all the lawyers in America occasionally go back to law school in one way or another nowadays, to bring themselves up-to-date on new developments in the profession. Much of what is dealt with in these short courses is, of course, of the "how-to-do-it" type, almost mechanical in character, involving forms, techniques, and procedures for dealing with one kind of special situation or another, such as the trial of personal injury cases, the development of an oil and gas lease program, the operation of a prosecuting attorney's office, the evaluation of lands to be taken by condemnation proceedings for public uses, or the like. These do not much change popular attitudes, or lawyer attitudes, about the nature of law and its function in society, but only help lawyers to do specific jobs a little better. Also, a lot of lawyers attend legal institutes and short courses primarily to get a tax deductible vacation, preferably on a football weekend. That is not typical, though. The fact remains, along with the "how-to-do-it" courses and the "fun-and-games" aspect of continuing legal education, that there is mixed into these lawyers' seminars a great deal of discussion calling for new analysis of the law's function in a changing society.

I have just reviewed the printed programs for some of these recent short courses conducted in our law schools. In a course on eminent domain, two hours were spent on the effect of jet airports on urban and suburban development and realty values, and another session dwelt on modern traffic problems in their relation to municipal parking facilities and to limited access highways. This obviously compelled the lawyers present to think for a little while about the changing character of our once rural, now urban society and the effect this change is having not only on the economics of property but upon the law of property. An institute on wills and estates includes consideration of the changed character of inherited estates in an insurance-oriented tax-supported modern society in which social security and retirement funds dominate much of our thinking and in which gifts to charity may take from an estate only a fraction of what the charity receives. One on labor arbitration and collective bargaining enters into a whole new field of economic rights and relationships that for practical purposes came into being after the New Deal period of the 1930s. One on criminal law enforcement included a panel on concepts of legal responsibility. There was a lawyers' seminar on world rule of law, another dealing with the concept of human freedom in the modern American economy, still another on water resources and the law. There was an institute on laws and regulations affecting small businesses which, in legal theory, may be no different from other businesses, but which certainly do have economic problems, and therefore legal problems, which are different from those facing either our corporate giants or the owners of corner groceries. There have been several institutes on legal problems arising out of the development of nuclear and atomic energy. Institutes on oil and gas law almost invariably include sessions on legal devices for achieving conservation and maximum utilization of the natural resource. Taxation seminars are conducted somewhere in the country every few days and, despite the super technicality with which they abound, every one of them deals somehow with the economic and political effects of the taxes and tax systems that are studied, and with the relative functions of free private enterprise and big government in our society. Seminars on personal injury litigation, held almost as frequently, deal inevitably with the new industrial revolution that has given us products liability, and with the liability insurance revolution that has turned automobile accident law into a kind of privately administered workers' compensation system with Monte Carlo side effects. Seminars on insurance law not only cross over into traffic safety and industrial safety programs but into old age retirement and pension plans, social security, the effect of insurance investments upon our national economy, and the relation between absentee ownership and professional management in large corporate industry. Legal institutes on the Uniform Commercial Code, now adopted in all but one of the 50 states, are enabling lawyers to learn about the banking business and about all sorts of consumer and equipment sales and financing with new forms of security devised to fit the needs of modern business rather than the traditions of the common law. The list could be multiplied. The point is that not only law students but practicing lawyers also are, under the aegis of the law schools, delving into some realities of law in modern life that are pretty far removed from the rules that we read in the law textbooks of the 1800s.

I referred near the beginning of my remarks to the spate of current criticism directed at our appellate courts for their alleged disregard of *stare decisis*, and for their willingness to

overturn old precedents and to liberalize the law. We know
that some judges are called "activists," because they are willing
to question old legal rules, not follow them blindly merely because they are old, and in some quarters "activist" is a nasty
word. In another group are judges who are loosely identified as
favoring judicial restraint. Their position, stated broadly, is
that judges should abide by precedent and established doctrine
as far as possible, and should in general leave to the legislatures the task of improving the law. This group itself readily
enough engages also in judicial renovation of the law, a bit
more slowly and subtly than the avowed activists, but just as
surely. They are more likely to do it by distinguishing older decisions, or by finding a thread of growth already present in
them, or by dropping warnings of prospective overrulings before the ultimate step is taken and then citing the warning as
authority for the final departure later. However they do it, I
am not much inclined to distinguish between great judges like
Schaefer and Traynor and great judges such as Cardozo, Hand,
and Holmes in a slightly earlier generation. All of them are or
were engaged in bringing our law up to date. Only in their judicial techniques do they differ.

None of them have sought to abandon the past. The past is
a part of the present. The past is a part of all of us today, and a
part of all our law today. No great judge urges that we should
abandon *stare decisis*, the rule of precedent, today or ever.
There may be some theorists who would be willing for justice
to be administered on a completely ad hoc basis, without law
as we know it save in statutory form. I do not know any major
jurists who advocate such a thing, despite occasional loose
talk, and I am certain that there are few if any appellate judges
in America who operate that way.

By the same token, on the other side of the scale of theo-
retic talk, there are lawyers and judges who say that they op-

pose all judicial change in the law. If you consider their talk, by itself, you would conclude that they oppose all judicial promulgation of rules that are not already firmly embedded in the concrete of prior adjudication. Yet a reading of the judicial opinions of judges who talk like that almost invariably reveals that what they really oppose are new directions in current societal change. The same judges are often quite willing to promulgate "strong opinions," going beyond what is required by earlier ones, in directions they do like, which quite often are toward societal views that have prevailed in times gone by.

There is no appellate judge in America who is not an "activist," in a realistic definition of the term. This is in the sense that the judge believes in improving the law, according to his lights, and affirmatively tries to do so. There are very real differences among judges, both as to what are the true directions toward where improvement lies, and as to the proper rate of judicial movement toward them. But there are more judges today who are willing to move with fair speed, and to admit that they do so, than there were a judicial generation ago.

What I have wanted to do is to relate this fact, this current trend toward frank engagement in the deliberate process of improving judge-made law, to the processes and methods of modern legal education. I have tried to relate the question-asking approach which, I like to think, dominates America's law schools today, to the question-asking approach which, bitterly attacked though it sometimes be, is beginning to prevail in America's appellate courts and in the common law today. They are of one piece, and one explains the other. It was inevitable, once the approach became standard in law study, that it would a little later become standard in appellate adjudication. I believe that is what has happened. Perhaps the nature of our American democratic society made it inevitable that this would happen.

The old "taught law" has ceased to be such "tough law" as it once was, as far as specific doctrine is concerned, and a new toughness of the taught question-asking technique is taking its place. It is the taught question "Why?" that toughly persists today.

Index